위아
중학듣기
모의고사 20회

3

In-Depth Lab 지음

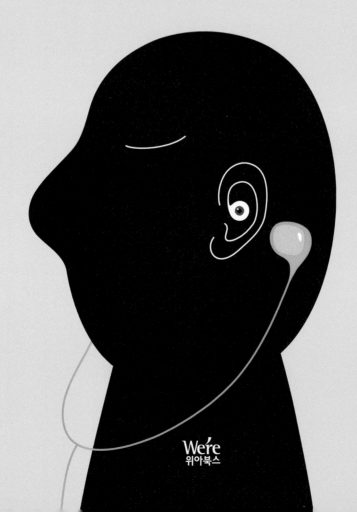

We're
위아북스

머리말 Preface

듣기가 안 되는 학생들의 경우에는 한두 개 들리는 단어들을 중심으로 전체 내용 또는 문제의 답을 상상하게 되는데, 말 그대로 상상이기 때문에 정답은 물론 내용에 대한 이해도 어렵다. 나중에 script를 보면서 정답을 맞추다 보면, 모르는 단어가 있었거나, 의미는 알지만 소리로 인식하지 못했거나, 연음되어 개별 단어들이 들리지 않았거나 등등의 여러가지 이유를 발견하게 된다. 그 외에도 잠시 딴 생각을 하느라, 지나간 단어에 집착하느라, 순간 집중력이 떨어져서 문제를 풀지 못하는 경우들도 있을 것이다. 하지만, 기본적으로 많은 학생들이 속도와 소리에 대한 적응, 그리고 듣는 동시에 머리로 내용을 이해하는 훈련 부족으로 인해 어려움을 겪는다고 볼 수 있다.

위에서 언급한 속도 적응, 소리 인식, 직청직해는 무엇보다도 반복된 청취를 통해서만 습득될 수 있는 것이기 때문에, 일반적이고 빈번한 주제들에 대해서 무수히 듣고 들을 내용을 확인하는 것 외에는 다른 방도가 없다고 해도 과언이 아닐 것이다. 이를 위해, 계속해서 새로운 청취 지문을 듣고 문제를 푸는 것도 좋은 방법이지만, 이보다 중요한 것은 각각의 지문으로 "완벽 청취" 훈련을 하는 것이다. 한 번 들을 때는 전체 지문에서 몇 가지의 단어만을 catch하게 되지만, 두 번 세 번 듣게 되면, 그 몇 가지의 단어들 주변에 있는 단어들이 들리고 서서히 구멍 난 부분들이 많이 채워지는 것을 느끼게 된다. 이렇게 많은 부분의 단어들이 채워지고 나면 전체 문장 또는 지문의 내용이 메워지는 것을 느끼며, 이때 비로소 내용에 대해 올바른 이해를 할 수 있게 된다. 또한 "완벽 청취" 훈련은 속도에 대한 적응, 소리에 대한 인식, 직청직해 훈련에도 효과적이다.

실질적인 실력 평가를 위해 많은 청취 시험들은 normal speed가 되어가고 있다. Normal이란 우리의 기준이 아닌, 원어민의 기준의 normal로 우리에게는 상당히 빠르게 느껴지는 속도이고, 이런 normal speed가 원어민이 가장 자연스럽게 느끼는 속도라고 했을 때 이에 따라 연음되는 발음들 또한 자연스럽게 많아질 것이다. 그렇기 때문에 더욱 많이 듣고, 익숙해지는 과정이 필요한데, 직청직해는 속도와 소리에 대한 적응 위에 가능할 수 있다.

본 교재는 중학 영어듣기 모의고사를 봐야 하는 학생들을 위한 것이다. 최근 5년간의 기출 문항들을 분석하여 주제나 문제 유형들을 최대한 반영하였고, 점차 길어지고 어려워지는 지문의 길이와 녹음 속도 등을 실정에 맞추었다. 한 번 듣고 문제만 풀고 넘어가는 것이 아니라, 여러 번 듣고 써 보는 훈련까지 하기를 당부한다.

역시 왕도는 없다. 반복해서 많이 듣는 것만이 방법이다. 하지만, 얼마나 다행인가? 어떤 특정 사람들만이 할 수 있는 비법이 아니라, 반복해서 많이 듣는 것은 누구나가 할 수 있는 방법이니 말이다.

In-Depth Lab

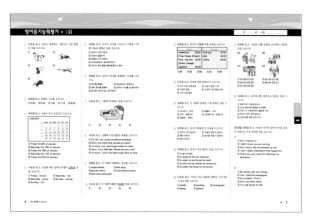

영어듣기능력평가 20회분

- 모의고사 20회 총 400문제로, 최근까지 출제된 시·도 영어듣기평가 유형들을 포함하여 출제 가능성이 있는 대부분의 유형들을 다루었습니다.

- 학교에서 실시되고 있는 듣기평가와 동일한 구성으로, 한 면에 시험문제가 모두 보이도록 하여 실전에 충실히 대비하게 했습니다.

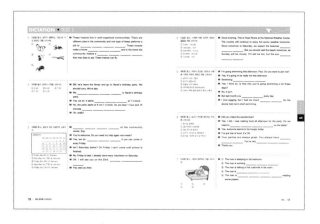

DICTATION

- Tape를 반복하여 들으며, 각 문제의 Script를 훑어보고 중요한 단어 및 표현, 문장을 빈칸에 채워 넣으며 전체 내용을 학습할 수 있습니다.

- 자신의 약점을 파악하여 취약부분을 집중적으로 연습할 수 있습니다.

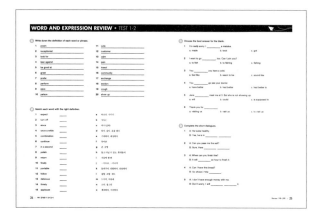

REVIEW

- 지문에서 가장 중요한 어휘를 골라 연습하는 코너입니다.

- 청취 학습의 기본기인 어휘 다지기를 위하여 모의고사 2회분마다 어휘, 숙어를 총정리하여 연습하도록 했습니다. (10회분)

CONTENTS

1 다음을 듣고, 남자가 설명하는 그림으로 가장 알맞은 것을 고르시오.

① ②

③ ④

⑤

2 대화를 듣고, 현재의 시각을 고르시오.
① 5:45 ② 6:45 ③ 7:00 ④ 7:15 ⑤ 8:00

3 대화를 듣고, 오늘이 무슨 요일인지 고르시오.

JANUARY						
SUN	MON	TUE	WED	THU	FRI	SAT
				1	2	3
4	5	6	7	8	9	10
11	12	13	14	15	16	17
18	19	20	21	22	23	24
25	26	27	28	29	30	31

① Friday the 9th of January
② Saturday the 10th of January
③ Friday the 16th of January
④ Saturday the 17th of January
⑤ Friday the 23rd of January

4 다음을 듣고, 요일에 따른 날씨의 연결이 잘못된 것은 고르시오.

① Friday - cloudy ② Saturday - hot
③ Saturday - sunny ④ Sunday - cloudy
⑤ Sunday - hot

5 대화를 듣고, 여자가 조깅을 그만두고 수영을 시작한 이유로 알맞은 것을 고르시오.
① 날씨가 너무 더워서
② 조깅이 싫증나서
③ 무릎이 너무 아파서
④ 다이어트에 더 효과적이어서
⑤ 의사가 허리 통증 완화에 좋다고 해서

6 대화를 듣고, 남자가 여자를 칭찬하는 이유를 고르시오.
① 청소를 잘해서 ② 샌드위치가 맛있어서
③ 파티 준비를 잘해서 ④ 남자의 식사를 늘 챙겨줘서
⑤ 음식을 가리지 않고 잘 먹어서

7 다음을 듣고, 그림과 일치하는 것을 고르시오.

① ② ③ ④ ⑤

8 다음을 듣고, 상황에 가장 알맞은 표현을 고르시오.
① It's OK, you could be behind schedule.
② Sorry, but what time should we meet?
③ I'm sorry, but I just forgot where to meet.
④ Sorry, I'm a little late. Where are you now?
⑤ I'm sorry. I won't be able to get here on time.

9 대화를 듣고, 두 사람이 대화하는 장소를 고르시오.
① supermarket ② fish shop
③ grocery store ④ convenience store
⑤ fast-food restaurant

10 다음을 듣고, 두 사람의 대화가 어색한 것을 고르시오.
① ② ③ ④ ⑤

11 대화를 듣고, 여자가 지불해야 할 금액을 고르시오.

Food		Drinks	
Sandwiches	$2.50	Soda pop	$1.50
(Tuna, Cheese, Chicken)		Milk	$1.00
Pizza - one slice	$3.00	Coffee	$2.00
(Potato, Sausage)			
Spaghetti	$5.00		

① $4 ② $5 ③ $6 ④ $7 ⑤ $8

12 다음을 듣고, 무엇에 관한 설명인지 고르시오.
① 인기 가요 순위 발표   ② 시상식 일정 소개
③ 수상자 발표   ④ 수상자 선정 방법 안내
⑤ 수상 소감 발표

13 대화를 듣고, 두 사람의 관계로 가장 알맞은 것을 고르시오.
① 아나운서 – 관객   ② 해설자 – 코치
③ 코치 – 운동선수   ④ 인터뷰기자 – 운동선수
⑤ 면접관 – 지원자

14 대화를 듣고, 여자가 병원에 간 이유를 고르시오.
① 감기가 낫지 않아서   ② 기침이 멈추지 않아서
③ 배가 아파서   ④ 음식을 먹을 수 없어서
⑤ 목이 아파서

15 대화를 듣고, 남자가 지금 하려는 일을 고르시오.
① to go to bed
② to study for the job interview
③ to wash up and brush his teeth
④ to pick out his clothes for tomorrow
⑤ to polish his shoes for tomorrow

16 다음을 듣고, 여자가 무슨 대회에 관하여 이야기하고 있는지를 고르시오.
① poetry   ② painting   ③ photograph
④ essay   ⑤ speech

17 대화를 듣고, 오늘의 여행 일정을 순서대로 나타낸 것을 고르시오.

(A)

(B)

(C)

(D)

① (A)-(B)-(C)-(D)   ② (A)-(D)-(C)-(B)
③ (A)-(C)-(D)-(B)   ④ (B)-(A)-(D)-(C)
⑤ (C)-(D)-(A)-(B)

18 대화를 듣고, 남자에 대한 설명으로 알맞은 것을 고르시오.
① 매일 탁구 수업을 받는다.
② 몇 달 전에 탁구클럽에 가입했다.
③ 주로 7시 이후에 탁구 클럽에 간다.
④ 학교가 아주 일찍 끝난다.
⑤ 오늘 밤에 영화 보러 간다.

[19-20] 대화를 듣고, 여자의 마지막 말에 이어질 남자의 응답으로 가장 적절한 것을 고르시오.

19
① Don't mention it.
② I didn't know you are coming.
③ Don't worry. No one showed up yet.
④ I don't really understand what happened.
⑤ Thank you very much for following my directions.

20
① Be careful with your things.
② Yes, I read the newspaper.
③ No problem. I'll do it.
④ Don't put them there!
⑤ You just saved my life.

1 다음을 듣고, 남자가 설명하는 그림으로 가장 알맞은 것을 고르시오.

① ② ③ ④ ⑤

M These insects live in well-organized communities. There are different jobs in the community and one type of these performs a job to _____ _____ _____ _____. These insects make a home _____ _____ _____ and in the home the community makes a _____ _____ _____ _____ that man likes to eat. These insects can fly.

2 대화를 듣고, 현재의 시각을 고르시오.
① 5:45   ② 6:45   ③ 7:00
④ 7:15   ⑤ 8:00

W Bill, let's leave the library and go to Sarah's birthday party. We should hurry. We're late.
M We _____ _____ _____ _____ to Sarah's birthday party.
W Yes, we do. It starts _____ _____ _____, at 7 o'clock.
M No, the party starts at 8 not 7 o'clock. So we have 1 hour and 15 minutes _____ _____ _____ _____.
W Oh, really?

3 대화를 듣고, 오늘이 무슨 요일인지 고르시오.

JANUARY						
SUN	MON	TUE	WED	THU	FRI	SAT
				1	2	3
4	5	6	7	8	9	10
11	12	13	14	15	16	17
18	19	20	21	22	23	24
25	26	27	28	29	30	

① Friday the 9th of January
② Saturday the 10th of January
③ Friday the 16th of January
④ Saturday the 17th of January
⑤ Friday the 23rd of January

M _____ _____ _____ _____ at the community center, Suji.
W You're welcome. Do you need my help again next week?
M Yes, we do. _____ _____ _____ if you can come in every Friday.
W Isn't Saturday better? On Friday I can't come until school is finished.
M No, Friday is best. I already have many volunteers on Saturday.
W OK. I will see you on the 23rd. _____ _____ _____.
M Yes, see you then.

4 다음을 듣고, 요일에 따른 날씨의 연결이 <u>잘못된</u> 것을 고르시오.

① Friday – cloudy
② Saturday – hot
③ Saturday – sunny
④ Sunday – cloudy
⑤ Sunday – hot

M Good evening. This is Ross Rivers at the National Weather Center. The country will continue to enjoy hot sunny weather tomorrow. Since tomorrow is Saturday, we expect the beaches _____ _____ _____. But you should visit the beach tomorrow, as Sunday will be cloudy. It'll still be hot, but the sun _____ _____ _____.

---

5 대화를 듣고, 여자가 조깅을 그만두고 수영을 시작한 이유로 알맞은 것을 고르시오.

① 날씨가 너무 더워서
② 조깅이 싫증나서
③ 무릎이 너무 아파서
④ 다이어트에 더 효과적이어서
⑤ 의사가 허리 통증 완화에 좋다고 해서

W I'm going swimming this afternoon, Paul. Do you want to join me?
M Yes, it's going to be really hot this afternoon.
W Swimming _____ _____ _____.
M Yes, I think so. Is that why you're going swimming a lot these days?
W No, it isn't.
M But last month you _____ _____ every day.
W I love jogging, but I had too much _____ _____. So the doctor told me to start swimming.

---

6 대화를 듣고, 남자가 여자를 칭찬하는 이유를 고르시오.

① 청소를 잘해서
② 샌드위치가 맛있어서
③ 파티 준비를 잘해서
④ 남자의 식사를 늘 챙겨줘서
⑤ 음식을 가리지 않고 잘 먹어서

M Did you make the sandwiches?
W Yes, I did. I was making food all afternoon for the party. Do we need to _____ _____ _____ _____ on the table?
M Yes, everyone seems to be hungry today.
W I've got lots of food. It's OK.
M Your parties are always great. You always have _____ _____ _____. You're very _____ _____ _____.
W Thank you.

---

7 다음을 듣고, 그림과 일치하는 것을 고르시오.

① ② ③
④ ⑤

M ① The man is sleeping in his bedroom.
② The man is working _____ _____ _____.
③ The man is talking to his customer in his room.
④ The man is _____ _____ _____.
⑤ The man is _____ _____ _____ _____ reading some papers.

8 다음을 듣고, 상황에 가장 알맞은 표현을 고르시오.

① It's OK, you could be behind schedule.
② Sorry, but what time should we meet?
③ I'm sorry, but I just forgot where to meet.
④ Sorry, I'm a little late. Where are you now?
⑤ I'm sorry. I won't be able to get here on time.

W You are supposed to meet a friend at 1 o'clock outside a fast-food restaurant. Unfortunately, you _____ _____ _____ you wanted to take. It's five minutes to 1 o'clock, but you are 20 minutes _____ _____ the restaurant. You won't get to the restaurant until 1:15. So you _____ _____ _____. In this situation, what would you say to your friend?

---

9 대화를 듣고, 두 사람이 대화하는 장소를 고르시오.

① supermarket
② fish shop
③ grocery store
④ convenience store
⑤ fast-food restaurant

M Yes, sir. How may I help you?
W I'd like a Happy Fishburger combination.
M OK. One Happy combo. _____ _____ _____ _____ would you like?
W Cola, please.
M That's $4.50.
W Here you are. Oh, could I get _____ _____ _____ of ketchup?

---

10 다음을 듣고, 두 사람의 대화가 <u>어색한</u> 것을 고르시오.

① ② ③
④ ⑤

① **M** I'd like to _____ _____, but I have to go.
　 W Thank you for coming to visit me.
② **M** Do you _____ _____ _____?
　 W Yes, it's 3:10.
③ **M** Thank you for the birthday present.
　 W _____ _____. I hope you like it.
④ **M** Can I see your passport, sir?
　 W He is over there. _____ _____ _____.
⑤ **M** You must turn off the lights when you leave a room.
　 W OK. I'll remember to do it.

---

11 대화를 듣고, 여자가 지불해야 할 금액을 고르시오.

Food		Drinks	
Sandwiches	$2.50	Soda pop	$1.50
(Tuna, Cheese, Chicken)		Milk	$1.00
Pizza - one slice	$3.00	Coffee	$2.00
(Potato, Sausage)			
Spaghetti	$5.00		

① $4　②$5　③$6
④ $7　⑤$8

M Can I _____ _____ _____, please?
W Yes, you can. I'd like one slice of pizza.
M What kind of pizza?
W Potato. Oh, no. Hmm... _____ _____ _____ _____ of pizza. One slice of potato pizza and one slice of sausage.
M _____ _____ _____?
W Yes, coffee please.
M OK. Two slices of pizza and coffee, is it right?

12 다음을 듣고, 무엇에 관한 설명인지 고르시오.

① 인기 가요 순위 발표
② 시상식 일정 소개
③ 수상자 발표
④ 수상자 선정 방법 안내
⑤ 수상 소감 발표

M If you are one of the lucky winners, please _____ _____ to the stage to _____ _____ _____. Finishing third is Minjung Lee. *[applause]* Stand over here, Minjung. And now _____ _____ _____ is Seongmi Park. *[applause]* And now the winner of the 10th annual Jeongdong Speech Contest is Hanna Jung. *[applause]* Now _____ _____ all of them. Then I'll give each person his or her prize.

13 대화를 듣고, 두 사람의 관계로 가장 알맞은 것을 고르시오.

① 아나운서 – 관객
② 해설자 – 코치
③ 코치 – 운동선수
④ 인터뷰기자 – 운동선수
⑤ 면접관 – 지원자

W David, David, come here for a short interview. *[pause]* You played a great game.
M Well, I _____ _____ _____. The coach wanted to be sure we were ready.
W I think you were ready. You _____ _____ _____.
M I hit the ball hard both times and I was lucky both shots went in.
W Can you say something to your fans before you go _____ _____ _____?
M Yes. Thanks for _____ _____ _____ so well.

14 대화를 듣고, 여자가 병원에 간 이유를 고르시오.

① 감기가 낫지 않아서
② 기침이 멈추지 않아서
③ 배가 아파서
④ 음식을 먹을 수 없어서
⑤ 목이 아파서

W Hello, doctor.
M Ah, Mrs. Bentz. _____ _____ you here today? Do you still have your cold?
W The cold _____ _____ _____. Well, I cough once a while, but I think I can get over with it soon.
M I'm happy to hear that. Now, what seems to be the problem, then?
W Well, I've been _____ _____ _____ for several days and I thought it was because of my cold.
M It might be.
W But it doesn't go away even after my cold has gone.
M Let's see what I can do. _____ _____ on the table. Have you eaten anything unusual lately?
W I think it might have started after I ate some seafood at a restaurant.

15 대화를 듣고, 남자가 지금 하려는 일을 고르시오.

① to go to bed
② to study for the job interview
③ to wash up and brush his teeth
④ to pick out his clothes for tomorrow
⑤ to polish his shoes for tomorrow

M I'm going to go to bed soon, Mom. I've got that big job interview tomorrow and I want to _____ _____.

W Good idea. Are your shoes polished?

M Yes, I just did that.

W What are you going to wear?

M That's the last thing I have to do. I'll do that right now before I _____ _____ and brush my teeth.

W I'll help you _____ _____ _____ _____. OK?

M Thanks, Mom.

16 다음을 듣고, 여자가 무슨 대회에 관하여 이야기하고 있는지를 고르시오.

① poetry
② painting
③ photograph
④ essay
⑤ speech

W Good morning, students. I'd like to tell you about a new contest for _____ _____ _____ _____. The city government is holding its 10th annual contest for middle school students. The contest will be held next Saturday afternoon _____ _____ _____ _____. You will be given a painting, then asked to _____ _____ _____ about the painting. Those wanting to enter the contest should get information from the school office. Thank you.

17 대화를 듣고, 오늘의 여행 일정을 순서대로 나타낸 것을 고르시오.

(A)   (B)

(C)   (D)

① (A)-(B)-(C)-(D) ② (A)-(D)-(C)-(B)
③ (A)-(C)-(D)-(B) ④ (B)-(A)-(D)-(C)
⑤ (C)-(D)-(A)-(B)

M What activities are on today's tour schedule?

W First, we're going to visit Gyeongbok Palace.

M Will we _____ _____ _____ at the Palace?

W Yes, you'll have time to tour the Palace then visit the museum.

M I guess we'll eat lunch at the Palace.

W No, we'll _____ _____ _____ _____ to a restaurant in Myeongdong. After lunch we'll go shopping in Myeongdong. And then in the late afternoon we're going to _____ _____ _____, 'Nanta.'

M It sounds like a busy day.

18 대화를 듣고, 남자에 대한 설명으로 알맞은 것을 고르시오.

① 매일 탁구 수업을 받는다.
② 몇 달 전에 탁구클럽에 가입했다.
③ 주로 7시 이후에 탁구 클럽에 간다.
④ 학교가 아주 일찍 끝난다.
⑤ 오늘 밤에 영화 보러 간다.

W Do you want to go _____ _____ _____ tonight?
M Sorry, I want to go play table tennis.
W Table tennis?
M Yes, a few weeks ago I joined a table tennis club at my _____ _____ _____. Last week I had a lesson.
W Do you have a lesson every time you go?
M No, I usually get there too late. There are no lessons after 7 o'clock. And my school never _____ _____ _____ _____ early. So I usually can't get to the table tennis club before 7 o'clock.

19 대화를 듣고, 여자의 마지막 말에 이어질 남자의 응답으로 가장 적절한 것을 고르시오.

① Don't mention it.
② I didn't know you are coming.
③ Don't worry. No one showed up yet.
④ I don't really understand what happened.
⑤ Thank you very much for following my directions.

[Doorbell rings.]
W Good evening, Minsung.
M Hi, Jihye. _____ _____ _____.
W Yes, I'm sorry I'm late. I _____ _____ _____ _____ getting here. I followed your directions, but I _____ _____ _____. I got on the wrong bus.
M _____

20 대화를 듣고, 여자의 마지막 말에 이어질 남자의 응답으로 가장 적절한 것을 고르시오.

① Be careful with your things.
② Yes, I read the newspaper.
③ No problem. I'll do it.
④ Don't put them there!
⑤ You just saved my life.

W _____ _____ _____ _____ now. Good bye, Mike.
M Bye, Anne. Hey, by the way, where are my glasses?
W Your glasses? Did you leave them _____ _____ _____?
M I don't see them. Can you _____ _____ _____ _____?
W Sure. [pause] Here they are. Under these old test papers.
M _____

1 다음을 듣고, 여자가 설명하는 그림으로 가장 알맞은 것을 고르시오.

①   ②

③   ④

⑤

2 대화를 듣고, 남자가 식당을 예약한 시각을 고르시오.

① 7:00 ② 7:30 ③ 8:00 ④ 8:30 ⑤ 9:00

3 다음을 듣고, MP3 플레이어에 대한 설명으로 옳지 <u>않은</u> 것을 고르시오.

MP3 player	Price	Storage space
iSong	$100	2GB
iLake	$200	8GB
iMachine	$325	16GB

①   ②   ③   ④   ⑤

4 다음을 듣고, 일기예보에 대한 설명으로 옳은 것을 고르시오.

① 오늘 오후에는 비가 온다.
② 4월에 눈이 온 적이 있었다.
③ 눈은 오래 내리지 않을 것이다.
④ 기온은 영상 5도로 떨어졌다.
⑤ 내일은 눈이 올 것이다.

5 대화를 듣고, 남자가 영화를 보러 가지 <u>못하는</u> 이유를 고르시오.

① 몸이 안 좋아서   ② 돈이 없어서
③ 아빠가 싫어하셔서서   ④ 시험공부를 해야 해서
⑤ 영화가 재미없어서

6 대화를 듣고, 여자가 겨울을 좋아하는 이유를 고르시오.

① 스키를 좋아해서
② 스노보드를 좋아해서
③ 방학이 길어서
④ 추운 계절을 좋아해서
⑤ 책을 읽지 않아도 되어서

7 다음을 듣고, 그림의 상황에 가장 어울리는 대화를 고르시오.

①   ②   ③   ④   ⑤

8 다음을 듣고, 상황에 가장 알맞은 표현을 고르시오.

① Thanks for inviting me.
② What's wrong with you?
③ I've heard a lot about you.
④ How is your vacation going?
⑤ It was nice meeting you.

9 대화를 듣고, 두 사람이 대화하는 장소를 고르시오.

① cafeteria
② laboratory
③ classroom
④ teacher's room
⑤ bookstore

10 다음을 듣고, 두 사람의 대화가 <u>어색한</u> 것을 고르시오.

①   ②   ③   ④   ⑤

11 대화를 듣고, 남자가 지불해야 할 금액을 고르시오.

DRINKS		ICE CREAM	
Coke	1,000 won	Vanilla	1,000 won
Milk	1,500 won	Strawberry	1,500 won
Ice tea	2,000 won	Chocolate	1,500 won

① 1,500 won
② 2,000 won
③ 3,000 won
④ 3,500 won
⑤ 4,000 won

12 다음을 듣고, 무엇에 관한 설명인지 고르시오.
① 재난 방송
② 응급 처치법
③ 지진 대피 요령
④ 소방 훈련
⑤ 산불 방지책

13 대화를 듣고, 두 사람의 관계로 가장 알맞은 것을 고르시오.
① clerk ..... shopper
② cook ..... customer
③ receptionist ..... guest
④ flight attendant ..... traveler
⑤ real estate agent ..... client

14 대화를 듣고, 여자가 치과의사가 되려는 이유를 고르시오.
① 돈을 많이 벌어서
② 규칙적인 시간에 일해서
③ 부모님이 원하셔서
④ 고등학교 때부터 꿈꾸던 일이어서
⑤ 응급실 의사가 되는 것보다 더 쉬워서

15 대화를 듣고, 두 사람이 지금 해야 할 일을 고르시오.
① 쇼핑하기
② 셔츠 교환하기
③ 식사하기
④ 집에 가기
⑤ 셔츠 사이즈 확인하기

16 다음을 듣고, 그림과 일치하는 것을 고르시오.

①   ②   ③   ④   ⑤

17 대화를 듣고, 무엇에 관한 내용인지 고르시오.
① 방 청소
② 용돈 절약
③ 화재 예방
④ 에너지 절약
⑤ 자연 보호

18 대화를 듣고, 내용과 일치하는 것을 고르시오.
① 박물관에 갔다, 관광안내소로 갈 것이다.
② 월요일에는 궁을 개방하지 않는다.
③ 커피를 마신 후, 관광안내소로 갈 것이다.
④ 택시를 타고, 박물관에 갈 것이다.
⑤ 박물관에 가서 커피를 마실 것이다.

[19-20] 대화를 듣고, 마지막 말에 이어질 응답으로 가장 적절한 것을 고르시오.

19
① Navy blue.
② Bright red.
③ Anything in yellow.
④ The color doesn't matter.
⑤ Bright colors suit you.

20
① Yes, she's still living.
② Yes, he's in good shape.
③ No, I don't know his age.
④ I eat healthy food every day.
⑤ Thanks for the picture.

T E S T 2

1 다음을 듣고, 여자가 설명하는 그림으로 가장 알맞은 것을 고르시오.

① ② ③ ④ ⑤

W While some types of these _____ _____ _____ _____, other ones cover our ears. These can be _____ _____ all kinds of electronic machines such as MP3 players, _____ _____ _____ or cell phones. These are used for listening to music or people talking. When we wear these, others cannot hear what we are listening to.

2 대화를 듣고, 남자가 식당을 예약한 시각을 고르시오.

① 7:00 ② 7:30 ③ 8:00
④ 8:30 ⑤ 9:00

W Hello, Neo Italian Restaurant. May I help you?
M Yes. I'd like to _____ _____ _____ for seven, please.
W We are full at seven.
M Sorry, I meant _____ _____ _____ _____ _____. I want the reservation for 8:30 or 9.
W _____ _____ _____ at 9 not 8:30.
M Perfect! Oh, my name is Bill Jones.

3 다음을 듣고, MP3 플레이어에 대한 설명으로 옳지 않은 것을 고르시오.

MP3 player	Price	Storage space
iSong	$100	2GB
iLake	$200	8GB
iMachine	$325	16GB

① ② ③
④ ⑤

W ① The iLake has _____ _____ _____ of the iMachine.
② The iMachine is _____ _____ _____ the iLake.
③ The iSong is half the price of the iLake.
④ The iLake has more storage space than the iSong.
⑤ The iMachine is _____ _____ _____ _____ the iLake.

4 다음을 듣고, 일기예보에 대한 설명으로 옳은 것을 고르시오.

① 오늘 오후에는 비가 온다.
② 4월에 눈이 온 적이 있었다.
③ 눈은 오래 내리지 않을 것이다.
④ 기온은 영상 5도로 떨어졌다.
⑤ 내일은 눈이 올 것이다.

W Good morning. I'm Mary Shriver for ZYX News and here is the weather forecast for April 9th. Cold northern winds will _____ _____ _____ the city this afternoon. It will be the first time in the history of the city that it has snowed in April. _____ _____ _____ _____ to minus 5. The snow, however, will not _____ _____. Tomorrow will be rainy not snowy.

5 대화를 듣고, 남자가 영화를 보러 가지 못하는 이유를 고르시오.

① 몸이 안 좋아서
② 돈이 없어서
③ 아빠가 싫어하셔서
④ 시험공부를 해야 해서
⑤ 영화가 재미없어서

W Let's go to a movie on Saturday.

M Really? I've asked you twice and both times you were busy.

W I was busy _____ _____. I had to study for exams. But Brad Pitt's new movie *Last Life* has just opened and I'd love to see it.

M Me too. But _____ _____ _____ _____ this week. I've already spent _____ _____ _____. And I can't ask my dad for some more. He'll get angry that I've spent it all already.

---

6 대화를 듣고, 여자가 겨울을 좋아하는 이유를 고르시오.

① 스키를 좋아해서
② 스노보드를 좋아해서
③ 방학이 길어서
④ 추운 계절을 좋아해서
⑤ 책을 읽지 않아도 되어서

M What is your _____ _____?

W Winter.

M Winter? So you like skiing or may be snowboarding.

W No, I don't ski. _____ _____ _____ _____.

M What do you like to do in winter?

W Nothing. I don't like cold weather. But I like winter because I get a long vacation. So I can rest at home and read the books since I don't have time to read _____ _____ _____ _____.

M OK. I got it.

---

7 다음을 듣고, 그림의 상황에 가장 어울리는 대화를 고르시오.

① ② ③
④ ⑤

① **W** Your seats are over here. _____ _____.
　M Thank you.

② **W** It was a great concert.
　M Yes, thank you _____ _____ _____.

③ **W** Yes, how may I help you?
　M Two tickets in A section, please.

④ **W** Did you _____ _____ _____?
　M Yes, thank you for giving me the tickets.

⑤ **W** Do you have a reservation?
　M Yes, I reserved a double room.

---

8 다음을 듣고, 상황에 가장 알맞은 표현을 고르시오.

① Thanks for inviting me.
② What's wrong with you?
③ I've heard a lot about you.
④ How is your vacation going?
⑤ It was nice meeting you.

M David meets a classmate, Jane, on the street while he is shopping downtown. He hasn't seen Jane since winter vacation began _____ _____ _____ _____. He is very glad to see her. _____ _____ _____. In this situation, what would he say to her?

9 대화를 듣고, 두 사람이 대화하는 장소를 고르시오.

① cafeteria ② laboratory
③ classroom ④ teacher's room
⑤ bookstore

M Your desk is at the front.

W Yes. It's good. I like to _____ _____ to the blackboard.

M Not me. I prefer the back.

W The teacher should be here _____ _____ _____.

M It takes a minute to walk from the teacher's room. What is our mathematics teacher like anyway?

W I heard he gives _____ _____ _____.

M Quick! Sit down at your desk. The teacher is here.

10 다음을 듣고, 두 사람의 대화가 <u>어색한</u> 것을 고르시오.

① ② ③
④ ⑤

① **M** What are you _____ _____?

  W I lost my homework. I cannot find it anywhere.

② **M** Help yourself to some more food.

  W Thank you. The cake is delicious.

③ **M** It's _____ _____.

  W You'd better take your umbrella.

④ **M** How did you go there?

  W I need to _____ _____ _____.

⑤ **M** How long are you going to study tonight?

  W For 3 hours. Until 10 p.m.

11 대화를 듣고, 남자가 지불해야 할 금액을 고르시오.

DRINKS		ICE CREAM	
Coke	1,000 won	Vanilla	1,000 won
Milk	1,500 won	Strawberry	1,500 won
Ice tea	2,000 won	Chocolate	1,500 won

① 1,500 won ② 2,000 won
③ 3,000 won ④ 3,500 won
⑤ 4,000 won

W Do you want to eat ice cream, Matthew?

M Sure. I'll have vanilla, Suyoung.

W Vanilla? Why don't you have a chocolate ice cream?

M Hmm… _____ _____ _____. Would you like some coke?

W I like coke very much. But now, I'll have some ice tea. _____ _____.

M How much are they? I'll _____ _____ _____.

12 다음을 듣고, 무엇에 관한 설명인지 고르시오.

① 재난 방송
② 응급 처치법
③ 지진 대피 요령
④ 소방 훈련
⑤ 산불 방지책

W OK, class. This is _____ _____ _____. We are practicing how to leave the school when there is a fire. No, _____ _____ _____! Stay calm. Don't bring your bag. There is no time. Now _____ _____ at the door. Is the door hot? If it's hot, don't open it. It's not hot. Now we will use _____ _____ _____ at the back of the school. Everyone, follow me.

---

13 대화를 듣고, 두 사람의 관계로 가장 알맞은 것을 고르시오.

① clerk ..... shopper
② cook ..... customer
③ receptionist ..... guest
④ flight attendant ..... traveler
⑤ real estate agent ..... client

W Your bed is on the second floor. Room D.
M How many beds are there in the room?
W There are eight beds in each room. You may _____ _____ _____ _____.
M Thank you. Is the TV room on the first floor?
W Yes, it is. This _____ _____ doesn't have a kitchen, though.
M That's OK. I don't want to cook. But I want to go to the TV room and talk to _____ _____.

---

14 대화를 듣고, 여자가 치과의사가 되려는 이유를 고르시오.

① 돈을 많이 벌어서
② 규칙적인 시간에 일해서
③ 부모님이 원하셔서
④ 고등학교 때부터 꿈꾸던 일이어서
⑤ 응급실 의사가 되는 것보다 더 쉬워서

W I will finish school in two months.
M Will you open your own dental clinic?
W _____ _____ _____.
M In high school, didn't you want to be an emergency doctor?
W Yes, but then I thought their working hours were too long. Dentists work _____ _____. It seems like a good job for me.
M Yes, I agree. They don't usually _____ _____ _____ in the middle of the night. They usually work 9 to 6.

---

15 대화를 듣고, 두 사람이 지금 해야 할 일을 고르시오.

① 쇼핑하기
② 셔츠 교환하기
③ 식사하기
④ 집에 가기
⑤ 셔츠 사이즈 확인하기

W Hey, I'm sorry I'm late. What did you buy?
M _____ _____ _____. You were a little late, so I started looking around at all the shops. This shirt was _____ _____.
W Nice color, but it looks really small. Jacob, it's a small.
M You think so? Oh, no. I should _____ _____ _____ _____ before I bought.
W Let's try and exchange it before we get something to eat.

16 다음을 듣고, 그림과 일치하는 것을 고르시오.

M ① The girl is _____ _____ _____.

② _____ _____ _____ _____ in front of the girl.

③ The girl is writing in her notebook.

④ The girl is _____ _____ the door.

⑤ The notebooks on the desk are closed.

①   ②   ③
④   ⑤

17 대화를 듣고, 무엇에 관한 내용인지 고르시오.

① 방 청소   ② 용돈 절약
③ 화재 예방   ④ 에너지 절약
⑤ 자연 보호

M Jennifer, you left your bedroom _____ _____.

W Oh, I'm sorry. I just forgot.

M You have to turn off lights when you're not in the room. We need to _____ _____.

W I know, Dad. I'm trying hard. Sometimes I _____ _____ _____ _____.

M That's a good girl.

18 대화를 듣고, 내용과 일치하는 것을 고르시오.

① 박물관에 갔다, 관광안내소로 갈 것이다.
② 월요일에는 궁을 개방하지 않는다.
③ 커피를 마신 후, 관광안내소로 갈 것이다.
④ 택시를 타고, 박물관에 갈 것이다.
⑤ 박물관에 가서 커피를 마실 것이다.

M The museum is closed on Monday.

W That's right. Let's go to _____ _____ _____ and check where else we can visit.

M Good idea. If we just go somewhere else, it might be closed too.

W I think all the _____ _____ _____ on Monday, but we should check.

M Let's take a taxi to the tourist information office.

W OK. But first I'd love a cup of coffee. _____ _____.

M OK. Let's go get some coffee.

19 대화를 듣고, 마지막 말에 이어질 응답으로 가장 적절한 것을 고르시오.

① Navy blue.
② Bright red.
③ Anything in yellow.
④ The color doesn't matter.
⑤ Bright colors suit you.

M I want to _____ _____ _____.

W Is there any problem with the jacket?

M I just don't like _____ _____. But my wife bought me a yellow jacket!

W Would you like to see some jackets in different colors?

M Definitely.

W Is there _____ _____ _____ you'd like?

M _____

20 대화를 듣고, 마지막 말에 이어질 응답으로 가장 적절한 것을 고르시오.

① Yes, she's still living.
② Yes, he's in good shape.
③ No, I don't know his age.
④ I eat healthy food every day.
⑤ Thanks for the picture.

M Can I _____ _____ _____ of your family?

W Sure, here is one over here. It was taken just a few weeks ago at a family dinner.

M _____ _____ _____. Is this your grandfather? How old is he?

W He's 64.

M He looks very healthy _____ _____ _____.

W _____

WORD AND EXPRESSION REVIEW • TEST 1-2

A Write down the definition of each word or phrase.

1 poem

2 receptionist

3 look for

4 lean against

5 be good at

6 greet

7 prefer

8 perform

9 save

10 palace

11 cute

12 customer

13 calm

14 pain

15 insect

16 community

17 exchange

18 section

19 cough

20 show up

B Match each word with the right definition.

1 expect ------

2 turn off ------

3 since ------

4 once a while ------

5 combination ------

6 continue ------

7 in a second ------

8 polish ------

9 return ------

10 finally ------

11 portable ------

12 follow ------

13 delicious ------

14 thirsty ------

15 applause ------

a 따르다, 지키다

b 맛있는

c 박수(갈채)

d 닦다, 갈다, 윤을 내다

e 기대하다, 예상하다

f 목마른

g 곧, 금방

h 들고 다닐 수 있는, 휴대용의

i 가끔씩 한 번

j ~이므로, ~이니까

k 돌려주다, 반환하다, 반송하다

l 결합, 조합, 세트

m 드디어, 마침내

n 끄다, 잠그다

o 계속하다, 지속하다

C Choose the best answer for the blank.

1 I'm really sorry. I _____ a mistake.

    a. made   b. took   c. got

2 I want to go _____, too. Can I join you?

    a. to fish   b. to fishing   c. fishing

3 You _____ you have a cold.

    a. feel like   b. seem to be   c. sound like

4 You _____ go see your doctor.

    a. have better   b. had better   c. had better to

5 Jane _____ meet me at 3. But she is not showing up.

    a. will   b. could   c. is supposed to

6 Thank you for _____.

    a. visiting us   b. visit us   c. to visit us

D Complete the short dialogues.

1 A: He looks healthy.

    B: Yes, he is in _____ _____.

2 A: Can you pass me the salt?

    B: Sure. Here _____ _____.

3 A: When can you finish this?

    B: It will _____ an hour to finish it.

4 A: Can I have this bread?

    B: Go ahead. Help _____.

5 A: I don't have enough money with me.

    B: Don't worry. I will _____ _____ it.

1 대화를 듣고, 남자가 설명하는 동물로 알맞은 것을 고르시오.

①
②
③
④
⑤

2 대화를 듣고, 여자의 장래 희망을 고르시오.

① nurse
② lawyer
③ doctor
④ pharmacist
⑤ professor

3 다음을 듣고, 표의 내용과 일치하지 않는 것을 고르시오.

	Bed time	Wake up time
Peter	10 p.m.	7 a.m.
Paul	9 p.m.	6 a.m.
John	11 p.m.	7:30 a.m.

① ② ③ ④ ⑤

4 다음을 듣고, 지금 세일하고 있는 물건을 고르시오.

① men's suits
② men's pants
③ men's dress shirts
④ men's dress shoes
⑤ men's neckties

5 다음을 듣고, 그림의 상황에 가장 어울리는 대화를 고르시오.

① ② ③ ④ ⑤

6 대화를 듣고, 두 사람이 지금 할 일로 알맞은 것을 고르시오.

① 놀이공원의 입장권을 산다
② 가게에서 우산을 산다
③ 은행에 들러서 돈을 찾는다
④ 식당에 가서 밥을 먹는다
⑤ 놀이기구를 탄다

7 다음을 듣고, 내용과 일치하지 않는 것을 고르시오.

① Bill Peterson은 대학 교수이다.
② 각 스피치는 3분간 이루어진다.
③ 청중은 스피치 중간에 박수를 칠 수 없다.
④ 대학생 영어 말하기 대회이다.
⑤ Bill Peterson은 심사위원장이다.

8 대화를 듣고, 그들이 이사를 가야 하는 이유를 고르시오.

① 새 친구들을 사귀려고
② 아빠의 직장이 너무 멀어서
③ 아빠의 직장이 이전을 해서
④ 아들의 학교 근처로 가려고
⑤ 살기 좋은 곳으로 가려고

9 대화를 듣고, 여자가 싫어하는 음악이라고 언급한 것을 고르시오.

① pop music
② folk music
③ Jazz
④ heavy metal
⑤ classical music

10 다음을 듣고, 무엇에 관한 내용인지 고르시오.

① 올바른 TV 시청 방법
② 방송 프로그램 선전
③ 성공적인 연애 노하우
④ 퀴즈쇼에 출연을 신청하는 방법
⑤ 9개의 방송 채널 안내

11 대화를 듣고, 남자가 엄마에게 전화를 건 이유를 고르시오.

① 아빠와 이야기하고 싶어서
② 열심히 공부한다는 것을 말하려고
③ 안부를 물으려고
④ 돈을 줘서 고맙다고 인사하려고
⑤ 돈이 필요해서

12 다음을 듣고, 상황에 가장 알맞은 표현을 고르시오.

① Can I have a fork, please?
② Please help yourself.
③ Everything looks delicious.
④ You don't have to help me.
⑤ Have you had enough?

13 대화를 듣고, 남자가 전화를 건 이유로 알맞은 것을 고르시오.

① Pauls 박사님과 통화하려고
② 회의시간이 변경되었음을 알리려고
③ 오늘 4시에 가겠다고 말하려고
④ 회의에 못 간다고 말하려고
⑤ 약속을 취소하려고

14 대화를 듣고, 남자가 하이킹을 가지 <u>않는</u> 이유를 고르시오.

① 감기에 걸릴 것 같아서
② 여자가 가지 말라고 해서
③ 급한 볼 일이 생겨서
④ 몸 상태가 별로 안 좋아서
⑤ 친구가 너무 아파서

15 다음을 듣고, 내일 학생들이 입을 수 있는 복장을 고르시오.

① 교복　　　② 사복　　　③ 정장
④ 한복　　　⑤ 학교 체육복

16 대화를 듣고, 남자가 여자의 집에서 나와야 하는 시각을 고르시오.

① 8:20　　　② 8:30　　　③ 8:40
④ 9:00　　　⑤ 9:20

17 대화를 듣고, 남자가 도서관에 온 이유를 고르시오.

① 친구를 만나러
② 집이 시끄러워서
③ 엄마가 가라고 해서
④ 공부 습관을 바꾸려고
⑤ 고모와 고모부를 만나러

18 대화를 듣고, 여자의 심정으로 가장 알맞은 것을 고르시오.

① jealousy　　　② proud
③ disappointed　　④ angry
⑤ comfortable

[19-20] 대화를 듣고, 여자의 마지막 말에 이어질 남자의 응답으로 가장 적절한 것을 고르시오.

19

① Two nights, three days.
② April 24th at 3 p.m.
③ It's a long way to Seorak Mountain.
④ We'll take a school bus.
⑤ It's my first time to Seorak Mountain.

20

① I love classical music.
② The Royal City Orchestra.
③ They play classical music.
④ The concert starts at 8 p.m.
⑤ Let's go now or we'll be late.

TEST
3

1 대화를 듣고, 남자가 설명하는 동물로 알맞은 것을 고르시오.

① ② ③ ④ ⑤

M I just watched a _____ _____ _____. Guess which animal the show was about.

W Does the animal live in Africa?

M No, it lives in Australia.

W Does it _____ _____ _____?

M No, it doesn't. But it does _____ _____ _____. And it is small and cute. It lives in trees and sleeps most of the day.

2 대화를 듣고, 여자의 장래 희망을 고르시오.

① nurse ② lawyer
③ doctor ④ pharmacist
⑤ professor

M Why do you think you'd be good at it?

W I'm very interested in the human body and _____ _____ _____ _____.

M And blood? Does the sight of blood scare you?

W No, not at all. I'd get a lot of pleasure from _____ _____ _____ _____ again.

M It's really good for you.

W And after graduating, I will volunteer in a hospital in a poor country that really needs my help.

3 다음을 듣고, 표의 내용과 일치하지 <u>않는</u> 것을 고르시오.

	Bed time	Wake up time
Peter	10 p.m.	7 a.m.
Paul	9 p.m.	6 a.m.
John	11 p.m.	7:30 a.m.

① ② ③
④ ⑤

M ① Peter _____ _____ _____ than John.

② Paul goes to bed later than Peter.

③ Peter and Paul wake up before John.

④ Paul _____ _____ than John.

⑤ John sleeps less than Peter.

4 다음을 듣고, 지금 세일하고 있는 물건을 고르시오.

① men's suits
② men's pants
③ men's dress shirts
④ men's dress shoes
⑤ men's neckties

W Good morning, shoppers! We hope you are enjoying your afternoon shopping at A-1 Department Store. _____ _____ _____ we are having a special one-hour sale on Men's dress shirts. We have many _____ _____ _____ that will _____ _____ almost any of the pants or suits you have or your husband has in his wardrobe. _____ _____ _____ _____ dress shirts are available, so hurry now to the men's clothing department.

5 다음을 듣고, 그림의 상황에 가장 어울리는 대화를 고르시오.

① ② ③
④ ⑤

① **W** We're lost.

　M Hmm... Yes. I wish I _____ _____ _____.

② **W** Excuse me, sir. Where is the museum?

　M I don't know. I am a tourist, too.

③ **W** That's $2 for the map.

　M Here you go. Thank you.

④ **W** I'll _____ _____ _____ _____.

　M OK. I'll stop the car.

⑤ **W** Can you see the museum on the map?

　M Yes, I can. I think it's _____ _____.

---

6 대화를 듣고, 두 사람이 지금 할 일로 알맞은 것을 고르시오.

① 놀이공원의 입장권을 산다
② 가게에서 우산을 산다
③ 은행에 들러서 돈을 찾는다
④ 식당에 가서 밥을 먹는다
⑤ 놀이기구를 탄다

M It's going to be a fun day at Wacky Wacky World Amusement Park.

W I hope so. Harold, do you have a jacket and an umbrella? _____ _____ _____.

M Yes, I do. Elizabeth, how much money do you _____ _____ _____?

W Not much. $10.

M We'd better stop at a bank and get some money then. I don't have much, either. Some restaurants _____ _____ _____ _____ don't take credit cards.

---

7 다음을 듣고, 내용과 일치하지 <u>않는</u> 것을 고르시오.

① Bill Peterson은 대학 교수이다.
② 각 스피치는 3분간 이루어진다.
③ 청중은 스피치 중간에 박수를 칠 수 없다.
④ 대학생 영어 말하기 대회이다.
⑤ Bill Peterson은 심사위원장이다.

M Good evening. Welcome to Middle School's English Speaking Contest. I'm _____ _____ _____, Bill Peterson. I teach at Hankook University and I'm very happy to be here. _____ _____ _____ _____ about the contest. Each student will get 3 minutes to give his or her speech. If a student speaks too long, I will stop him or her. Please keep the 3-minute rule. And everyone in the audience _____ _____ _____ _____ until each speech is finished. Thank you.

8 대화를 듣고, 그들이 이사를 가야 하는 이 유를 고르시오.

① 새 친구들을 사귀려고
② 아빠의 직장이 너무 멀어서
③ 아빠의 직장이 이전을 해서
④ 아들의 학교 근처로 가려고
⑤ 살기 좋은 곳으로 가려고

M I don't want to _____ _____ _____. I don't want to move!

W Don't worry, dear. I'm sure you'll make new friends.

M But it's not easy to make friends.

W Namsu, your dad spends too much time traveling to and from work. He has _____ _____ _____ _____ for a long time.

M I know, Mom. I'm trying to understand. But my friends.

W Three hours is too long to travel to and from work every day. We must _____ _____ _____ Dad's office.

9 대화를 듣고, 여자가 싫어하는 음악이라고 언급한 것을 고르시오.

① pop music ② folk music
③ Jazz ④ heavy metal
⑤ classical music

W Can you please _____ _____ _____ _____ ?

M Oh, I thought you liked to listen to music.

W I do. I love to listen to folk music and pop music, especially boy bands.

M No thanks! _____ _____ for me!

W Is this CD that you like to listen to?

M Not really. My brother left it _____ _____ _____. I like classical music and Jazz actually.

W Well, change the CD then. I don't like heavy metal music. Does your brother like it?

M Yes, he loves it.

10 다음을 듣고, 무엇에 관한 내용인지 고르시오.

① 올바른 TV 시청 방법
② 방송 프로그램 선전
③ 성공적인 연애 노하우
④ 퀴즈쇼에 출연을 신청하는 방법
⑤ 9개의 방송 채널 안내

M _____ _____ _____ _____ _____, *Days of the Week*. Will Bill marry Jennifer? Does Sam still love Jennifer? You'll have to watch tonight _____ _____ _____. After *Days of the Week*, there will be an exciting new game show, *The Million Dollar Question*. Watch channel nine. We bring you _____ _____ _____ _____.

11 대화를 듣고, 남자가 엄마에게 전화를 건 이유를 고르시오.

① 아빠와 이야기하고 싶어서
② 열심히 공부한다는 것을 말하려고
③ 안부를 물으려고
④ 돈을 줘서 고맙다고 인사하려고
⑤ 돈이 필요해서

[Telephone rings.]

W Hello.

M Hi, Mom, it's me. How is it going? How about Dad?

W Not bad. By the way, you sound tired. _____ _____?

M Actually I _____ _____ _____.

W What happened? Are you studying hard?

M Umm. I need some more money this month.

W OK. I will talk to Dad tonight. How much?

M _____ _____ _____. 100,000 won.

W That's not a little!

---

12 다음을 듣고, 상황에 가장 알맞은 표현을 고르시오.

① Can I have a fork, please?
② Please help yourself.
③ Everything looks delicious.
④ You don't have to help me.
⑤ Have you had enough?

W Minji invites an American friend, Paula, to her house _____ _____ _____. Minji's mother makes a typical Korean meal, bulgogi, rice, and soup with _____ _____ _____ _____ including kimchi. Minji, her father and mother _____ _____ _____ _____. After short conversation with Paula, Minji's father starts to eat. What does Minji say to Paula in this situation?

---

13 대화를 듣고, 남자가 전화를 건 이유로 알맞은 것을 고르시오.

① Pauls 박사님과 통화하려고
② 회의시간이 변경되었음을 알리려고
③ 오늘 4시에 가겠다고 말하려고
④ 회의에 못 간다고 말하려고
⑤ 약속을 취소하려고

[Telephone rings.]

W Hello. Watson Medical Center.

M Hello. My name is John Holmes. I _____ _____ _____ at 4 with Dr. Pauls.

W Yes, Mr. Holmes.

M Well, my boss has changed the time of _____ _____ _____ this afternoon.

W So you won't be able to come at 4?

M _____ _____.

W Do you want to make a new appointment now?

M No, I will phone tomorrow.

14 대화를 듣고, 남자가 하이킹을 가지 <u>않는</u> 이유를 고르시오.

① 감기에 걸릴 것 같아서
② 여자가 가지 말라고 해서
③ 급한 볼 일이 생겨서
④ 몸 상태가 별로 안 좋아서
⑤ 친구가 너무 아파서

W Do you have any plans for Sunday?
M Not really. Paul wants me to _____ _____ _____ him.
W But you don't want to go?
M I don't think I should go. I still have _____ _____ _____ _____ a cold. I might get sick again. I think I need to rest.
W You're _____ _____. You were very sick on Wednesday and Thursday.

15 다음을 듣고, 내일 학생들이 입을 수 있는 복장을 고르시오.

① 교복
② 사복
③ 정장
④ 한복
⑤ 학교 체육복

M Class, do you remember we have _____ _____ tomorrow? We will go to the Korean Folk Village. We will see examples of Korean _____ _____. You may come to school later _____ _____. The buses will leave at 9. Don't be late. And you shouldn't be wearing your uniform for this trip. Bye. See you tomorrow.

16 대화를 듣고, 남자가 여자의 집에서 나와야 하는 시각을 고르시오.

① 8:20
② 8:30
③ 8:40
④ 9:00
⑤ 9:20

W When do you have to go?
M At 9:00. I must be home by 9.
W When do you _____ _____ _____ my house then?
M Well, _____ _____ 20 minutes to walk home.
W So, you're leaving at 8:30?
M Well, I will just leave _____ _____ _____ _____.

17 대화를 듣고, 남자가 도서관에 온 이유를 고르시오.

① 친구를 만나러
② 집이 시끄러워서
③ 엄마가 가라고 해서
④ 공부 습관을 바꾸려고
⑤ 고모와 고모부를 만나러

W Hi, Minsung. I don't usually see you in the library at night.
M Well, I used to be able to study at home.
W What happened?
M My aunt and uncle are living with us _____ _____ _____. They are moving to Seoul and _____ _____.
W That's nice of your family to help them.
M Yes, it is. But the house is too noisy now. I need _____ _____ _____ _____.
W Well, that's why you come here.

18 대화를 듣고, 여자의 심정으로 가장 알맞은 것을 고르시오.

① jealousy
② proud
③ disappointed
④ angry
⑤ comfortable

M Is Carolyn's TV show about to start?

W Yes, it is. It's almost 8:00. Hurry up! *[pause]*

M I'm here. I'm so happy for her. She _____ _____ _____ her dream of being an actress.

W And we always encouraged her to do something she enjoyed. And now our daughter is _____ _____ _____ on a TV drama.

M All my friends are watching. I _____ _____ _____ when I told them she was on TV.

W I'm sure the drama will be successful. She's a great actress.

19 대화를 듣고, 여자의 마지막 말에 이어질 남자의 응답으로 가장 적절한 것을 고르시오.

① Two nights, three days.
② April 24th at 3 p.m.
③ It's a long way to Seorak Mountain.
④ We'll take a school bus.
⑤ It's my first time to Seorak Mountain.

M Mom, our school trip is next week.

W To Seorak Mountain?

M Yes. Third year students _____ _____ _____.

W You'll _____ _____.

M I hope so.

W _____ _____ _____ doesn't say how long the trip is.

M _____.

20 대화를 듣고, 여자의 마지막 말에 이어질 남자의 응답으로 가장 적절한 것을 고르시오.

① I love classical music.
② The Royal City Orchestra.
③ They play classical music.
④ The concert starts at 8 p.m.
⑤ Let's go now or we'll be late.

W Can you go to a movie tonight?

M I _____ _____ _____ _____ a concert, a classical music concert.

W Is there _____ _____?

M Yes, there is one at the Royal Elizabeth Concert Hall.

W Do you know _____ _____ _____?

M _____.

1 대화를 듣고, 상황에 알맞은 표지판을 고르시오.

①   ②

③   ④

⑤

2 대화를 듣고, 여자의 현재 직업을 고르시오.

① computer engineer
② programmer
③ reporter
④ writer
⑤ actress

3 대화를 듣고, 남자가 전화를 건 목적을 고르시오.

① 과학 실습 작품을 학교에 가져와달라고
② 과학 박람회를 보러 와달라고
③ 차로 데리러 와달라고
④ 과학 실습 작품 만드는 것을 도와달라고
⑤ 같이 교외로 드라이브 가자고

4 대화를 듣고, 여자가 남자에게 충고하고 있는 것으로 알맞은 것을 고르시오.

① to see a doctor
② to buy a new chair
③ to sit properly
④ to ask his mom
⑤ to sit and study all day

5 다음 자동응답기의 내용을 듣고, 질문에 답하시오.

① press 1   ② press 2   ③ press 3
④ press 4   ⑤ press 5

6 대화를 듣고, 여자가 하루 동안 복용할 약의 양과 복용 횟수를 고르시오.

① 한 스푼씩 – 하루에 한 번
② 한 스푼씩 – 하루에 두 번
③ 한 스푼씩 – 하루에 세 번
④ 두 스푼씩 – 하루에 한 번
⑤ 두 스푼씩 – 하루에 두 번

7 다음을 듣고, 비행기가 이륙할 시각을 고르시오.

① 3:00
② 3:30
③ 4:13
④ 4:30
⑤ 5:13

8 다음을 듣고, 수도의 오늘 날씨를 고르시오.

①   ②

③   ④

⑤

9 대화를 듣고, 대화가 일어나고 있는 장소로 가장 알맞은 것을 고르시오.

① beach
② fire station
③ swimming pool
④ cosmetic shop
⑤ amusement park

10 다음을 듣고, 두 사람의 대화가 <u>어색한</u> 것을 고르시오.

①   ②   ③   ④   ⑤

11 대화를 듣고, 여자의 심정으로 가장 알맞은 것을 고르시오.

① bored
② worried
③ surprised
④ satisfied
⑤ curious

12 대화를 듣고, 두 사람의 관계로 가장 알맞은 것을 고르시오.

① 매표소 직원 – 관객
② 항공사 직원 – 승객
③ 디자이너 – 모델
④ 의류 판매원 – 손님
⑤ 식당 점원 – 손님

13 대화를 듣고, 두 사람이 지불할 총 금액을 고르시오.

① $10
② $11.5
③ $12
④ $15
⑤ $18

14 다음을 듣고, 내용과 일치하지 <u>않는</u> 것을 고르시오.

① 학교에 체육관이 없다.
② 학생수가 800명이 넘는다.
③ 체육수업은 교실에서 한다.
④ 강당에서 학생들이 연극을 공연한다.
⑤ 공부하기 싫어하는 학생들을 더욱 격려한다.

15 대화를 듣고, 여자가 기름진 음식을 먹지 <u>않는</u> 이유를 고르시오.

① 맛이 없어서
② 살이 찔까봐
③ 저혈압이 있어서
④ 심장에 문제가 있어서
⑤ 의사가 먹지 말라고 해서

16 대화를 듣고, 여자의 직업으로 가장 알맞은 것을 고르시오.

① principal
② pharmacist
③ nurse
④ dentist
⑤ personal trainer

17 대화를 듣고, 이어지는 질문에 가장 알맞은 답을 고르시오.

① 색상이 마음에 안 들어서
② 남자친구가 싫어해서
③ 사이즈가 작아서
④ 사이즈가 커서
⑤ 디자인이 마음에 안 들어서

[18-19] 대화를 듣고, 여자의 마지막 말에 대한 남자의 응답으로 가장 적절한 것을 고르시오.

18

① That's okay. Never mind.
② No, I don't think he has a funny name.
③ Yes, I will connect you now.
④ Thank you very much for calling.
⑤ Yes, that's his name. I made a mistake.

19

① Where did she go?
② When will Susie be home?
③ Can you dial later, please?
④ Oh, I'm sorry to trouble you.
⑤ So then, please call Susie.

20 다음을 듣고, 상황에 가장 알맞은 표현을 고르시오.

① Can you finish the plan by this Sunday?
② I want you to meet my family this Sunday.
③ Would you like to join us this Sunday?
④ What time will your friends be ready on Sunday?
⑤ Do you have time to go to swimming pool this Sunday?

1 대화를 듣고, 상황에 알맞은 표지판을 고르 시오.

① ② ③ ④ ⑤

M Why did you _____ _____ _____ there?

W Oh, don't worry. Someone else will _____ _____ _____.

M That's a terrible attitude. And you could _____ _____ _____.

W A fine?

M That sign says there is a $50 fine for throwing garbage on the street.

W Hmm... I'd better pick it up. I know it's wrong. I will try to fix my _____ _____.

2 대화를 듣고, 여자의 현재 직업을 고르시오.

① computer engineer
② programmer
③ reporter
④ writer
⑤ actress

M Do you work at home?

W Yes, I get up and work in front of the computer for five or six hours. Sometimes I get a whole chapter done. Other times just _____ _____ _____.

M Then you take a break.

W Yes. I _____ _____ _____ in front of the computer after dinner and work for another 6 hours.

M Do you only write novels?

W No, I've also written _____ _____ _____.

3 대화를 듣고, 남자가 전화를 건 목적을 고르시오.

① 과학 실습 작품을 학교에 가져와달라고
② 과학 박람회를 보러 와달라고
③ 차로 데리러 와달라고
④ 과학 실습 작품 만드는 것을 도와달라고
⑤ 같이 교외로 드라이브 가자고

[Telephone rings.]

W Hello.

M Hi, Mom. It's me.

W Hi, William, are you coming home?

M I want to bring _____ _____ _____ home today.

W OK.

M The science _____ _____ _____ and there's no room to keep it in the classroom.

W I'm sure you can keep it in your bedroom.

M But it's a little big and heavy to carry _____ _____ _____ _____. Can you drive me home today?

W OK. I'll be there in 15 minutes.

4 대화를 듣고, 여자가 남자에게 충고하고 있는 것으로 알맞은 것을 고르시오.

① to see a doctor
② to buy a new chair
③ to sit properly
④ to ask his mom
⑤ to sit and study all day

M Oh, my back hurts. _____ _____ _____ _____ .

W You've been sitting and studying all day.

M These chairs are not comfortable. I need a new chair.

W Not really. That won't _____ _____ _____ . It might help, but to solve the problem, you have to sit properly. You don't sit _____ _____ _____ _____ .

M Ahh! You sound like my mom. 'Sit straight!' 'Sit straight!'

W Well, your mom is right!

---

5 다음 자동응답기의 내용을 듣고, 질문에 답하시오.

① press 1
② press 2
③ press 3
④ press 4
⑤ press 5

M Thank you for calling Westwood Middle School. It is past five o'clock and the school office is closed. If you want to _____ _____ _____ for the school office, press 1. If you want the phone to ring in the teacher's room, press 2. If you want _____ _____ _____ , press 3. To learn about school events, press 4. If you want to talk to _____ _____ _____ , press 5.

Q What should you press to see if the Art teacher is working at his desk?

---

6 대화를 듣고, 여자가 하루 동안 복용할 약의 양과 복용 횟수를 고르시오.

① 한 스푼씩 – 하루에 한 번
② 한 스푼씩 – 하루에 두 번
③ 한 스푼씩 – 하루에 세 번
④ 두 스푼씩 – 하루에 한 번
⑤ 두 스푼씩 – 하루에 두 번

M You take this _____ _____ .

W Should I take the medicine three times a day?

M Oh, no. Twice a day.

W But I'd like to recover from this cold since I have exams next week. Is it _____ _____ _____ take it after every meal?

M It's strong medicine. You only need to take it in the morning and at night.

W When I wake up and before I go to bed?

M That's right.

W _____ _____ _____ _____ _____ ?

M Just one teaspoon of cough syrup each time.

W OK. Thanks.

7 다음을 듣고, 비행기가 이륙할 시각을 고르시오.

① 3:00
② 3:30
③ 4:13
④ 4:30
⑤ 5:13

M Hello, Wonderful Airline passengers. I am sorry for the problems. The flight will not _____ _____ at 3:00 as planned. The icy, cold weather means we must be careful. The plane must _____ _____ _____ _____ _____. It takes time to remove the ice from the plane. The plane _____ _____ _____ to take off an hour and half later than it was scheduled. Please _____ _____ until we call you to get on the plane.

8 다음을 듣고, 수도의 오늘 날씨를 고르시오.

①
②
③
④
⑤

W Good morning. I'm Alice Smith _____ _____ _____ _____ weather reports. Good news for our nation's capital. The hurricane that hit the southern part of the country yesterday will not reach the capital. The hurricane _____ _____ _____ _____. The capital area will be windy and rainy today. But we must help people living in the south _____ _____. The hurricane _____ _____ _____ there.

9 대화를 듣고, 대화가 일어나고 있는 장소로 가장 알맞은 것을 고르시오.

① beach
② fire station
③ swimming pool
④ cosmetic shop
⑤ amusement park

M Ouch! _____ _____ _____.

W Put some more suntan lotion on your back.

M Can you help me out with that?

W Sure. Have you seen our son, Billy? Where is he?

M He's swimming in the ocean _____ _____ _____ _____ boys over there.

W Good. _____ _____ _____ he is having fun.

10 다음을 듣고, 두 사람의 대화가 <u>어색한</u> 것을 고르시오.

①   ②   ③
④   ⑤

① **M** Ted is in the hospital. He broke his leg.

　W Oh, really? I think he is nice to his friends.

② **M** Seongmin's grandmother _____ _____ yesterday.

　W I'm sorry to hear that.

③ **M** How do you like the movie?

　W The story is great. _____ _____ _____ _____.

④ **M** What do you do on weekends?

　W I help my parents _____ _____ _____. Then I play with my sister.

⑤ **M** I _____ _____ _____ _____ on the test.

　W Good for you. You studied very hard.

11 대화를 듣고, 여자의 심정으로 가장 알맞은 것을 고르시오.

① bored
② worried
③ surprised
④ satisfied
⑤ curious

M Mom, can I have some money _____ _____ _____ ?

W Jacob, I gave you some money for pens last week.

M Umm... I lost my pencil case.

W And you _____ _____ _____ _____ sneakers last week, too. You must be more careful!

M I can just buy new ones.

W Jacob! That's _____ _____ _____ . Don't talk like that! I don't have a lot of money. I'm very unhappy with you.

12 대화를 듣고, 두 사람의 관계로 가장 알맞은 것을 고르시오.

① 매표소 직원 – 관객
② 항공사 직원 – 승객
③ 디자이너 – 모델
④ 의류 판매원 – 손님
⑤ 식당 점원 – 손님

W How much _____ _____ _____ _____ ?

M 32 dollars and 25 cents, ma'am.

W _____ _____ _____ ?

M That's right.

W Wait a moment. I really think I should get that muffler for my mother.

M The one in red you just tried on?

W No, the one _____ _____ _____ . You told me that it's on sale, right?

M That's correct, ma'am.

W Please _____ _____ _____ .

M Certainly. Do you want me to put that in the same bag?

13 대화를 듣고, 두 사람이 지불할 총 금액을 고르시오.

① $10   ② $11.5   ③ $12
④ $15   ⑤ $18

W That was a nice meal. The food is great at this new restaurant.

M _____ _____ _____ _____ .

W So what does the total bill _____ _____ ?

M $10.

W I thought it would be at least $15. Is that _____ _____ _____ ?

M Yes, but I'll leave a 15% tip.

W _____ _____ 20%. The service was really good.

M Okay.

14 다음을 듣고, 내용과 일치하지 <u>않는</u> 것을 고르시오.

① 학교에 체육관이 없다.
② 학생수가 800명이 넘는다.
③ 체육수업은 교실에서 한다.
④ 강당에서 학생들이 연극을 공연한다.
⑤ 공부하기 싫어하는 학생들을 더욱 격려한다.

M Hello. I'm John Smith, the principal of Sweet Valley Middle School. I have over 800 students in my school. Some like to study hard, but some do not. I _____ _____ _____ those who don't like to study hard. I try to make learning fun. We don't _____ _____ _____ at our school, so students take physical education classes outside. But we have a nice theater. Students _____ _____ _____ every semester.

15 대화를 듣고, 여자가 기름진 음식을 먹지 않는 이유를 고르시오.

① 맛이 없어서
② 살이 찔까봐
③ 저혈압이 있어서
④ 심장에 문제가 있어서
⑤ 의사가 먹지 말라고 해서

M Why don't we have fried chicken?
W _____ _____, I don't want fried chicken. Let's find another place to eat.
M Fried chicken _____ _____.
W But it's not healthy.
M You don't have to worry. You're really thin.
W I may be thin, but my doctor said I shouldn't eat _____ _____.
M Do you have a heart problem?
W I have _____ _____ _____. I will have a problem if I'm not careful.

16 대화를 듣고, 여자의 직업으로 가장 알맞은 것을 고르시오.

① principal
② pharmacist
③ nurse
④ dentist
⑤ personal trainer

M Will it hurt?
W No, it doesn't really hurt.
M But _____ _____ is so long.
W Don't worry, _____ _____ will help you feel better. Your cold will _____ _____ _____.
M OK. *[pause]* Ah...
W _____ _____. *[pause]* We're almost there. That's it.

17 대화를 듣고, 이어지는 질문에 가장 알맞은 답을 고르시오.

① 색상이 마음에 안 들어서
② 남자친구가 싫어해서
③ 사이즈가 작아서
④ 사이즈가 커서
⑤ 디자인이 마음에 안 들어서

M Hello, ma'am. May I help you?

W Yes, please. I'd like to _____ _____ _____. It was a present from my boyfriend.

M Is it the wrong color?

W No, it's not the color. _____ _____ _____. He bought a medium.

M So you want to exchange it for a smaller one. Is that correct?

W Yes, _____ _____ _____ _____ you have this sweater in a small size?

Q Why does she want to exchange the sweater?

---

18 대화를 듣고, 여자의 마지막 말에 대한 남자의 응답으로 가장 적절한 것을 고르시오.

① That's okay. Never mind.
② No, I don't think he has a funny name.
③ Yes, I will connect you now.
④ Thank you very much for calling.
⑤ Yes, that's his name. I made a mistake.

[Telephone rings.]

W Hello. Can I help you?

M Yes, I _____ _____ _____ _____ Mr. Cairns.

W Cairns? Mr. Cairns doesn't _____ _____.

M _____ _____ _____. He is a manager.

W Do you mean Mr. Carson?

M _____

---

19 대화를 듣고, 여자의 마지막 말에 대한 남자의 응답으로 가장 적절한 것을 고르시오.

① Where did she go?
② When will Susie be home?
③ Can you dial later, please?
④ Oh, I'm sorry to trouble you.
⑤ So then, please call Susie.

[Telephone rings.]

W Hello.

M Hello. Can I please talk to Susie?

W Susie? No one _____ _____ _____ lives here.

M Is this 9-3-6-2-2-0-1?

W No, you _____ _____ _____ _____. It's 9-3-6-2-2-0-2.

M _____

---

20 다음을 듣고, 상황에 가장 알맞은 표현을 고르시오.

① Can you finish the plan by this Sunday?
② I want you to meet my family this Sunday.
③ Would you like to join us this Sunday?
④ What time will your friends be ready on Sunday?
⑤ Do you have time to go to swimming pool this Sunday?

W You and two other friends are going to the beach this Sunday morning. Then you remember that another friend of yours, Bill, likes swimming and _____ _____ _____ _____ very much. You want to ask Bill _____ _____ _____ this Sunday. You tell Bill about the plans to go to the beach. After telling Bill your plan to go to the beach, what _____ _____ _____ _____?

WORD AND EXPRESSION REVIEW • TEST 3-4

A Write down the definition of each word or phrase.

1	pouch	11	attitude	
2	graduate	12	passenger	
3	volunteer	13	take off	
4	clap	14	remove	
5	typical	15	patiently	
6	appointment	16	direction	
7	traditional	17	pass away	
8	encourage	18	owe	
9	notice	19	bill	
10	garbage	20	come along	

B Match each word with the right definition.

1	fine	_____	a	~을 겁나게 하다, 위협하다
2	grade	_____	b	현재, 바로 지금
3	disease	_____	c	이용할 수 있는, 가능한
4	gymnasium	_____	d	판사, 심판관, 심사원
5	available	_____	e	(소리를) 줄이다
6	turn down	_____	f	발견하다, 찾아내다, 해결하다
7	find out	_____	g	가져오다, 데려오다
8	bring	_____	h	벌금, 과태료
9	judge	_____	i	소설
10	include	_____	j	적당히, 알맞게, 올바르게
11	scare	_____	k	교장, 사장, 회장, 우두머리
12	at the moment	_____	l	점수, 성적, 평가
13	properly	_____	m	~을 포함하다
14	principal	_____	n	체육관, (실내) 경기장
15	novel	_____	o	병, 질병

C Choose the best answer for the blank.

1 This tie goes _____ this jacket.

   a. to   b. on   c. with

2 They are about _____ dinner.

   a. eat   b. to eat   c. eating

3 Stay here _____ you want to.

   a. as long as   b. as far as   c. as good as

4 Would you _____ a message?

   a. leave   b. have   c. make

5 I can't stop _____ while I'm watching the show.

   a. laugh   b. to laugh   c. laughing

6 It was nice _____ you to help me.

   a. for   b. to   c. of

D Complete the short dialogues.

1 A: I was in New York last summer.

   B: So _____ _____.

2 A: It is 8:40 now.

   B: Yes, it is 20 _____ 9.

3 A: _____ did you like the movie?

   B: It was great. What about you?

4 A: Look! This CD is 20% off.

   B: Right. It's _____ _____.

5 A: Do you live in Jongno?

   B: No. I _____ _____ live there, but now I live in Gangnam.

1 대화를 듣고, 여자가 본 표지판을 고르시오.

①
②
③
④
⑤

2 대화를 듣고, 미스 영국으로 선발된 여성의 몸무게를 고르시오.

① 35 kg   ② 45 kg   ③ 60 kg
④ 70 kg   ⑤ 80 kg

3 대화를 듣고, 남자가 가고자 하는 곳을 고르시오.

4 대화를 듣고, 두 사람의 대화가 이루어지고 있는 장소로 알맞은 것을 고르시오.

① stationery store   ② post office
③ hospital   ④ bank
⑤ butcher's

5 대화를 듣고, 남자가 병원에 가는 이유로 알맞은 것을 고르시오.

① 정기검진 받으러   ② 취직하러
③ 아파서   ④ 예방접종 맞으러
⑤ 근처에 볼 일이 있어서

6 대화를 듣고, 남자의 심정으로 가장 알맞은 것을 고르시오.

① thankful   ② worried
③ jealous   ④ relieved
⑤ pleased

7 대화를 듣고, 여자가 전화를 건 목적으로 알맞은 것을 고르시오.

① 책을 가져가라고
② 책을 반납하려고
③ 책을 주문하려고
④ 책의 품절을 알리려고
⑤ 찾는 책이 있는지 확인하려고

8 다음 자동응답기의 내용을 듣고, 질문에 답하시오.

① 1   ② 2   ③ 3   ④ 4   ⑤ 5

9 대화를 듣고, 여자가 지불해야 할 총 금액이 얼마인지 고르시오.

① 4,000원   ② 4,100원
③ 4,200원   ④ 4,500원
⑤ 5,000원

10 다음을 듣고, 무엇에 관한 내용인지 고르시오.

① 교장실에서는 정숙하기
② 교실에서 조용히 책 읽고 있기
③ 수업시간에 게임을 한 학생들 혼내기
④ 말썽 피운 학생들을 교장실로 데려가기
⑤ 수업 중에 떠들고 돌아다닌 학생들 벌주기

11 대화를 듣고, 내용과 일치하지 <u>않는</u> 것을 고르시오.

① 남자는 주말에 수업 준비를 해야 한다.
② 남자는 주말에 시험지를 채점해야 한다.
③ 남자는 가족과 함께 승마를 계획 중이다.
④ 여자는 주말에 바빠서 말을 타러 가지 못한다.
⑤ 남자는 여자에게 말 타러 가자고 제안하고 있다.

12 다음을 듣고, 그림의 상황에 가장 어울리는 대화를 고르시오.

① 　　② 　　③ 　　④ 　　⑤

13 대화를 듣고, 여자의 직업으로 알맞은 것을 고르시오.

① flight attendant 　　② taxi driver
③ veterinarian 　　④ cashier
⑤ bank teller

14 다음을 듣고, 병에 걸리지 않으려면 어떻게 해야 하는지 고르시오.

① 친구들과 눈을 마주치지 말아야 한다.
② 병원에 가서 주사를 받아야 한다.
③ 눈을 절대 비비지 말아야 한다.
④ 손을 자주 씻어야 한다.
⑤ 학교에 나오지 말고, 집에 있어야 한다.

15 대화를 듣고, 내용과 일치하지 <u>않는</u> 것을 고르시오.

① The man didn't know about White Day.
② The man and the woman are just friends.
③ The man will go to meet his girlfriend right now.
④ The man will buy the woman some candies.
⑤ The woman explains the man about White Day.

16 대화를 듣고, 무엇에 관한 내용인지 고르시오.

① 에너지 절약 　　② 폭설 대비
③ 기후 변화 　　④ 환경 보호
⑤ 일기예보

17 다음을 듣고, 이어지는 질문에 알맞은 답을 고르시오.

① 학교 컴퓨터실을 구비하려고
② 현장 학습 비용 마련을 위해
③ 학생들에게 장학금을 주기 위해
④ 학교 운동회 비용을 충당하려고
⑤ 불우이웃돕기 성금을 마련하려고

[18-19] 대화를 듣고, 남자의 마지막 말에 이어질 여자의 응답으로 가장 적절한 것을 고르시오.

18

① Yes, it's No. 45.
② Every 15 minutes.
③ It's 8:30.
④ No, it's the wrong bus.
⑤ Bus No. 35 not 45.

19

① I like the teacher who teaches it.
② We are studying European history now.
③ Our country has a long history.
④ I have a history test next week.
⑤ My sister is good at history.

20 다음을 듣고, 상황에 가장 어울리는 표현을 고르시오.

① I'll hold the door for you.
② Do you have my notebook?
③ What's today's homework?
④ Be careful or you'll drop something.
⑤ You shouldn't carry so many things.

TEST **5**

1 대화를 듣고, 여자가 본 표지판을 고르시오.

① ② ③ ④ ⑤

W There is _____ _____ _____ . Which way should I turn?

M Keep going straight.

W I can't. The sign _____ _____ _____ means I must turn left or right.

M Oh, sorry. I didn't see the sign. Turn left. You've got to go north on Route 66.

W OK. _____ _____ _____ .

2 대화를 듣고, 미스 영국으로 선발된 여성의 몸무게를 고르시오.

① 35 kg
② 45 kg
③ 60 kg
④ 70 kg
⑤ 80 kg

M Wow! Look at this picture in the newspaper. Her name is Chloe. She is _____ _____ _____ of the beauty contest to be Miss England.

W Oh, I know the story. She is a little fat. The story says she weighs 25kg more than the other girls.

M 25kg more than the other girls? Wow!

W Yes. Beauty is in the _____ _____ _____ _____ , you know.

M OK. How much does she weigh?

W Well, most of _____ _____ _____ weigh 45kg.

3 대화를 듣고, 남자가 가고자 하는 곳을 고르시오.

M Excuse me, could you please tell me where the Queen Elizabeth Theater is?

W It's not too far away. _____ _____ for one block and then turn left.

M Straight for one block. Turn left.

W Then it'll be _____ _____ _____ in the middle of the block.

M On my right or left? Could you _____ _____ _____ ?

W On your right.

M I see. Thank you very much.

W You're welcome.

4 대화를 듣고, 두 사람의 대화가 이루어지고 있는 장소로 알맞은 것을 고르시오.

① stationery store
② post office
③ hospital
④ bank
⑤ butcher's

W Can I help you?

M Yes, please. Is there any way I can have this delivered tomorrow?

W Only if you send it _____ _____ _____.

M Thank god! How much will that be?

W _____ _____ _____ how much it weighs. I'll check it now. *[pause]* $9.00.

M Well, that's a lot more than I expected. Well, I guess I have no other choice. Here you go.

W I'm really sorry. I _____ _____ 100 dollar bill. Do you have anything smaller?

M I only have five dollars with me. Well, how long will it take if it is _____ _____ _____?

W It usually takes 3 business days. And it is 4 dollars and five cents.

5 대화를 듣고, 남자가 병원에 가는 이유로 알맞은 것을 고르시오.

① 정기검진 받으러
② 취직하러
③ 아파서
④ 예방접종 맞으러
⑤ 근처에 볼 일이 있어서

M Which bus goes near the Broadway Medical Center?

W Bus No. 56. Are you sick?

M No, _____ _____. I am traveling with my family to Cambodia next vacation. They have _____ _____ _____ _____ that we don't get here anymore.

W On, really? I didn't know that. So?

M We need _____ _____ _____ so we won't get sick while we are there.

6 대화를 듣고, 남자의 심정으로 가장 알맞은 것을 고르시오.

① thankful
② worried
③ jealous
④ relieved
⑤ pleased

W He's a really handsome actor. I'd love to meet him one day.

M Maybe you'd like to _____ _____ _____ _____ tonight instead of me.

W Of course I would.

M What?

W Richard, _____ _____. It's my imagination. I know it'll never happen. No one is going to _____ _____ _____ from you.

M _____ _____ _____ if I said the same thing.

7 대화를 듣고, 여자가 전화를 건 목적으로 알맞은 것을 고르시오.

① 책을 가져가라고
② 책을 반납하려고
③ 책을 주문하려고
④ 책의 품절을 알리려고
⑤ 찾는 책이 있는지 확인하려고

[Telephone rings.]

M Hello.

W Hello. May I please speak with Jinsung Lee.

M _____ _____ _____ _____ .

W This is the Best Bookstore. The book _____ _____ _____ last week arrived this morning.

M Oh, that's great news.

W You can come down and pick it up _____ _____ _____ .

M Thank you. I'll be down to pick it up later today.

W You're welcome. Bye.

---

8 다음 자동응답기의 내용을 듣고, 질문에 답하시오.

① 1
② 2
③ 3
④ 4
⑤ 5

W Thank you for calling High1 Hotel in Seoul. Press 1 to learn about our rooms and what is in each room. Press 2 to learn about _____ _____ _____ _____ in each of our rooms. Press 3 to talk to a _____ _____ so that you can make a reservation. Press 4 _____ _____ _____ to the hotel's buffet restaurant. Press 5 to be connected to the hotel's coffee shop. Thank you for calling High 1 Hotel.

Q What should you press to reserve a room?

---

9 대화를 듣고, 여자가 지불해야 할 총 금액이 얼마인지 고르시오.

① 4,000원
② 4,100원
③ 4,200원
④ 4,500원
⑤ 5,000원

M _____ _____ _____ ?

W Yes, it is.

M So you have two notebooks, _____ _____ 800 won, two pens, oh, this pen is 1,000 won and the other one is 1,500.

W So how much do I owe you?

M 4,100 won. Do you need a bag?

W Yes, please.

M _____ _____ _____ is 100 won.

W OK. Here is 5,000 won.

---

10 다음을 듣고, 무엇에 관한 내용인지 고르시오.

① 교장실에서는 정숙하기
② 교실에서 조용히 책 읽고 있기
③ 수업시간에 게임을 한 학생들 혼내기
④ 말썽 피운 학생들을 교장실로 데려가기
⑤ 수업 중에 떠들고 돌아다닌 학생들 벌주기

M OK. Class, I have to go down to the principal's office _____ _____ _____ _____ . I want you to read the story on pages 46 and 47. _____ _____ ! _____ ! Last time I left the classroom for 10 minutes, you guys weren't studying. When I came back, some students were standing and talking. You were playing games. This time you must study _____ _____ _____ _____ !

11 대화를 듣고, 내용과 일치하지 <u>않는</u> 것을 고르시오.

① 남자는 주말에 수업 준비를 해야 한다.
② 남자는 주말에 시험지를 채점해야 한다.
③ 남자는 가족과 함께 승마를 계획 중이다.
④ 여자는 주말에 바빠서 말을 타러 가지 못한다.
⑤ 남자는 여자에게 말 타러 가자고 제안하고 있다.

M What are you going to do this weekend, Paula?
W I have to _____ _____ _____.
M Oh, so do I. And I have to prepare some lessons for next week. But I was thinking of going _____ _____ with my family.
W Sounds like fun.
M _____ _____ _____ I am asking. Does your family want to join my family? After horseback riding, we can go eat in a restaurant.
W I'll ask my husband and son tonight.

12 다음을 듣고, 그림의 상황에 가장 어울리는 대화를 고르시오.

① ② ③
④ ⑤

① **W** This show is really boring.
　M _____ _____ _____ then. I don't want to watch it either.
② **W** Jim, where are you now?
　M I'm in the kitchen. I'm _____ _____ _____ for dinner.
③ **W** _____ _____. The food was delicious.
　M Are you sure you don't want anymore?
④ **W** Would you tell me how long it takes to fly to LA?
　M It takes 12 hours from Seoul.
⑤ **W** Nice to meet you. Where are you from?
　M I'm from Vancouver, Canada.

13 대화를 듣고, 여자의 직업으로 알맞은 것을 고르시오.

① flight attendant
② taxi driver
③ veterinarian
④ cashier
⑤ bank teller

W How is it going, Mr. Ford?
M Hi. Mendy.
W Are you going somewhere? Why do you need all these?
M I'm going away for a while with my dog to visit my friends in Seattle.
W I see. Do you need a bag for these?
M That will be nice. May I _____ _____ _____ _____?
W Sure. Here you go.
M Thanks.
W Is there anything else you're looking for?
M No, _____ _____ _____ _____.
W All right. *[pause]* The total is $45.75.
M Do you accept cards?
W Sure. Sign right here. *[pause]* _____ _____ _____.

14 다음을 듣고, 병에 걸리지 않으려면 어떻게 해야 하는지 고르시오.

① 친구들과 눈을 마주치지 말아야 한다.
② 병원에 가서 주사를 받아야 한다.
③ 눈을 절대 비비지 말아야 한다.
④ 손을 자주 씻어야 한다.
⑤ 학교에 나오지 말고, 집에 있어야 한다.

W Students, please _____ _____. Many students are sick. Their eyes are red and they are not at school. You can get this disease easily. Everyone touches their eyes _____ _____ _____. It's hard to stop doing that. So if you don't want to get sick, you must _____ _____ _____ _____. If you have clean hands, you may not get sick.

15 대화를 듣고, 내용과 일치하지 않는 것을 고르시오.

① The man didn't know about White Day.
② The man and the woman are just friends.
③ The man will go to meet his girlfriend right now.
④ The man will buy the woman some candies.
⑤ The woman explains the man about White Day.

M White Day! What's that, Jihyun?
W On White Day men give women candies. On Valentine's Day women give men chocolates.
M _____ _____. In America there is no White Day.
W Really? Well, today is White Day, Ted, do you have some candies for me?
M We're just friends.
W Friends give friends candies. _____ _____ here in Korea. Giving candies is not only about love. It's about friendship.
M Hmm... OK, _____ _____ _____ candy store?

16 대화를 듣고, 무엇에 관한 내용인지 고르시오.

① 에너지 절약
② 폭설 대비
③ 기후 변화
④ 환경 보호
⑤ 일기예보

M Winters were colder when I was a child.
W But winter is cold now, Daddy.
M It was much colder when I was a kid. We had ten times _____ _____ in winter. Not one or two.
W Oh, I know. We learned about this in school. The earth's _____ _____.
M Some scientists say it is.
W What about summers? Are they hotter now?
M I don't know. I spend my summer days _____ _____ _____ _____.

17 다음을 듣고, 이어지는 질문에 알맞은 답을 고르시오.

① 학교 컴퓨터실을 구비하려고
② 현장 학습 비용 마련을 위해
③ 학생들에게 장학금을 주기 위해
④ 학교 운동회 비용을 충당하려고
⑤ 불우이웃돕기 성금을 마련하려고

M Buy a ticket to _____ _____ _____ to win a computer! Hurry! Before all the tickets are sold. Tickets are $5. The money will be used to _____ _____ our school field trip to Jeju Island. The winners will get a new laptop computer. Since only 300 tickets _____ _____ _____, you'll have a good chance to win. Hurry!

Q Why are they trying to _____ _____?

18 대화를 듣고, 남자의 마지막 말에 이어질 여자의 응답으로 가장 적절한 것을 고르시오.

① Yes, it's No. 45.
② Every 15 minutes.
③ It's 8:30.
④ No, it's the wrong bus.
⑤ Bus No. 35 not 45.

M Which bus do I take to go to the Northend?

W Number 45. It stops right here.

M How often does it _____ _____ _____ _____?

W I don't know. But it says on the bus schedule sign right there.

M I can't see it. Can you _____ _____ _____ _____, please?

W _____

19 대화를 듣고, 남자의 마지막 말에 이어질 여자의 응답으로 가장 적절한 것을 고르시오.

① I like the teacher who teaches it.
② We are studying European history now.
③ Our country has a long history.
④ I have a history test next week.
⑤ My sister is good at history.

M What is your _____ _____ at school?

W I liked English before. But now history is my favorite.

M History? I don't like history. You have to remember too many _____ _____ _____.

W Well, I wouldn't say 'too many,' but you do have to remember a lot.

M Why do you like it then?

W _____

20 다음을 듣고, 상황에 가장 어울리는 표현을 고르시오.

① I'll hold the door for you.
② Do you have my notebook?
③ What's today's homework?
④ Be careful or you'll drop something.
⑤ You shouldn't carry so many things.

W You are _____ _____ _____ at lunchtime. One of your teachers is walking down the hallway. _____ _____ _____ many books and lots of notebooks. She is going to put them in the classroom. You see that the teacher won't be able to _____ _____ _____ _____ because she is carrying too many things. You want to _____ _____ _____ _____. In this situation, what would you say to the teacher?

1 다음을 듣고, 남자가 설명하는 그림으로 가장 알맞은 것을 고르시오.

①
②

③
④

⑤

2 대화를 듣고, 남자가 사진을 찾을 수 있는 시각을 고르시오.

① 2:00 p.m.　　② 2:13 p.m.
③ 2:30 p.m.　　④ 2:43 p.m.
⑤ 3:00 p.m.

3 다음을 듣고, 표의 내용과 <u>다른</u> 것을 고르시오.

<Average amount of weekly allowance spent and saved>

	Allowance	Money spent	Money saved
John	$10	$7	$3
Terry	$15	$15	0
Bob	$10	$5	$5

① ② ③ ④ ⑤

4 다음을 듣고, 요일별 날씨가 바르게 연결된 것을 고르시오.

① today - cloudy　　② today - foggy
③ tomorrow - rainy　④ tomorrow - windy
⑤ tomorrow - warm

5 대화를 듣고, 엄마가 아침식사를 준비하지 <u>못하는</u> 이유를 고르시오.

① 병원에 입원해서　　② 너무 바빠서
③ 늦잠을 자서　　　　④ 감기에 걸려서
⑤ 일찍 출근해서

6 대화를 듣고, 여자가 머리를 짧게 자른 이유를 고르시오.

① 긴 머리가 싫증나서
② 날씨가 너무 더워서
③ 짧은 머리가 더 잘 어울려서
④ 분위기를 바꿔보려고
⑤ 짧은 머리가 유행이어서

7 다음을 듣고, 그림의 상황에 가장 어울리는 대화를 고르시오.

① ② ③ ④ ⑤

8 다음을 듣고, 상황에 가장 알맞은 표현을 고르시오.

① Jisun, do you still have my pencil?
② Jisun, it's OK. I'll lend you a pencil.
③ Jisun, do you have an extra pencil?
④ I'm sorry, but I haven't got your pencil.
⑤ Jisun, what do you think about this new pencil?

9 대화를 듣고, 두 사람이 대화하는 장소를 고르시오.

① playground
② fitness club
③ mountain
④ aerobics center
⑤ swimming pool

10 다음을 듣고, 두 사람의 대화가 <u>어색한</u> 것을 고르시오.

① ② ③ ④ ⑤

11 대화를 듣고, 남자가 지불해야 할 금액을 고르시오.

Ernie's Ice Cream	
Double Cone	$2.00
Single Cone	$1.50
Double Cup	$2.30
Single Cup	$1.80

① $3.30   ② $3.50   ③ $3.80
④ $4.10   ⑤ $4.30

12 다음을 듣고, 남자의 설명과 일치하는 것을 고르시오.

① 육식보다 채식이 좋다.
② 과자보다 과일이 좋다.
③ 과일보다 우유가 좋다.
④ 과자보다 고기가 좋다.
⑤ 우유보다 소다수가 좋다.

13 대화를 듣고, 두 사람의 관계로 가장 알맞은 것을 고르시오.

① 선생님 – 학생   ② 아빠 – 딸
③ 학생 – 학생   ④ 선생님 – 선생님
⑤ 엄마 – 아들

14 대화를 듣고, 두 사람이 지금 하려고 하는 일을 고르시오.

① to go on a picnic
② to go shopping
③ to sing a song
④ to practice driving
⑤ to find where to park

15 대화를 듣고, 여자가 남자에게 부탁한 일을 고르시오.

① to feed the dog
② to pack their bags
③ to go skiing with her
④ to shut the windows
⑤ to invite his friend to his condominium

16 다음을 듣고, 그림과 일치하는 것을 고르시오.

①   ②   ③   ④   ⑤

17 다음을 듣고, 남자가 싫어하는 운동을 고르시오.

① soccer   ② basketball
③ volleyball   ④ baseball
⑤ table tennis

18 대화를 듣고, 여자가 남자에게 방을 청소하라고 한 이유를 고르시오.

① 사촌동생들이 지저분하게 어질러놓아서
② 친척들이랑 같이 방에서 자야 하니까
③ 사촌동생들이 물건을 깨뜨리지 않도록 하려고
④ 깨끗한 모습으로 손님을 맞이하려고
⑤ 깨진 물건들이 바닥에 흐트러져 있어서

[19-20] 대화를 듣고, 여자의 마지막 말에 이어질 남자의 응답으로 가장 적절한 것을 고르시오.

19
① Write to me often.
② No, you aren't going.
③ Too bad you're going.
④ That's a good idea.
⑤ OK. I will send you a package.

20
① You must go take some rest.
② Why do you look terrible?
③ Can you turn up the heat?
④ Do you have more tissues?
⑤ That's none of my business.

T E S T
6

1 다음을 듣고, 남자가 설명하는 그림으로 가장 알맞은 것을 고르시오.

① ② ③ ④ ⑤

M This building is symbolized by a _____ _____ _____. The people working in this building try to _____ _____ _____ sick people. The people being helped often sleep in this building overnight, because they are not perfectly healthy so they _____ _____ _____ _____.

2 대화를 듣고, 남자가 사진을 찾을 수 있는 시각을 고르시오.

① 2:00 p.m.
② 2:13 p.m.
③ 2:30 p.m.
④ 2:43 p.m.
⑤ 3:00 p.m.

W Good morning, sir. May I help you?
M Yes, I am here to _____ _____ _____ _____.
W What is your name, sir?
M Derek Benson. *[pause]*
W I'm sorry, sir, but your pictures are _____ _____ _____.
M I was told to pick them up at 2. It's 2:30. When can I _____ _____ _____?
W I'm sorry. We had a problem. They'll be ready in 30 minutes.

3 다음을 듣고, 표의 내용과 <u>다른</u> 것을 고르시오.

〈Average amount of weekly allowance spent and saved〉

	Allowance	Money spent	Money saved
John	$10	$7	$3
Terry	$15	$15	0
Bob	$10	$5	$5

① ② ③
④ ⑤

M ① John and Bob _____ _____ _____ _____ of money each week to spend.
② Bob saves the most money among the three.
③ Terry spends _____ _____ _____ _____ each week.
④ John spends more money than Bob each week.
⑤ Bob _____ _____ _____ than Terry.

4 다음을 듣고, 요일별 날씨가 바르게 연결된 것을 고르시오.

① today – cloudy
② today – foggy
③ tomorrow – rainy
④ tomorrow – windy
⑤ tomorrow – warm

W Good morning. This is Beth Benson with the weather report. We'll have warm weather and sunny skies today. A perfect day _____ _____ _____ in the park. Tomorrow, however, it'll be cloudy and windy. It will _____ _____ _____ for outdoor activities. So do something today before the weather changes. If you'll look at this _____ _____, you'll be able to see those clouds moving in from the north.

5 대화를 듣고, 엄마가 아침식사를 준비하지 <u>못하는</u> 이유를 고르시오.

① 병원에 입원해서
② 너무 바빠서
③ 늦잠을 자서
④ 감기에 걸려서
⑤ 일찍 출근해서

M _____ _____ in here.
W I'm making pancakes for breakfast.
M Really? I didn't know you could make pancakes.
W I _____ _____ _____ last year.
M So why don't you make them more often?
W Mom usually cooks us a nice breakfast, but she can't today.
M Where is mom?
W She's sick. She's got a bad cold, so just _____ _____ _____.

6 대화를 듣고, 여자가 머리를 짧게 자른 이유를 고르시오.

① 긴 머리가 싫증나서
② 날씨가 너무 더워서
③ 짧은 머리가 더 잘 어울려서
④ 분위기를 바꿔보려고
⑤ 짧은 머리가 유행이어서

W How's my hair look?
M You look good _____ _____ _____. It's my first time to see you with short hair.
W Actually I love having long hair.
M I don't understand then.
W The problem is _____ _____. This summer is too hot. I don't feel cool with long hair.
M Well, you should _____ _____ _____.
W I hope so.

T E S T 6

7 다음을 듣고, 그림의 상황에 가장 어울리는 대화를 고르시오.

① ② ③
④ ⑤

① W Where are you going?
  M To my bedroom. I'm tired.
② W _____ _____ _____.
  M Thank you, I will.
③ W Are you crying, too?
  M Yes, it's a sad movie.
④ W I'll miss you.
  M _____ _____ _____, Sweetie. I'll be home soon.
⑤ W I _____ _____ _____.
  M OK. You can go now.

8 다음을 듣고, 상황에 가장 알맞은 표현을 고르시오.

① Jisun, do you still have my pencil?
② Jisun, it's OK. I'll lend you a pencil.
③ Jisun, do you have an extra pencil?
④ I'm sorry, but I haven't got your pencil.
⑤ Jisun, what do you think about this new pencil?

W Jihye comes to class and _____ _____ _____. She takes out her books and notebooks to get ready _____ _____ _____. Then she looks for her pencil case. She can't find it. She turns to the student _____ _____ to her, Jisun. In this situation, what would Jihye say to Jisun?

9 대화를 듣고, 두 사람이 대화하는 장소를 고르시오.

① playground
② fitness club
③ mountain
④ aerobics center
⑤ swimming pool

M How far did you run?
W Just 5 km.
M Isn't it boring running _____ _____ _____?
W Kind of. But I must exercise and it's too cold to _____ _____.
M Why don't you _____ _____ _____?
W You have to pay extra for those classes. I don't have the extra money these days.
M Well, spring is coming soon. You'll be outside soon.

10 다음을 듣고, 두 사람의 대화가 <u>어색한</u> 것을 고르시오.

① ② ③
④ ⑤

① M Do you have time?
  W Yes, I can _____ _____ with you.
② M Who are you waiting for?
  W For 20 minutes.
③ M I can't understand this math problem.
  W I will explain it to you.
④ M What did you think of the science test?
  W It was hard. I _____ _____ _____.
⑤ M Mom, I'm cold.
  W Then put on a sweater, dear. We cannot _____ _____ _____ _____.

11 대화를 듣고, 남자가 지불해야 할 금액을 고르시오.

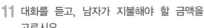

Ernie's Ice Cream	
Double Cone	$2.00
Single Cone	$1.50
Double Cup	$2.30
Single Cup	$1.80

① $3.30
② $3.50
③ $3.80
④ $4.10
⑤ $4.30

W May I help you, sir?

M Yes, please. I'd like a double cone. _____ _____ of chocolate and one scoop of strawberry.

W OK. [pause] _____ _____ _____.

M And my girlfriend will have a double cup. Two scoops of cherry ice cream.

W OK, a double cone of cherry ice cream?

M Oh, no. _____ _____ _____.

W Well, I'm sorry. [pause] Here you are.

M Thank you. How much do I owe you?

---

12 다음을 듣고, 남자의 설명과 일치하는 것을 고르시오.

① 육식보다 채식이 좋다.
② 과자보다 과일이 좋다.
③ 과일보다 우유가 좋다.
④ 과자보다 고기가 좋다.
⑤ 우유보다 소다수가 좋다.

M As you may know, most snack foods are _____ _____. Snacks don't have enough vitamins, I mean _____ _____. If you want to study hard, you should make your body healthier. So you can fight diseases better. And you won't have to see me often. To make your body stronger, you have to eat _____ _____ _____ _____ at snack time. And low-fat milk is much better than any kinds of soda.

---

13 대화를 듣고, 두 사람의 관계로 가장 알맞은 것을 고르시오.

① 선생님 – 학생
② 아빠 – 딸
③ 학생 – 학생
④ 선생님 – 선생님
⑤ 엄마 – 아들

W Are you done with your homework?

M Yes. I just finished homework for math and English.

W I hope you did your homework _____ _____ _____. Sometimes you don't do your homework carefully.

M You can _____ _____.

W No, that's OK. If you're finished, you can play computer games. _____ _____ _____ when dinner is ready.

M OK.

14 대화를 듣고, 두 사람이 지금 하려고 하는 일을 고르시오.

① to go on a picnic
② to go shopping
③ to sing a song
④ to practice driving
⑤ to find where to park

W There are _____ _____ _____.
M Yes, some small shops are building these big discount shopping malls.
W Well, stop and let's do some shopping.
M Armanda, we decided to _____ _____ _____ in the countryside today. We both said we wanted some fresh air.
W OK. Don't worry. Keep driving until you find _____ _____ _____ for a picnic.
M Yes, I need to hear birds singing _____ _____ _____.

15 대화를 듣고, 여자가 남자에게 부탁한 일을 고르시오.

① to feed the dog
② to pack their bags
③ to go skiing with her
④ to shut the windows
⑤ to invite his friend to his condominium

W We are all ready to go. _____ _____ _____ _____, the lights are off, and the windows are shut.
M I can't wait. I haven't been skiing in a long time.
W It's nice of your friend to invite us to stay with them _____ _____ _____.
M Right. Oh, Janice. Did you give the dog lots of food? We won't be home tonight.
W Oh no! I didn't. Can you do it, please?
M OK. _____ _____ _____ his food bowl and give him lots of water.

16 다음을 듣고, 그림과 일치하는 것을 고르시오.

① ② ③
④ ⑤

W ① The boy is watching a game.
② The boy is _____ _____ _____.
③ The boy is wearing a baseball cap _____.
④ The boy is wearing a plain white T-shirt.
⑤ The boy is _____ _____ _____ in the schoolyard.

17 다음을 듣고, 남자가 싫어하는 운동을 고르시오.

① soccer
② basketball
③ volleyball
④ baseball
⑤ table tennis

M I love to play sports. I am a little short and heavy, but I run fast. Almost every sport is fun for me. When I play soccer, I run a lot so _____ _____ _____. I also love to play basketball. I'm shorter but faster than others. I _____ _____ them quickly. The only sport I am not _____ _____ in is baseball. It's too slow for me. It is not exciting to wait for the ball to be hit.

18 대화를 듣고, 여자가 남자에게 방을 청소하라고 한 이유를 고르시오.

① 사촌동생들이 지저분하게 어질러놓아서
② 친척들이랑 같이 방에서 자야 하니까
③ 사촌동생들이 물건을 깨뜨리지 않도록 하려고
④ 깨끗한 모습으로 손님을 맞이하려고
⑤ 깨진 물건들이 바닥에 흐트러져 있어서

W They will be here any minute.

M I'm ready.

W No, you're not. I asked you to _____ _____ your room.

M Do I have to? It's not _____ _____ .

W Your aunt, uncle and cousins are coming to visit. _____ _____ _____ will play in your room. They might break something if you don't _____ _____ _____ .

M OK. I'll put everything away so nothing gets broken.

W Now that's a good boy. Thanks.

---

19 대화를 듣고, 여자의 마지막 말에 이어질 남자의 응답으로 가장 적절한 것을 고르시오.

① Write to me often.
② No, you aren't going.
③ Too bad you're going.
④ That's a good idea.
⑤ OK. I will send you a package.

W I am so sad. This English summer camp is over.

M Me too. I hope we can _____ _____ _____ .

W I hope so, too.

M We live _____ _____ . But we can write to each other.

W Writing... Hmm... Isn't e-mail better?

M _____

---

20 대화를 듣고, 여자의 마지막 말에 이어질 남자의 응답으로 가장 적절한 것을 고르시오.

① You must go take some rest.
② Why do you look terrible?
③ Can you turn up the heat?
④ Do you have more tissues?
⑤ That's none of my business.

W Do you have a tissue?

M I think I do. Wait. Here you go.

W Thanks.

M _____ _____ _____ . Did you catch a bad cold?

W I'm not sure.

M What do you mean? Did you see your doctor?

W Not yet. I'm _____ _____ _____ it is a cold or not. It's an _____ _____ .

M _____

A Write down the definition of each word or phrase.

1	intersection	11	heal
2	weigh	12	release
3	deliver	13	allowance
4	imagination	14	activity
5	happen	15	satellite
6	prepare	16	borrow
7	accept	17	kind of
8	receipt	18	feed
9	raise	19	plain
10	symbolize	20	awkward

B Match each word with the right definition.

1	bowl	a	주사
2	lend	b	주문하다
3	pick up	c	(짐을) 꾸리다, 싸다, 포장하다
4	come by	d	치료하다, 고치다
5	carry	e	~을 가득 채우다
6	shot	f	길이
7	cure	g	오다, 들르다
8	pack	h	양
9	average	i	그 대신에
10	order	j	~의 냄새가 나다
11	smell	k	~을 빌려주다
12	instead	l	평균의, 보통 수준의
13	length	m	되찾다, 입수하다, 마중 나가다, 중간에 태우다
14	fill up	n	나르다, 들고 가다, 가지고 가다
15	amount	o	주발, 사발, 공기

C Choose the best answer for the blank.

1 Keep _____ straight.

a. go   b. to go   c. going

2 I'd like to _____ a reservation for a flight to New York.

a. take   b. make   c. keep

3 You _____ happy today.

a. look   b. look like   c. look at

4 She's got a bad cold, so just let her _____ .

a. sleep   b. to sleep   c. sleeping

5 It depends _____ how much it weighs.

a. of   b. in   c. on

6 She came _____ my absence.

a. while   b. during   c. when

D Complete the short dialogues.

1 A: I don't enjoy golf.

B: I don't, _____ .

2 A: What time is it now?

B: It's 8. You must hurry, _____ you'll be late.

3 A: What are you doing now?

B: I'm _____ _____ my key. I thought I put it on my desk, but I couldn't find it.

4 A: Why don't you exercise regularly?

B: I want to, but it's _____ busy to exercise these days.

5 A: Mom, I'm cold.

B: Then _____ on a sweater.

1 다음을 듣고, 남자가 설명하는 교통수단으로 가장 알맞은 것을 고르시오.

2 대화를 듣고, 남자가 찾아가고자 하는 곳을 지도에서 고르시오.

3 대화를 듣고, 두 사람이 대화하는 장소를 고르시오.

① grocery store
② photo studio
③ dental clinic
④ gymnasium
⑤ flower shop

4 대화를 듣고, 연극이 시작하는 시각을 고르시오.

① 6:00   ② 6:30   ③ 7:00
④ 7:30   ⑤ 8:00

5 대화를 듣고, 여자가 남자에게 전화를 건 목적으로 알맞은 것을 고르시오.

① 같이 축구 시합을 하려고
② TV 수리를 부탁하려고
③ 축구경기 정보를 물어보려고
④ 축구 시합을 함께 보자고
⑤ 새로 산 TV를 자랑하려고

6 대화를 듣고, 남자의 태도로 가장 알맞은 것을 고르시오.

① greedy   ② introvert
③ sensitive   ④ thoughtful
⑤ irresponsible

7 대화를 듣고, 두 사람의 관계로 알맞은 것을 고르시오.

① 점원 – 사장
② 약사 – 손님
③ 선생님 – 학생
④ 간호사 – 환자
⑤ 보험사 직원 – 피보험인

8 다음을 듣고, 두 사람의 대화가 <u>어색한</u> 것을 고르시오.

①   ②   ③   ④   ⑤

9 다음을 듣고, 여자가 영화 동아리를 좋아하지 <u>않는</u> 이유를 고르시오

① 작년에도 영화 동아리였기 때문에
② 공포영화를 보고 싶지 않아서
③ 좋아하는 영화를 볼 수 없어서
④ 학생들이 영화를 직접 고를 수 없어서
⑤ 볼링 동아리에 다시 가입하고 싶어서

10 대화를 듣고, 여자가 현재 배우고 있는 악기를 고르시오.

① piano   ② guitar   ③ drum
④ violin   ⑤ flute

11 대화를 듣고, 두 사람이 노래방에 가려는 의도를 고르시오.

① 노래 연습을 하기 위해
② 사장님의 기분을 풀어주기 위해
③ 기분전환을 위해
④ 새로 만난 직원과 어색함을 없애기 위해
⑤ 두고 온 물건을 찾기 위해

12 대화를 듣고, 남자가 지금 바로 해야 할 일로 알맞은 것을 고르시오.

① to go play basketball
② to go buy some cereal
③ to have breakfast
④ to take out the waste
⑤ to get ready to go outside

13 대화를 듣고, 남자가 지불할 금액을 고르시오.

① $10 　② $15 　③ $20
④ $25 　⑤ $30

14 대화를 듣고, 여자가 아기 돌보는 일을 하는 이유를 고르시오.

① 너무 즐겁고 적성에 맞아서
② 사람들이 자꾸 부탁해서
③ 생활비를 벌기 위해서
④ 전자사전을 사려고
⑤ 엄마가 하라고 시켜서

15 다음을 듣고, 무엇에 관한 내용인지 고르시오.

① 심해지는 기상 악화
② 크리스마스 파티
③ 항공 운항 재개
④ 공항 버스 운행
⑤ 공항 폐쇄 안내

16 대화를 듣고, 여자의 침실 벽에 붙어 있는 것을 고르시오.

① 남자 친구의 사진
② 좋아하는 가수의 포스터
③ 달력
④ 영화 포스터
⑤ 그녀가 그린 그림

17 대화를 듣고, 내용에 어울리는 속담으로 알맞은 것을 고르시오.

① Walls have ears.
② Practice makes perfect.
③ Kill two birds with one stone.
④ A little knowledge is a dangerous thing.
⑤ Good luck does not always repeat itself.

18 다음을 듣고, 이어서 들려주는 질문에 알맞은 답을 고르시오.

① bears 　② deer 　③ beavers
④ squirrels 　⑤ racoons

[19-20] 대화를 듣고, 남자의 마지막 말에 이어질 여자의 응답으로 가장 적절한 것을 고르시오.

19

① Yes, you must practice hard.
② Yes, it'll be interesting.
③ Yes, you did a good job.
④ No! Go get some exercise.
⑤ Who will you play with?

20

① Mark James, the class president.
② I agree with you. He's kind.
③ He gives too much homework.
④ Mr. Smith. He's very funny.
⑤ Math is my favorite class.

TEST 7

1 다음을 듣고, 남자가 설명하는 교통수단으로 가장 알맞은 것을 고르시오.

① ② ③ ④ ⑤

M People living on small islands use this a lot. People living on large islands usually _____ _____ _____ to fly to the mainland, but people living on small islands usually do not. They must go down _____ _____ _____ and walk, ride a bicycle or drive their car onto it. It takes you from the island to the mainland by _____ _____ _____ _____.

2 대화를 듣고, 남자가 찾아가고자 하는 곳을 지도에서 고르시오.

M Can you tell me where the nearest post office is?

W Hmm… _____ _____ _____ for one minute. Walk straight for two blocks.

M OK. And then what?

W Then you turn right and walk straight for _____ _____ _____.

M So… Is it on the left or the right side?

W On the left side. It's so big that you can't miss it.

M Thank you very much.

W _____ _____.

3 대화를 듣고, 두 사람이 대화하는 장소를 고르시오.

① grocery store
② photo studio
③ dental clinic
④ gymnasium
⑤ flower shop

M Stay still. I need to give you this shot.

W Why?

M To _____ _____ _____.

W Before you pull out my tooth?

M Yes, this will freeze your mouth so I can remove _____ _____ _____ on the left.

W Will it be painful?

M A little. But that wisdom tooth will cause you more pain in the future if I don't _____ _____ _____.

4 대화를 듣고, 연극이 시작하는 시각을 고르시오.

① 6:00
② 6:30
③ 7:00
④ 7:30
⑤ 8:00

M Why are you taking _____ _____?

W I'm getting ready.

M The play starts in an hour. And it takes _____ _____ _____ to drive there.

W What time is it now?

M It is 6:30.

W Oh, _____ _____ _____? I thought it was 6 o'clock.

M No, you are wrong. It's half past six.

W I'll hurry. I'll be one more minute, then.

---

5 대화를 듣고, 여자가 남자에게 전화를 건 목적으로 알맞은 것을 고르시오.

① 같이 축구 시합을 하려고
② TV 수리를 부탁하려고
③ 축구경기 정보를 물어보려고
④ 축구 시합을 함께 보자고
⑤ 새로 산 TV를 자랑하려고

[Telephone rings.]

M Hello.

W Hi, Jimmy. This is Rachel.

M Hi, Rachel. _____ _____ _____?

W What are you doing now? We're just _____ _____ _____ watch the soccer game.

M Me too.

W You know, we've just got this new super big LCD television screen.

M Yeah. You told me last time.

W So why don't you _____ _____ _____ and watch the game with us?

M Thanks. I'd love to.

---

6 대화를 듣고, 남자의 태도로 가장 알맞은 것을 고르시오.

① greedy
② introvert
③ sensitive
④ thoughtful
⑤ irresponsible

W Wow! There is a big chocolate bar.

M That chocolate bar on the table is mine. Don't open it!

W I just want _____ _____ _____. It's a big bar of chocolate.

M I want to save it for later. So you can't have any.

W When I have food, I always _____ _____ _____ _____. You're my brother! Come on!

M No, it's a special chocolate bar.

W You're _____ _____!

7 대화를 듣고, 두 사람의 관계로 알맞은 것을 고르시오.

① 점원 – 사장
② 약사 – 손님
③ 선생님 – 학생
④ 간호사 – 환자
⑤ 보험사 직원 – 피보험인

M Hello. I need this _____ _____.

W Do you have your _____ _____?

M Yes, here it is.

W Wait five minutes, Mr. Hanson. *[pause]* Here you go.

M So, how often do I take these?

W 3 times a day _____ _____ _____. 30 minutes after meals.

M Thank you.

8 다음을 듣고, 두 사람의 대화가 <u>어색한</u> 것을 고르시오.

①　　　　②　　　　③
④　　　　⑤

① **M** I'd like a cola, large please.

　W That'll be $1.50.

② **M** How have you been?

　W I've been _____ _____.

③ **M** Are you going to the show?

　W The next bus will come _____ _____ _____.

④ **M** When should we meet?

　W At 3:00. In front of the Post Office on 4th Street.

⑤ **M** Let's meet at 7:00.

　W OK. I will _____ _____ _____ _____. See you then.

9 다음을 듣고, 여자가 영화 동아리를 좋아하지 <u>않는</u> 이유를 고르시오

① 작년에도 영화 동아리였기 때문에
② 공포영화를 보고 싶지 않아서
③ 좋아하는 영화를 볼 수 없어서
④ 학생들이 영화를 직접 고를 수 없어서
⑤ 볼링 동아리에 다시 가입하고 싶어서

W Once a month every student in our school _____ _____ an extra-curricular activity. We call it club day. Last year I was _____ _____ _____ _____. It wasn't much fun. This year I am in the movie club. But it's not much fun either, because I never get to choose a movie. Everyone in the club chooses it together. Well, I like _____ _____ but no one else does. So we never watch horror movies.

10 대화를 듣고, 여자가 현재 배우고 있는 악기를 고르시오.

① piano
② guitar
③ drum
④ violin
⑤ flute

M Can you meet me after class?

W No, sorry, I _____ _____ _____ with my friend.

M What is it?

W My friend and I want to learn how to _____ _____ _____. So we plan to go find out where we can learn.

M I play the guitar. I am taking lessons every Saturday.

W I'd like to hear you play sometime. I've been playing the violin for 3 years.

M Wow! That's a long time, you must be very good.

W Not really. It's a _____ _____ to play. The piano is much easier.

11 대화를 듣고, 두 사람이 노래방에 가려는 의도를 고르시오.

① 노래 연습을 하기 위해
② 사장님의 기분을 풀어주기 위해
③ 기분전환을 위해
④ 새로 만난 직원과 어색함을 없애기 위해
⑤ 두고 온 물건을 찾기 위해

W Bad day? You look tired.
M I've been working _____ _____ _____. And my boss was angry all day today.
W Maybe you need a new job.
M It's hard to _____ _____ _____ _____ these days.
W Come on, honey. Don't worry so much. Let's go singing. After an hour in the singing room, you'll be feeling better.
M Good idea. It always _____ _____ _____.

12 대화를 듣고, 남자가 지금 바로 해야 할 일로 알맞은 것을 고르시오.

① to go play basketball
② to go buy some cereal
③ to have breakfast
④ to take out the waste
⑤ to get ready to go outside

W You got up early this morning. You look like you're ready to _____ _____ _____ _____.
M I'm meeting my friends at the park for a game of basketball.
W OK. Have you taken out _____ _____ _____ yet?
M Oh, I forgot.
W You have to do that before you can go play basketball. Did you have some breakfast?
M Yes, I had some cereal _____ _____ _____ _____, Mom. I'll take the garbage out now. See you in a minute.

13 대화를 듣고, 남자가 지불할 금액을 고르시오.

① $10
② $15
③ $20
④ $25
⑤ $30

W Hi, how may I help you?
M Well, I want a _____ _____ for my mother.
W How about a bag? We have many bags ladies like these days.
M Oh, I don't have much money.
W Then _____ _____ would be nice. This purple one is $10. And this red one is $20.
M How much is that one?
W The blue one is $30.
M I'll _____ _____ _____ _____. I only have $15.
W Should I _____ _____ _____ for you?

14 대화를 듣고, 여자가 아기 돌보는 일을 하는 이유를 고르시오.

① 너무 즐겁고 적성에 맞아서
② 사람들이 자꾸 부탁해서
③ 생활비를 벌기 위해서
④ 전자사전을 사려고
⑤ 엄마가 하라고 시켜서

M Can you meet us tonight for ice cream at the cafe?

W No, _____ _____.

M Again! Wow, you are doing a lot of babysitting these days.

W Yes, I am. I told my mom to tell all the moms _____ _____ _____ that I could babysit.

M Do you enjoy it?

W Hmm... Sometimes, but I'm doing because I want to save money to buy a new _____ _____.

M It shouldn't be hard to save that much money.

15 다음을 듣고, 무엇에 관한 내용인지 고르시오.

① 심해지는 기상 악화
② 크리스마스 파티
③ 항공 운항 재개
④ 공항 버스 운행
⑤ 공항 폐쇄 안내

M Passengers, can I have your attention please? The storm outside has stopped. You will get home for Christmas. The airport was closed for 30 hours. But _____ _____ _____ now. Look at the _____ _____ to see which flights will leave first. Thank you for _____ _____.

16 대화를 듣고, 여자의 침실 벽에 붙어 있는 것을 고르시오.

① 남자 친구의 사진
② 좋아하는 가수의 포스터
③ 달력
④ 영화 포스터
⑤ 그녀가 그린 그림

M Hi, Susan. What are you dong?

W I'm listening to music. As you know, I like News Kids.

M Do you have a poster of News Kids _____ _____ _____ _____ ?

W No, actually I don't. I keep their pictures _____ _____ _____.

M So you don't have any pictures of them in your bedroom?

W Well, _____ _____ _____ _____ on my desk. On my bedroom wall, there used to be a calendar. But I have a poster of my favorite movie now.

M _____ _____ _____ ?

W Yeah, of the movie *Love Everlasting*.

17 대화를 듣고, 내용에 어울리는 속담으로 알맞은 것을 고르시오.

① Walls have ears.
② Practice makes perfect.
③ Kill two birds with one stone.
④ A little knowledge is a dangerous thing.
⑤ Good luck does not always repeat itself.

M Barbara, you're doing well. _____ _____ _____ carefully.
W I'm writing my name, Dad. You taught me yesterday.
M For a six-year-old, you write letters really well.
W Ahh! Look! It's not good.
M It's OK. _____ _____ _____ ... [pause] See? Yours is OK.
W No, it's not. _____ _____ .
M Well, copy that letter again and again and again until it looks like mine. You can do it.

---

18 다음을 듣고, 이어서 들려주는 질문에 알맞은 답을 고르시오.

① bears
② deer
③ beavers
④ squirrels
⑤ racoons

M Welcome to Blackstone National Park. I'm _____ _____ _____ and I am here to tell you a little bit about the park. There are no bears in this park, so you don't have to worry about them. But there are many other animals in the park: _____ , _____ , squirrels and lots of others. But there is only one animal you have to worry about. _____ ! They will come near your campsite and try to take your food.
Q What animal do they have to _____ _____ _____ ?

---

19 대화를 듣고, 남자의 마지막 말에 이어질 여자의 응답으로 가장 적절한 것을 고르시오.

① Yes, you must practice hard.
② Yes, it'll be interesting.
③ Yes, you did a good job.
④ No! Go get some exercise.
⑤ Who will you play with?

W I'm worried that you are watching too much TV.
M _____ _____ _____ _____ , Mom.
W Turn off the TV. I think you'd better go play sports with your friends. It is unhealthy for you to _____ _____ and watch TV all day.
M Mom, it's _____ _____ _____ . Can I just play computer games?
W _____

---

20 대화를 듣고, 남자의 마지막 말에 이어질 여자의 응답으로 가장 적절한 것을 고르시오.

① Mark James, the class president.
② I agree with you. He's kind.
③ He gives too much homework.
④ Mr. Smith. He's very funny.
⑤ Math is my favorite class.

W Who is your favorite teacher?
M My math teacher, Mr. White.
W _____ _____ _____ ?
M He is kind and he always helps students _____ _____ _____ . And he knows all the names of students. Every student _____ _____ . Who is your favorite teacher?
W _____

1 다음을 듣고, 남자가 설명하는 그림으로 가장 알맞은 것을 고르시오.

①   ②

③   ④

⑤

2 대화를 듣고, 여자의 직업으로 가장 알맞은 것을 고르시오.

① cook   ② fire fighter
③ engineer   ④ waitress
⑤ delivery person

3 대화를 듣고, 여자가 전화를 건 목적을 고르시오.

① 빵을 좀 사오라고
② 걸어서 집에 오라고
③ 계란을 사오라고
④ 어디에 있는지 확인하려고
⑤ 은행에서 돈을 좀 찾아오라고

4 대화를 듣고, 남자의 직업으로 가장 알맞은 것을 고르시오.

① movie star
② producer
③ comedian
④ TV talk show host
⑤ home shopping host

5 다음을 듣고, this가 가리키는 나라를 고르시오.

① China   ② Canada   ③ America
④ France   ⑤ England

6 대화를 듣고, 남자가 사려는 물건과 할인율로 알맞게 짝지어진 것을 고르시오.

① 셔츠 – 20%   ② 신발 – 30%
③ 스웨터 – 20%   ④ 바지 – 30%
⑤ 양복 – 30%

7 다음을 듣고, 점심시간이 몇 시부터인지 고르시오.

① 12:30   ② 12:35
③ 12:40   ④ 12:45
⑤ 12:50

8 다음을 듣고, 모레의 날씨를 고르시오.

① windy   ② snowy
③ rainy   ④ sunny
⑤ cloudy

9 대화를 듣고, 대화가 일어나고 있는 장소로 가장 알맞은 것을 고르시오.

① zoo
② fish store
③ electronics store
④ butcher shop
⑤ fast-food restaurant

10 다음을 듣고, 두 사람의 대화가 <u>어색한</u> 것을 고르시오.

①   ②   ③   ④   ⑤

11 대화를 듣고, 남자의 심정으로 가장 알맞은 것을 고르시오.

① patient   ② relieved
③ depressed   ④ worried
⑤ anxious

12 대화를 듣고, 두 사람의 관계로 가장 알맞은 것을 고르시오.

① 택시기사 – 승객
② 웨이터 – 손님
③ 선생님 – 학부모
④ 간호사 – 환자
⑤ 요리사 – 웨이트리스

13 다음을 듣고, 상황의 순서가 바르게 나열된 것을 고르시오.

(A) 　　　　(B)

(C)

① (A)-(B)-(C)　　　　② (A)-(C)-(B)
③ (B)-(C)-(A)　　　　④ (B)-(A)-(C)
⑤ (C)-(A)-(B)

14 다음을 듣고, 내용과 일치하지 않는 것을 고르시오.

① 1시간 후에 세일을 시작한다.
② 줄에서 이탈하면, 자리를 잃게 된다.
③ 1시간 동안 가게 문을 열지 않는다.
④ 다른 사람이 대신 자리를 맡아둘 수 있다.
⑤ 말다툼이 생기면, 가게에 들어가지 못한다.

15 대화를 듣고, Billy가 영화를 보다가 그만둔 이유를 고르시오.

① 영화가 너무 재미없어서
② 너무 피곤하고 졸려서
③ 화질이 너무 안 좋아서
④ DVD 플레이어가 고장이 나서
⑤ 엄마가 보지 말라고 화를 내서

16 대화를 듣고, 남자가 할 일이 아닌 것을 고르시오.

① 숙제하기
② 친구 만나기
③ 쇼핑몰에 가기
④ 대신 책 반납하기
⑤ 미술 과제 용품 사기

17 대화를 듣고, 이어지는 질문에 가장 알맞은 답을 고르시오.

① 필통　　　② 책가방　　　③ 인형
④ 파인애플　　　⑤ 양말

[18-19] 대화를 듣고, 남자의 마지막 말에 대한 여자의 응답으로 가장 적절한 것을 고르시오.

18
① you bought me a new one.
② I will go get it right now.
③ I will tell you the story.
④ I forgive you.
⑤ but you shouldn't do that.

19
① I'll be finished soon.
② Yesterday at 5 p.m.
③ Monday evening at 8 p.m.
④ It's 8 o'clock now.
⑤ Class finishes at 8 on Monday.

20 다음을 듣고, 상황에 가장 어울리는 표현을 고르시오.

① Do you always eat rice for dinner?
② How much do you usually eat?
③ Can I have another bowl, please?
④ Can you buy some more rice?
⑤ Are you still hungry?

TEST 8

1 다음을 듣고, 남자가 설명하는 그림으로 가장 알맞은 것을 고르시오.

① ② ③ ④ ⑤

M This makes cooking the main food of every Korean meal easy. It is usually stored on the kitchen _____ _____ . Rice is washed and put in it. _____ _____ cooks the rice perfectly. Rice is often burned when cooked _____ _____ _____ _____ , but not when cooked using one of these. Of course we can cook other things like chicken in it, but it is mainly used for rice.

2 대화를 듣고, 여자의 직업으로 가장 알맞은 것을 고르시오.

① cook
② fire fighter
③ engineer
④ waitress
⑤ delivery person

M Excuse me?

W Yes, sir. Is something wrong?

M I ordered a well-done steak, but this _____ _____ _____ _____ .

W I'm sorry, sir. I'll _____ _____ _____ to the kitchen.

M Thank you. And I'd like some more water, too.

W One minute, sir.

3 대화를 듣고, 여자가 전화를 건 목적을 고르시오.

① 빵을 좀 사오라고
② 걸어서 집에 오라고
③ 계란을 사오라고
④ 어디에 있는지 확인하려고
⑤ 은행에서 돈을 좀 찾아오라고

[Telephone rings.]

M Hi.

W Hello, Howard. It's Mom. Are you walking home now?

M Yes, I left school a minute ago.

W Well, I'm _____ _____ _____ and I don't have eggs.

M Do you want me to buy some on my way home?

W Yes, _____ _____ what I'd like you to do.

M Oh, should I buy some bread? I think I ate them last night.

W You don't _____ _____ . I bought some this morning.

M OK. No problem.

4 대화를 듣고, 남자의 직업으로 가장 알맞은 것을 고르시오.

① movie star
② producer
③ comedian
④ TV talk show host
⑤ home shopping host

M Everyone, let's _____ _____ _____ to Jenny Jones. [applause] Welcome!

W It's a pleasure to be here.

M _____ _____ _____ . Will you tell us about your new movie?

W Yes, it's a comedy with Bill Benson. _____ _____ _____ .

M Yes, I like him too. He was on the show two weeks ago.

W I know. He told me that, and a lot about you also.

5 다음을 듣고, this가 가리키는 나라를 고르시오.

① China
② Canada
③ America
④ France
⑤ England

M After Russia, this is the second largest country in the world. This country shares the world's _____ _____ _____ with the United States of America. And most of the people who live in this country live in the south near the border with the United States. There are _____ _____ _____ : French and English. _____ _____ is Ottawa.

6 대화를 듣고, 남자가 사려는 물건과 할인율로 알맞게 짝지어진 것을 고르시오.

① 셔츠 – 20%
② 신발 – 30%
③ 스웨터 – 20%
④ 바지 – 30%
⑤ 양복 – 30%

M I'll take these two right here.
W Would you like some shirts to _____ _____ _____ ?
M No, thank you. I think I have lots of shirts at home that will go with these.
W Well, how about some pants? They are on sale. 30% off. Did you know _____ _____ _____ are on sale, too? 20% off!
M I _____ _____ _____ , but I don't need any sweaters.
W OK. How would you like to pay for these?

7 다음을 듣고, 점심시간이 몇 시부터인지 고르시오.

① 12:30
② 12:35
③ 12:40
④ 12:45
⑤ 12:50

M Sit down! Everyone, sit down! And please _____ _____ . It is 12:35 and it is not lunchtime. The bell rings in 5 minutes and then you can _____ _____ _____ . At 12:40 you have a 50-minute break for lunch. Please _____ _____ _____ _____ you can go for lunch before the bell rings. Keep doing your work until the bell rings. Now be quiet, everyone!

8 다음을 듣고, 모레의 날씨를 고르시오.

① windy
② snowy
③ rainy
④ sunny
⑤ cloudy

W Good evening. I'm Lisa Gibbons with the weather report. We will have _____ _____ _____ weather tomorrow. It will be cool and windy. A great day for flying a kite. And you should try hard to get to the park tomorrow, because _____ _____ _____ will be cold and rainy. You'll probably want to _____ _____ that day.

9 대화를 듣고, 대화가 일어나고 있는 장소로 가장 알맞은 것을 고르시오.

① zoo
② fish store
③ electronics store
④ butcher shop
⑤ fast-food restaurant

M Do you have _____ _____?

W Yes, we have nice rib and sirloin steaks.

M How much are the rib steaks?

W $20 a kilo. And the sirloin is _____ _____ _____, $30 a kilo.

M I'll take 10 rib steaks. I'm having a BBQ party tomorrow.

W Well, the weather is perfect. And it should be nice tomorrow, too.

M I also need _____ _____ _____ for hamburgers for the kids.

W We have ground beef right over here.

---

10 다음을 듣고, 두 사람의 대화가 어색한 것을 고르시오.

①   ②   ③
④   ⑤

① **W** What do you want to drink with your pizza?

   M Potato pizza, please.

② **W** How many children do you have?

   M I have two daughters and one son.

③ **W** _____ _____ _____ _____ your steak done?

   M Well-done, please.

④ **W** Can you please _____ _____?

   M Sure. Listen carefully this time.

⑤ **W** Your sister is in the second grade of high school. What about you?

   M I'm _____ _____ _____ _____ of middle school.

---

11 대화를 듣고, 남자의 심정으로 가장 알맞은 것을 고르시오.

① patient
② relieved
③ depressed
④ worried
⑤ anxious

M Did you sleep well last night? I was _____ _____ _____ _____.

W Sometimes you can't sleep when you have an exam the next day.

M But this is different. We have waited to get to the beach in the Philippines for a long time.

W We should have a good time _____ _____ _____.

M It'll be great. Swimming, scuba diving... It's going to be lots of fun.

W _____ _____. We aren't even at the airport yet.

12 대화를 듣고, 두 사람의 관계로 가장 알맞은 것을 고르시오.

① 택시기사 – 승객
② 웨이터 – 손님
③ 선생님 – 학부모
④ 간호사 – 환자
⑤ 요리사 – 웨이트리스

M Let me take these dishes _____ _____ _____ _____.

W Thank you.

M I hope everything was fine.

W _____. I like the atmosphere here and _____ _____. Of course, the food was the greatest part. We would both like something for dessert, though. Do you have _____ _____ _____?

M Yes, we do. I'll go and get it for you. Is there anything else I can help you with?

W No, thanks.

13 다음을 듣고, 상황의 순서가 바르게 나열된 것을 고르시오.

(A)   (B)

(C)

① (A)-(B)-(C)   ② (A)-(C)-(B)
③ (B)-(C)-(A)   ④ (B)-(A)-(C)
⑤ (C)-(A)-(B)

W I had the strangest dream last night. _____ _____ _____ _____ was chasing me in the street. I _____ _____ a lake, because I thought the monster couldn't swim. But he could! So he followed me. I got out of the lake and ran _____ _____ _____. The monster caught me. We started fighting. We _____ _____ _____ _____.
Then I woke up. I was holding my teddy bear.

14 다음을 듣고, 내용과 일치하지 <u>않는</u> 것을 고르시오.

① 1시간 후에 세일을 시작한다.
② 줄에서 이탈하면, 자리를 잃게 된다.
③ 1시간 동안 가게 문을 열지 않는다.
④ 다른 사람이 대신 자리를 맡아둘 수 있다.
⑤ 말다툼이 생기면, 가게에 들어가지 못한다.

M Shoppers! May I have your attention? The store will not open for 1 hour. Then our Sale of the Year will begin. _____ _____ _____ and wait quietly. If you leave the line, you will lose your place. Others cannot _____ _____ _____. If there are _____ _____, store employees will not let you enter the store. Thank you.

15 대화를 듣고, Billy가 영화를 보다가 <u>그만</u> <u>둔</u> 이유를 고르시오.

① 영화가 너무 재미없어서
② 너무 피곤하고 졸려서
③ 화질이 너무 안 좋아서
④ DVD 플레이어가 고장이 나서
⑤ 엄마가 보지 말라고 화를 내서

W Billy, is the movie finished already?

M No, it's not finished, Mom. That's what _____ _____ _____.

W Isn't it interesting to you?

M It is interesting. I can't wait to _____ _____ _____, though I'm a little tired and sleepy.

W Then, what is it that makes you angry?

M It stopped.

W Stopped? Oh, don't tell me that the player doesn't work again.

M I think it is broken again. _____ _____ _____ _____, but it doesn't play.

W I'll take it to _____ _____ _____ tomorrow.

16 대화를 듣고, 남자가 할 일이 <u>아닌</u> 것을 고르시오.

① 숙제하기
② 친구 만나기
③ 쇼핑몰에 가기
④ 대신 책 반납하기
⑤ 미술 과제 용품 사기

M I'm going to Eaglewood shopping mall. I need to buy things _____ _____ _____ _____. Do you want to come? One of my friends is coming, too.

W I can't. I have a lot of homework tonight.

M I see.

W Is Eaglewood shopping mall next to the library?

M Yes, it is.

W Then, can you return this book for me? I have to return it tomorrow but I won't have time.

M OK. I'll _____ _____ _____.

17 대화를 듣고, 이어지는 질문에 가장 알맞은 답을 고르시오.

① 필통
② 책가방
③ 인형
④ 파인애플
⑤ 양말

M What does Jihye want for her birthday?

W She didn't say. But she likes things with _____ _____ _____ on them.

M Pineapple Girl?

W Yes, Pineapple Girl. She loves Pineapple Girl. _____ _____ _____ _____ _____ and a school bag with Pineapple Girl on them.

M I saw a Pineapple Girl doll in a shop near the school.

W That sounds like a good idea. We can _____ _____ _____.

Q What present will they buy for a friend?

18 대화를 듣고, 남자의 마지막 말에 대한 여자의 응답으로 가장 적절한 것을 고르시오.

① you bought me a new one.
② I will go get it right now.
③ I will tell you the story.
④ I forgive you.
⑤ but you shouldn't do that.

M Do you have my book _____ _____ last week?
W I'm really sorry, but I left it in my mom's house.
M Oh, no. I really _____ _____ _____ today.
W I didn't know you would need it this soon.
M _____ _____ _____ _____ to write this week and I need it for the paper.
W Don't worry, _____

---

19 대화를 듣고, 남자의 마지막 말에 대한 여자의 응답으로 가장 적절한 것을 고르시오.

① I'll be finished soon.
② Yesterday at 5 p.m.
③ Monday evening at 8 p.m.
④ It's 8 o'clock now.
⑤ Class finishes at 8 on Monday.

M Thank you for letting me _____ _____ _____.
W You're welcome. You asked me so many times.
M You promised me that I can learn the guitar if I study hard.
W Yes, _____ _____ are OK. So I let you take guitar lessons. I met a guitar teacher today. _____ _____ _____ _____.
M Oh, that's great. When will he come?
W _____

---

20 다음을 듣고, 상황에 가장 어울리는 표현을 고르시오.

① Do you always eat rice for dinner?
② How much do you usually eat?
③ Can I have another bowl, please?
④ Can you buy some more rice?
⑤ Are you still hungry?

M You are _____ _____ with your mother and father. You are really hungry because _____ _____ _____ for a couple of hours after school. You have eaten _____ _____ _____ _____. You are still hungry and you want some more. In this situation, what would you say to your mother?

A Write down the definition of each word or phrase.

1	opportunity	11	everlasting
2	freeze	12	respect
3	remove	13	pleasure
4	go over	14	border
5	greedy	15	prescription
6	prescription	16	anxious
7	insurance card	17	atmosphere
8	instrument	18	store
9	lately	19	argument
10	departure	20	employee

B Match each word with the right definition.

1	broken	_____	a	정지한, 움직이지 않는
2	chase	_____	b	뽑다, 빼다
3	spin	_____	c	아픈, 고통스러운
4	line up	_____	d	위로하다, 기분 좋게 하다
5	favorite	_____	e	뒤쫓다, 추격하다
6	still (adj.)	_____	f	무방비의
7	pull out	_____	g	난로
8	dock	_____	h	지면, 땅, 흙
9	forgive	_____	i	한 줄로 늘어서다
10	painful	_____	j	~을 보관하다, 맡아두다
11	undefended	_____	k	망가진, 고장이 난
12	save	_____	l	뱅뱅 돌다
13	ground (n.)	_____	m	선창, 부두
14	stove	_____	n	용서하다
15	cheer up	_____	o	마음에 드는, 매우 좋아하는

C Choose the best answer for the blank.

1 Hello. I need this prescription _____.

a. filling   b. to fill   c. filled

2 Once a month every student participates _____ an extra-curricular activity.

a. in   b. on   c. with

3 Do you want me to buy some bread _____ my way home?

a. in   b. on   c. with

4 They stopped _____ and studied hard.

a. talk   b. to talk   c. talking

5 That's what _____ me angry.

a. gives   b. makes   c. lets

6 I'll _____ my sister the teddy bear for her birthday present.

a. get   b. borrow   c. have

D Complete the short dialogues.

1 A: Is the bank on the left or the right side?

B: On the left side. It's so big you can't _____ it.

2 A: Would you like your steak rare?

B: No, I'd like my steak _____.

3 A: My Canadian friend, Tom, speaks two languages, English and French.

B: There are two _____ languages in Canada.

4 A: You have to slow down in the school zone.

B: I agree _____ you.

5 A: The DVD player is broken again. It spins and spins, but it doesn't play.

B: I'll _____ it to the repair shop tomorrow.

1 대화를 듣고, 남자가 설명하는 교통수단으로 알맞은 것을 고르시오.

① 　②

③ 　④

⑤

2 다음을 듣고, 그림의 상황에 가장 어울리는 대화를 고르시오.

①　②　③　④　⑤

3 대화를 듣고, 두 사람이 대화하는 장소로 알맞은 곳을 고르시오.

① 호텔　　② 식당　　③ 은행
④ 주유소　⑤ 식료품점

4 대화를 듣고, 남자가 전화를 건 목적으로 알맞은 것을 고르시오.

① 여자를 파티에 초대하려고
② 호텔에 객실을 예약하려고
③ 식당에 테이블을 예약하려고
④ 식당 예약을 취소하려고
⑤ 예약 시간을 변경하려고

5 다음을 듣고, 잃어버린 아이가 입고 있는 바지 색깔을 고르시오.

① 갈색　　② 파란색　　③ 검은색
④ 흰색　　⑤ 회색

6 대화를 듣고, 내용에 어울리는 속담으로 알맞은 것을 고르시오.

① Slow and steady wins the race.
② Hard work never killed anyone.
③ All work and no play makes Jack a dull boy.
④ A penny saved is a penny earned.
⑤ There is no substitute for hard work.

7 대화를 듣고, 여자가 전화를 한 목적으로 알맞은 것을 고르시오.

① 셔츠를 교환하려고
② 셔츠를 주문하려고
③ 주문에 대해 불평하려고
④ 소포 발송에 대해 문의하려고
⑤ 계산서를 지불하려고

8 대화를 듣고, 현재 시각으로 알맞은 것을 고르시오.

① 7:30　　② 7:50　　③ 8:12
④ 8:20　　⑤ 8:30

9 다음을 듣고, 표의 내용과 일치하지 <u>않는</u> 것을 고르시오.

Name	Number of text messages sent each day	Number of phone calls made each day
Emily	9	4
Rachel	20	12
Sue	38	6

①　②　③　④　⑤

10 다음을 듣고, 체육 수업이 <u>취소된</u> 이유를 고르시오.

① 비바람　　② 무더위　　③ 황사
④ 혹한　　⑤ 체육관 공사

11 다음을 듣고, 두 사람의 대화가 <u>어색한</u> 것을 고르시오.

① ② ③ ④ ⑤

12 대화를 듣고, 남자의 심정으로 가장 알맞은 것을 고르시오.

① happy ② scared
③ jealous ④ proud
⑤ disappointed

13 대화를 듣고, 두 사람의 관계로 알맞은 것을 고르시오.

① tour guide ..... tourist
② hotel receptionist ..... guest
③ real estate agent ..... client
④ grocery store clerk ..... customer
⑤ manager ..... bank teller

14 대화를 듣고, 남자가 지불해야 할 금액으로 알맞은 것을 고르시오.

① $19.50 ② $20.00 ③ $20.50
④ $56.00 ⑤ $67.00

15 다음을 듣고, 지켜야 할 사항으로 언급되지 <u>않은</u> 것을 고르시오.

① 휴대전화를 꺼라.
② 연극이 끝나면 박수를 쳐라.
③ 연극이 끝나기 전에 자리를 떠나지 마라.
④ 아이들이 나올 때마다 박수를 쳐라.
⑤ 연극이 진행되는 동안 말하지 마라.

16 다음을 듣고, 영화에 대한 내용과 일치하지 <u>않는</u> 것을 고르시오.

① It's an horror movie.
② It was released last week.
③ The creature lives in a lake.
④ People are scared of it.
⑤ The creature kills many people.

[17~18] 대화를 듣고, 이어지는 질문에 가장 알맞은 답을 고르시오.

17
① 음식 ② 참가자 ③ 벌레
④ 활동 ⑤ 야영지

18
① after buying some food
② after 30 minutes
③ after she finishes shopping
④ after he finishes his homework
⑤ after he eats dinner

[19-20] 대화를 듣고, 남자의 마지막 말에 이어질 여자의 응답으로 가장 적절한 것을 고르시오.

19
① I also forgot about it.
② Can you buy my things, too?
③ Biology is our favorite class.
④ You should come with me.
⑤ Where are you going?

20
① Really? Could you fix it for me?
② I'm good at computers, too.
③ May I use your computer?
④ Was anyone hurt in the crash?
⑤ Thanks for fixing it for me.

TEST 9

1 대화를 듣고, 남자가 설명하는 교통수단으로 알맞은 것을 고르시오.

① ② ③ ④ ⑤

M I'm thinking of _____ _____. Can you guess which one it is?

W Does it have _____ _____?

M No, it has four wheels. And people _____ _____ _____ _____ it.

W People pay to ride in it. OK. Is it a bus?

M No, it isn't. It is smaller than a bus.

2 다음을 듣고, 그림의 상황에 가장 어울리는 대화를 고르시오.

① ② ③
④ ⑤

① **M** Can I _____ _____ _____?
  W I'll have the fish and vegetable salad.

② **M** Here is your steak and salad.
  W Oh, _____ _____ you made a mistake. I ordered the fish and soup.

③ **M** Would you like to sit here?
  W OK. It's a nice table _____ _____ _____ _____.

④ **M** What will you cook for dinner?
  W I'll cook the fish we bought yesterday.

⑤ **M** _____ _____ _____. How was the food?
  W It was a nice meal. Thank you.

3 대화를 듣고, 두 사람이 대화하는 장소로 알맞은 곳을 고르시오.

① 호텔 ② 식당 ③ 은행
④ 주유소 ⑤ 식료품점

M Can I please have your _____ _____?

W Yes, here it is.

M You forgot to sign right here. By the way, you _____ _____ _____ 100,000 won. But there is only 50,000 won in your account.

W Oh, really. Oh, I forgot that I spent some money _____ _____ _____ yesterday.

M Then how much would you like to withdraw right now?

4 대화를 듣고, 남자가 전화를 건 목적으로 알맞은 것을 고르시오.

① 여자를 파티에 초대하려고
② 호텔에 객실을 예약하려고
③ 식당에 테이블을 예약하려고
④ 식당 예약을 취소하려고
⑤ 예약 시간을 변경하려고

[Telephone rings.]

W Hello. Beijing Chinese Restaurant.

M Hello. Is it still possible to _____ _____ _____ for tonight?

W Yes, sir. What time would you like to make a reservation for?

M At 8 o'clock.

W Yes, _____ _____ _____ at eight o'clock. How many people are _____ _____ _____ ?

M Six. And the name is Frank Jones. J-O-N-E-S.

W OK. Mr. Jones, _____ _____ _____ at 8 tonight.

---

5 다음을 듣고, 잃어버린 아이가 입고 있는 바지 색깔을 고르시오.

① 갈색
② 파란색
③ 검은색
④ 흰색
⑤ 회색

M Good afternoon, shoppers. _____ _____ _____ is looking for her son, Peter. Peter was shopping with his mother in the children's _____ . She stopped to look at some clothes and he walked away. Peter is 9 years old. He has brown hair and blue eyes. And he is wearing black pants, a white sweater and _____ _____ . If you see him, please bring him to the _____ _____ _____ on the 5th floor.

---

6 대화를 듣고, 내용에 어울리는 속담으로 알맞은 것을 고르시오.

① Slow and steady wins the race.
② Hard work never killed anyone.
③ All work and no play makes Jack a dull boy.
④ A penny saved is a penny earned.
⑤ There is no substitute for hard work.

W I'm thinking of buying a new bag.

M What is wrong with the bag you have now? Is it _____ _____ ?

W It is not that. It is just that I'm kind of tired of it.

M What are you talking about? You just bought it a few months ago.

W That's exactly _____ _____ _____ . It has been months.

M Come on! Didn't you tell me that you have two part-time jobs at night to _____ _____ _____ for your future?

W Yeah. But it is _____ _____ _____ that I want to buy, not something that is expensive.

M I really don't think you should spend money on things you don't really need.

W Well, you're right.

7 대화를 듣고, 여자가 전화를 한 목적으로 알맞은 것을 고르시오.

① 셔츠를 교환하려고
② 셔츠를 주문하려고
③ 주문에 대해 불평하려고
④ 소포 발송에 대해 문의하려고
⑤ 계산서를 지불하려고

[Telephone rings.]

M Hello. GGG Home Shopping.

W Hello. I'd like to order the set of _____ _____ _____ on TV now.

M Yes, ma'am. One minute. The Davinci dress shirts, is that correct?

W Yes, _____ _____. I ordered something else in a small size last time and I had to exchange it.

M So you want to order mediums this time?

W Yes. That's correct. Then my husband _____ _____.

M You told me that you have ordered from us before?

W Yes, I have. My name is Betty White.

---

8 대화를 듣고, 현재 시각으로 알맞은 것을 고르시오.

① 7:30   ② 7:50   ③ 8:12
④ 8:20   ⑤ 8:30

W Dad, we have to hurry up.

M We've got _____ _____ _____. That clock says 7:30.

W 7:30? Dad, that clock is broken. It needs _____ _____ _____.

M So what time is it?

W Look at that clock over there. It's 20 past eight. I'm leaving for school now. The class begins at 8:30.

M Whoops, _____ _____ _____ _____!

---

9 다음을 듣고, 표의 내용과 일치하지 <u>않는</u> 것을 고르시오.

	Number of text messages sent each day	Number of phone calls made each day
Emily	9	4
Rachel	20	12
Sue	38	6

①   ②   ③
④   ⑤

W ① Rachel sends more text messages than Sue.

② Rachel makes the most _____ _____ _____ of the three girls.

③ Emily sends _____ _____ _____ than Sue.

④ Sue makes more cell phone calls than Emily.

⑤ Emily makes the fewest cell phone calls.

---

10 다음을 듣고, 체육 수업이 <u>취소된</u> 이유를 고르시오.

① 비바람
② 무더위
③ 황사
④ 혹한
⑤ 체육관 공사

M Students, today we will not have physical education classes. There is a big _____ _____ _____. I don't want you to get sick. I don't want you to run outside for a long time when _____ _____ _____ _____ yellow dust everywhere. I wish our school had an indoor gymnasium, but it does not. Please study in your classroom _____ _____ _____ _____.

11 다음을 듣고, 두 사람의 대화가 <u>어색한</u> 것을 고르시오.
① ② ③
④ ⑤

① **M** How many brothers and sisters do you have?
　W None. I'm _____ _____ _____.
② **M** Sue, can you stop talking in class?
　W Yes. I'm sorry, Mr. Smith.
③ **M** Will you _____ _____ _____ or a credit card?
　W Thanks. Here's your change.
④ **M** Thank you for _____ _____ _____ _____.
　W You're welcome.
⑤ **M** Are you ready for dinner?
　W Yes, I am. I've already washed my hands.

12 대화를 듣고, 남자의 심정으로 가장 알맞은 것을 고르시오.
① happy
② scared
③ jealous
④ proud
⑤ disappointed

W So, is everyone here?
M No, I don't think so. Amy is not here yet.
W Oh, I didn't tell you. Amy couldn't come. She's helping her grandmother tonight.
M Oh, really? _____ _____ _____. I really wanted to talk to her tonight.
W _____ _____ _____ _____ at school tomorrow?
M Yes, but I _____ _____ _____ _____ to her for a long time tonight. You know I really like her.

13 대화를 듣고, 두 사람의 관계로 알맞은 것을 고르시오.
① tour guide ..... tourist
② hotel receptionist ..... guest
③ real estate agent ..... client
④ grocery store clerk ..... customer
⑤ manager ..... bank teller

M Did you _____ _____ _____ with us?
W Yes, I did. I had a nice view of the city from my room.
M That's good. You stayed three nights and the room you had is $75 a night.
W I also ordered some food _____ _____ _____.
M Yes, you did. So your total bill is $280. _____ _____ _____.

14 대화를 듣고, 남자가 지불해야 할 금액으로 알맞은 것을 고르시오.

① $19.50
② $20.00
③ $20.50
④ $56.00
⑤ $67.00

M Excuse me, I'm _____ _____ _____ _____ for my girlfriend.

W Well, how about this one?

M How much is it?

W It's $15.50

M It's expensive but beautiful. And _____ _____ _____. How much are they?

W They are $5.50.

M OK. I'll take both the necklace and the earrings. Could you _____ _____ a little bit?

W Well... I can _____ _____ one dollar.

M Oh, thanks. Here they are.

15 다음을 듣고, 지켜야 할 사항으로 언급되지 않은 것을 고르시오.

① 휴대전화를 꺼라.
② 연극이 끝나면 박수를 쳐라.
③ 연극이 끝나기 전에 자리를 떠나지 마라.
④ 아이들이 나올 때마다 박수를 쳐라.
⑤ 연극이 진행되는 동안 말하지 마라.

W Welcome to Melville High School's _____ _____ _____ of *West Side Story*. Before the play begins, please turn off your cell phones. Also I'd like to ask you _____ _____ _____ when your child appears. You can clap at the end of the play. And do not leave before the _____ _____ _____ _____. Finally, do not talk during the show.

16 다음을 듣고, 영화에 대한 내용과 일치하지 않는 것을 고르시오.

① It's an horror movie.
② It was released last week.
③ The creature lives in a lake.
④ People are scared of it.
⑤ The creature kills many people.

M *The Creature* is an horror movie. _____ _____ _____ last week. I saw it _____ _____ _____ because I love horror movies. *The Creature* is a monster which lives in a lake. It's actually very kind, but people _____ _____ _____ it because it's so ugly. People decide to kill the monster.

17 대화를 듣고, 이어지는 질문에 가장 알맞은 답을 고르시오.

① 음식
② 참가자
③ 벌레
④ 활동
⑤ 야영지

W My summer vacation was great. How about yours?

M It was good. I went to a summer camp _____ _____ _____.

W Oh, did you have lots of fun?

M I did. The camp was great. There were good food and _____ _____ _____. And I made many good friends.

W Good for you.

M I loved everything _____ _____ _____. I got too many _____ _____.

Q What was one thing that he didn't like during the summer camp?

18 대화를 듣고, 이어지는 질문에 가장 알맞은 답을 고르시오.

① after buying some food
② after 30 minutes
③ after she finishes shopping
④ after he finishes his homework
⑤ after he eats dinner

W Did you finish your homework?

M Not yet. It will take one more hour to finish.

W I have to go shopping for 30 minutes and buy some food for dinner.

M Okay, Mom.

W _____ _____ _____ that computer and play computer games until your homework is finished.

M I promise I won't touch my computer _____ _____ _____.

W Okay. I'll see you soon. Do you want chicken tonight?

M _____ _____.

Q When can he play computer games?

19 대화를 듣고, 남자의 마지막 말에 이어질 여자의 응답으로 가장 적절한 것을 고르시오.

① I also forgot about it.
② Can you buy my things, too?
③ Biology is our favorite class.
④ You should come with me.
⑤ Where are you going?

W Hi, Mark! Where are you going?

M Hi, Susie! I'm going home from a swimming lesson. Where are you going?

W I have to buy some things for _____ _____ _____ _____.

M Which class?

W _____ _____. Don't you remember?

M Oh, I take biology with you. I forgot the teacher asked us to buy some things.

W _____

20 대화를 듣고, 남자의 마지막 말에 이어질 여자의 응답으로 가장 적절한 것을 고르시오.

① Really? Could you fix it for me?
② I'm good at computers, too.
③ May I use your computer?
④ Was anyone hurt in the crash?
⑤ Thanks for fixing it for me.

W My computer _____ _____ _____ _____ again. I have to finish this report today.

M Oh, that's too bad.

W Yeah. I don't know anything about computers. Do you know _____ _____ _____ my computer?

M Well, I am _____ _____ _____ computers.

W _____

1 대화를 듣고, 남자가 오늘 밤에 할 일을 고르시오.

2 대화를 듣고, 남자가 하루에 먹어야 할 약의 양과 횟수를 고르시오.

① three pills — twice a day
② four pills — twice a day
③ six pills — twice a day
④ four pills — three times a day
⑤ three pills — three times day

3 대화를 듣고, 여자가 가려고 하는 곳을 고르시오.

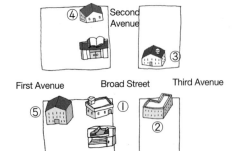

4 대화를 듣고, 두 사람의 대화가 이루어지고 있는 장소를 고르시오.

① 세탁소　　② 탈의실　　③ 옷 가게
④ 수영장　　⑤ 옷 수선집

5 대화를 듣고, 두 사람이 과학관에 가는 이유를 고르시오.

① 비가 와서
② 어제 다녀왔는데, 너무 좋아서
③ 활동적인 하루를 보낼 수 있어서
④ 방학 숙제를 해야 해서
⑤ 남자가 로봇을 좋아해서

6 대화를 듣고, 남자의 심정으로 가장 적절한 것을 고르시오.

① lonely　　② comfortable　③ indifferent
④ nervous　　⑤ disturbed

7 대화를 듣고, 남자가 전화를 건 목적으로 알맞은 것을 고르시오.

① 약속을 취소하려고
② 약속 시간을 변경하려고
③ 약속 시간을 확인하려고
④ 약속 장소를 변경하려고
⑤ 약속 장소를 물어보려고

8 다음 자동응답기의 내용을 듣고, 질문에 답하시오.

① 1　　　② 2　　　③ 3　　　④ 4　　　⑤ 5

9 대화를 듣고, 두 사람의 관계로 가장 알맞은 것을 고르시오.

① judge ..... defendant
② policeman ..... victim
③ lawyer ..... witness
④ taxi driver ..... passenger
⑤ security guard ..... bank teller

10 다음을 듣고, 무엇에 관한 내용인지를 고르시오.

① 쓰레기 분리 수거 잘하기
② 급식 중단 안내
③ 편식하지 않기
④ 음식물 버리지 않기
⑤ 식당의 위생과 청결 검사

11 다음을 듣고, 내용과 일치하지 <u>않는</u> 것을 고르시오.

① 버스에 탄 학생수는 35명이다.
② 학교까지는 보통 1시간 반 정도 소요된다.
③ 버스 안에서는 한 번도 노래를 부르지 않았다.
④ 길이 막히면, 학교까지 3시간 정도 걸릴 수 있다.
⑤ 학교에 도착할 때까지 잠을 자라고 권하고 있다.

12 다음을 듣고, 그림의 상황에 가장 어울리는 대화를 고르시오.

① ② ③ ④ ⑤

13 대화를 듣고, 남자의 직업으로 가장 적절한 것을 고르시오.

① refrigerator repairman
② fashion model
③ hotel cashier
④ electronics salesman
⑤ deliveryman

14 대화를 듣고, 남자가 방과 후에 할 일을 고르시오.

① cleaning the classroom
② having a detention
③ getting extra help
④ helping Mr. Lee with math problems
⑤ reading a book

15 대화를 듣고, 내용과 어울리는 속담을 고르시오.

① Well begun, half done.
② Easy come, easy go.
③ Birds of a feather flock together.
④ Every dog has his day.
⑤ Look before you leap.

16 대화를 듣고, 무엇에 관한 내용인지 고르시오.

① borrowing money from a bank
② buying a house
③ getting a job as a real estate agent
④ commuting by public transportation
⑤ reserving three rooms at a hotel

[17-18] 다음을 듣고, 이어지는 질문에 답하시오.

17

① 전자제품 전원 끄기
② 안전벨트 착용하기
③ 양식 작성하기
④ 비행기에서 신속하게 내리기
⑤ 면세제품 구입하기

18

① 날씨가 너무 안 좋아서
② 관중들이 던진 물건들을 치우려고
③ 공정한 경기가 이루어지지 않아서
④ 편파 판정으로 선수들이 시합을 거부해서
⑤ 선수들이 심판에게 항의해서

[19-20] 대화를 듣고, 여자의 마지막 말에 이어질 남자의 응답으로 가장 적절한 것을 고르시오.

19

① I play with my sister after dinner.
② I usually do it before dinner.
③ I watch TV when I get home.
④ I am very busy all day long.
⑤ What is our science homework today?

20

① I hate the design. I like the latest one.
② It's 50% off. You can buy it.
③ I understand. I'll get it then.
④ It's too expensive. Let's find another.
⑤ Is that why you bought it?

T E S T 10

1 대화를 듣고, 남자가 오늘 밤에 할 일을 고르시오.

① ② ③ ④ ⑤

M Hi, Sarah. Did you want to see me? _____ _____ you were looking for me.

W Hi, Paul. Are you busy this evening?

M Yes. I'm busy all this week. What happened?

W Oh, that's too bad. I just wanted to _____ _____ _____ _____ with you.

M I can't. I must study math tonight. We have _____ _____ next week.

W That's right. Maybe I should study, too.

M You can _____ _____ _____ my house tonight if you want. Cathy and Brian are coming, too.

W Thank you. It's nice of you _____ _____.

2 대화를 듣고, 남자가 하루에 먹어야 할 약의 양과 횟수를 고르시오.

① three pills — twice a day
② four pills — twice a day
③ six pills — twice a day
④ four pills — three times a day
⑤ three pills — three times day

W Here is _____ _____, sir.

M Thank you. Do I take one or two pills each time?

W Inside the box, there are 18 _____ _____ _____. If you have three meals a day, you will be taking 6 pills per day for 3 days.

M Does that mean it's okay to _____ _____ _____ _____ if I have two meals?

W Right. Just make sure that you take two at a time, 30 minutes after each meal. And if the condition is not getting better, you will have to see your doctor again.

M OK. Thank you very much.

W You're welcome. I hope you will _____ _____ soon.

3 대화를 듣고, 여자가 가려고 하는 곳을 고르시오.

Main Street
④ Second Avenue
③
First Avenue   Broad Street   Third Avenue
⑤   ①   ②

W _____ _____. Is there a bakery around here?

M Yes, there is one on the corner of Broad Street and Second Avenue.

W On the corner? Oh, I remember now.

M Do you mean the store which is _____ _____ _____?

W Right! Across from a bookstore.

M And next to a shoe store. _____ _____ _____?

W Yes, thank you very much.

4 대화를 듣고, 두 사람의 대화가 이루어지고 있는 장소를 고르시오.

① 세탁소
② 탈의실
③ 옷 가게
④ 수영장
⑤ 옷 수선집

M The waist seems _____ _____.

W So you'll need a larger size.

M Yes, I think so. Do you have one with a 32cm waist?

W One minute. *[pause]* Here you are, sir.

M Thank you. I'll go back to _____ _____ _____ and try them on.

W Those pants would look great _____ _____ _____.

M OK. _____ _____ _____ the shirt, too.

---

5 대화를 듣고, 두 사람이 과학관에 가는 이유를 고르시오.

① 비가 와서
② 어제 다녀왔는데, 너무 좋아서
③ 활동적인 하루를 보낼 수 있어서
④ 방학 숙제를 해야 해서
⑤ 남자가 로봇을 좋아해서

M What a terrible day! I don't like the rainy season.

W I know. What do you want to do today then?

M Well, I don't want to _____ _____ _____ _____. We did that yesterday. The National Art Museum was nice, but I want something more active today.

W I know... But because we have to do the vacation homework, let's visit the Science Pavilion. They are having _____ _____ _____. The robots fight each other.

M Hmm... I have _____ _____.

---

6 대화를 듣고, 남자의 심정으로 가장 적절한 것을 고르시오.

① lonely
② comfortable
③ indifferent
④ nervous
⑤ disturbed

M Sarah, I'm the only Korean student at this university, you know.

W Then, you must make many American friends, Sangjin.

M But it's hard. I haven't met anyone yet. I saw a movie yesterday _____ _____.

W I'm sorry, I was so busy I couldn't go with you.

M Maybe I should _____ _____ _____ _____. Right now I am in one by myself.

W That might be good idea. You _____ _____ _____ all the time.

7 대화를 듣고, 남자가 전화를 건 목적으로 알맞은 것을 고르시오.

① 약속을 취소하려고
② 약속 시간을 변경하려고
③ 약속 시간을 확인하려고
④ 약속 장소를 변경하려고
⑤ 약속 장소를 물어보려고

[Telephone rings.]

W Hi. Wendy speaking.

M Wendy, it's Fred.

W Oh! Hi, Fred. What's up? We're still going out tonight, aren't we?

M Yes, of course.

W Oh, I thought maybe you phoned to _____ _____ _____ .

M No, it's not that. Actually, I feel _____ _____ _____ . But did we make an appointment for 7 or 7:30?

W We said we'd meet at 7:30.

M I thought so. But I was scared of _____ _____ _____ .

8 다음 자동응답기의 내용을 듣고, 질문에 답하시오.

① 1   ② 2   ③ 3
④ 4   ⑤ 5

M Thank you for calling Megaplex 20 Theater. Press 1 if you want to hear what each movie is about. Press 2 if you want to _____ _____ _____ each movie starts and finishes. Press 3 if you want to know about _____ _____ . Press 4 to learn if a movie is _____ _____ . Press 5 to learn how to make a reservation on the Internet.

Q What should you press to learn when a movie is over?

9 대화를 듣고, 두 사람의 관계로 가장 알맞은 것을 고르시오.

① judge ..... defendant
② policeman ..... victim
③ lawyer ..... witness
④ taxi driver ..... passenger
⑤ security guard ..... bank teller

M Did a man _____ _____ _____ and run away?

W Yes, I had just gotten some money from the ATM.

M How much did you have? A lot of money?

W 100,000 won. I _____ _____ the street and _____ _____ _____ .

M What did he look like?

W He was young, about 23, tall, _____ _____ _____ .

10 다음을 듣고, 무엇에 관한 내용인지를 고르시오.

① 쓰레기 분리 수거 잘하기
② 급식 중단 안내
③ 편식하지 않기
④ 음식물 버리지 않기
⑤ 식당의 위생과 청결 검사

M Good morning, students. This is the principal speaking. We have a problem _____ _____ _____ . You take rice, kimchi, and other food and then you don't eat it. You throw it in the garbage. You don't think _____ _____ _____ . And that really makes me sad. _____ _____ _____ in the garbage is wrong. You have to change your habits.

11 다음을 듣고, 내용과 일치하지 <u>않는</u> 것을 고르시오.

① 버스에 탄 학생수는 35명이다.
② 학교까지는 보통 1시간 반 정도 소요된다.
③ 버스 안에서는 한 번도 노래를 부르지 않았다.
④ 길이 막히면, 학교까지 3시간 정도 걸릴 수 있다.
⑤ 학교에 도착할 때까지 잠을 자라고 권하고 있다.

W 33, 34, 35, OK, everyone is _____ _____ _____. We are ready to go back to our school. It will take about an hour and a half. But if there is _____ _____ _____, it will take a lot longer. Maybe 3 hours. The bus driver also said you may not use the karaoke machine. You were _____ _____ _____. Everyone must be tired. I suggest you sleep until _____ _____ _____ to the school.

12 다음을 듣고, 그림의 상황에 가장 어울리는 대화를 고르시오.

① ② ③
④ ⑤

① **W** Excuse me, sir, I don't understand.
  M OK. No problem. _____ _____ _____ _____.
② **W** Let's go to the beach this weekend.
  M OK. The forecast _____ _____ _____.
③ **W** What kind of movies do you like to watch?
  M I like _____ _____. How about you?
④ **W** Excuse me, may I sit down here?
  M No, I'm sorry. I'm saving it for someone.
⑤ **W** How much did it cost you?
  M I don't remember that exactly. Maybe twenty dollars.

13 대화를 듣고, 남자의 직업으로 가장 적절한 것을 고르시오.

① refrigerator repairman
② fashion model
③ hotel cashier
④ electronics salesman
⑤ deliveryman

M Good afternoon. How may I help you today, ma'am? TV, stereo...
W No, I need a _____ _____.
M Our refrigerators are over here.
W Thank you. Is this _____ _____ _____?
M Yes, it is. The design is very nice.
W _____ _____. How much is it?
M $1,000. But I can give you a 10% discount.

14 대화를 듣고, 남자가 방과 후에 할 일을 고르시오.

① cleaning the classroom
② having a detention
③ getting extra help
④ helping Mr. Lee with math problems
⑤ reading a book

M Can you wait for thirty minutes or after school finishes?
W Do you have to clean the classroom again?
M No, it was my turn last week.
W I thought so. Do you _____ _____ _____?
M No, it's not that. Mr. Lee promised to help me with a few math problems. I did _____ _____ on the last test.
W Oh, you're getting _____ _____ _____. I'll read in the classroom and wait for you.
M Thanks.

15 대화를 듣고, 내용과 어울리는 속담을 고르시오.

① Well begun, half done.
② Easy come, easy go.
③ Birds of a feather flock together.
④ Every dog has his day.
⑤ Look before you leap.

M Hey, Namwon is always talking to the new student. He doesn't talk to us much. Hey, what's the new student's name?
W Seonghyun. And yes, Namwon and Seonghyun are _____ _____.
M They became friends _____.
W They both love the _____ _____ _____ character. They talk about comic books all the time.
M Really? I didn't know that.
W Yes, I don't like to read comic books. I don't know what they are talking about.

16 대화를 듣고, 무엇에 관한 내용인지 고르시오.

① borrowing money from a bank
② buying a house
③ getting a job as a real estate agent
④ commuting by public transportation
⑤ reserving three rooms at a hotel

M I think this is the best. Let's buy it. How about you?
W It's the right size for our family. Three bedrooms.
M Yes, and it's a _____ _____.
W It's close to a subway stop and there are many buses in front of the apartment.
M Is it too expensive? Do we have the money?
W Yes, if we are careful. We will borrow some money from the bank. Then we will _____ _____ _____ _____.
M OK. Phone _____ _____ _____ agent.

17 다음을 듣고, 이어지는 질문에 답하시오.

① 전자제품 전원 끄기
② 안전벨트 착용하기
③ 양식 작성하기
④ 비행기에서 신속하게 내리기
⑤ 면세제품 구입하기

W Attention, everyone. This is the chief _____ _____, Mindy Marshall speaking. We will land in Seoul in 30 minutes. Before we land, you must _____ _____ a customs and _____ _____. Please do it right now. Then you'll be able to _____ _____ _____ quickly. If you have any questions about the form, just ask a flight attendant. Thank you for flying Fast Flyers Airlines.

Q What does the flight attendant want passengers to do right now?

18 다음을 듣고, 이어지는 질문에 답하시오.

① 날씨가 너무 안 좋아서
② 관중들이 던진 물건들을 치우려고
③ 공정한 경기가 이루어지지 않아서
④ 편파 판정으로 선수들이 시합을 거부해서
⑤ 선수들이 심판에게 항의해서

M Sports fans, _____ _____ has stopped the soccer game. We played 30 minutes. The game is not over. But it is raining too hard. And now _____ _____ _____, too. One player was hurt a few minutes ago when another player _____ _____ _____. The players can't control themselves. They are hurting each other. The referee has made _____ _____ _____.

Q Why has the game stopped?

19 대화를 듣고, 여자의 마지막 말에 이어질 남자의 응답으로 가장 적절한 것을 고르시오.

① I play with my sister after dinner.
② I usually do it before dinner.
③ I watch TV when I get home.
④ I am very busy all day long.
⑤ What is our science homework today?

M I usually play soccer in the school yard after school. What do you do _____ _____?
W I have a piano lesson after school everyday.
M Do you _____ _____ _____ in the evening after dinner?
W Yes, I do. How about you?
M _____

20 대화를 듣고, 여자의 마지막 말에 이어질 남자의 응답으로 가장 적절한 것을 고르시오.

① I hate the design. I like the latest one.
② It's 50% off. You can buy it.
③ I understand. I'll get it then.
④ It's too expensive. Let's find another.
⑤ Is that why you bought it?

W Minsu, you should get it. That MP3 player is very nice.
M Yes, I need a new one. But it's too expensive. It's $150, but I only have $100.
W This one is _____ _____ _____, but it is cheaper.
M Why is that? Isn't it strange?
W Maybe you can _____ _____ _____ on it. It's only $75.
M _____

A Write down the definition of each word or phrase.

1	vehicle	11	insect
2	withdraw	12	prescription
3	paycheck	13	offer
4	security	14	refrigerator
5	worn-out	15	detention
6	steady	16	fill out
7	substitute	17	customs
8	physical education	18	immigration
9	real estate agent	19	referee
10	clap	20	accidentally

B Match each word with the right definition.

1	sold out	___	a	나가다, 나타나다, 얼굴을 내보이다
2	release	___	b	계좌
3	crash	___	c	돈을 넣다, 예금하다
4	show up	___	d	빈 공간, 여유
5	pill	___	e	일행, 모임
6	account	___	f	~을 데려오다, 가져오다
7	land	___	g	~에 싫증이 나다
8	party	___	h	잔돈, 거스름돈
9	room	___	i	접수원
10	deposit	___	j	(값을) 깎다
11	be tired of	___	k	~을 개봉하다
12	change	___	l	(컴퓨터가) 갑자기 기능을 멈추다, 다운되다
13	receptionist	___	m	알약
14	knock off	___	n	매진된, 품절된
15	bring	___	o	착륙하다, 도착하다

C Choose the best answer for the blank.

1   Don't forget _____ the door before you go out.

     a. lock   b. to lock   c. locking

2   He decided _____ his house.

     a. sell   b. to sell   c. selling

3   Do you mean the store which is across _____ a bookstore?

     a. of   b. with   c. from

4   Would you please _____ the door open?

     a. hold   b. give   c. put

5   Can you ask Sophia _____ she's free on Friday?

     a. what   b. when   c. if

6   Don't play computer games _____ your homework is finished.

     a. whether   b. until   c. by

D Complete the short dialogues.

1   A: Have you decided what to do in the future?

     B: Yes, I've _____ a decision I will become a doctor.

2   A: These pants would look great with this shirt.

     B: OK. I'll go to the changing room and _____ _____ the shirt.

3   A: Do you live with your family?

     B: No, I live _____ myself.

4   A: What did you do last night?

     B: I had lots of homework, so I _____ my homework all night.

5   A: What did he _____ _____ ?

     B: He was young, about 23, tall, with short hair.

1 다음을 듣고, 남자가 설명하는 그림으로 가장 알맞은 것을 고르시오.

①

②

③

④

⑤

2 대화를 듣고, 여자가 감량한 체중을 고르시오.
① 1 kg　　② 2 kg　　③ 3 kg
④ 4 kg　　⑤ 5 kg

3 대화를 듣고, 여동생의 생일 파티를 계획하고 있는 요일과 날짜를 고르시오.

DECEMBER						
SUN	MON	TUE	WED	THU	FRI	SAT
	1	2	3	4	5	6
7	8	9	10	11	12	13
14	15	16	17	18	19	20
21	22	23	24	25	26	27
28	29	30				

① Friday the 12th
② Saturday the 13th
③ Sunday the 14th
④ Monday the 15th
⑤ Friday the 19th

4 다음을 듣고, 내일과 모레의 날씨로 바르게 짝지어진 것을 고르시오.
① wet - hot　　　② windy - cloudy
③ stormy - rainy　④ rainy - sunny
⑤ cold - stormy

5 대화를 듣고, 지성이가 학교에 가지 <u>못하는</u> 이유를 고르시오.
① 감기에 걸려서　　② 축구 대회에 나가서
③ 병원에 입원해서　④ 배탈이 나서
⑤ 팔이 부러져서

6 대화를 듣고, 여자가 인터넷 채팅을 하는 이유를 고르시오.
① 영어를 배우려고
② 고민을 상담하려고
③ 많은 친구들을 사귀려고
④ 다른 나라에 대해 배우려고
⑤ 새로운 사람들과 이야기하는 것이 좋아서

7 다음을 듣고, 그림의 상황에 가장 어울리는 대화를 고르시오.

①　　②　　③　　④　　⑤

8 다음을 듣고, 상황에 가장 알맞은 표현을 고르시오.
① Don't worry. I'll do better next time.
② Congratulations! Let's go get ice cream.
③ It was a hard test. It'll be easier next time.
④ Cheer for me loudly when it's my turn.
⑤ You can say that again. They did their best.

9 대화를 듣고, 두 사람이 대화하는 장소를 고르시오.
① computer store　　② library
③ bookstore　　　　④ classroom
⑤ convenience store

10 다음을 듣고, 두 사람의 대화가 <u>어색한</u> 것을 고르시오.
①　　②　　③　　④　　⑤

11 대화를 듣고, 남자가 지불해야 할 금액을 고르시오.

Pop Concert

(Everyday until July 28th)

Gold Tickets $22
Silver Tickets $17

* $5 off on Monday through Thursday
* $3 off on any holidays

① $15　　　② $24　　　③ $34
④ $36　　　⑤ $51

12 다음을 듣고, 무엇에 관한 설명인지 고르시오.
① 어린이들의 교통 사망률
② 학교보호구역 표지판 설치의 중요성
③ 운전면허 시험 요령
④ 고속도로 운전시 주의 사항
⑤ 학교보호구역 내에서의 주의 운전

13 대화를 듣고, 두 사람의 관계로 가장 알맞은 것을 고르시오.
① 선생님 – 학생　　　② 면접관 – 지원자
③ 학생 – 학생　　　④ 의사 – 환자
⑤ 감독 – 선수

14 대화를 듣고, 여자가 남자에게 전화 건 목적을 고르시오.
① 집에 오라고 말하려고
② 영화 시간을 물어보려고
③ 고모가 찾는다고 말하려고
④ 늦는다고 말하려고
⑤ 영화 보러 못 간다고 말하려고

15 대화를 듣고, 두 사람이 제일 먼저 할 일로 알맞은 것을 고르시오.
① to buy tickets　　　② to go to a restaurant
③ to see the concert　　　④ to drive home
⑤ to pick up the tickets from David

16 다음을 듣고, 표와 일치하지 <u>않는</u> 것을 고르시오.

	Fred (M)	Ted (M)	Jane (F)	Sandra (F)
Age (year)	17	18	16	15
Height (cm)	175	170	172	165
Weight (kg)	75	65	54	49

①　　②　　③　　④　　⑤

17 다음을 듣고, 무엇에 관한 내용인지 고르시오.
① 차량 정체　　　② 황사 현상
③ 지구 온난화　　　④ 대기 오염
⑤ 에너지 절약

18 대화를 듣고, 두 사람의 대화 내용과 일치하지 <u>않는</u> 것을 고르시오.
① 슈퍼 주니어 팬클럽을 창단하려고 한다.
② 일주일에 한 번씩 다른 팬들과 만날 것이다.
③ '아이 러브 슈퍼 주니어' 홈페이지를 개설할 것이다.
④ 홈페이지를 통해 팬클럽 활동을 시작할 것이다.
⑤ 두 사람의 이메일 주소를 홈페이지에 남길 것이다.

[19-20] 대화를 듣고, 남자의 마지막 말에 이어질 여자의 응답으로 가장 적절한 것을 고르시오.

19
① Yes, I'd appreciate it.
② What's wrong with you?
③ I can't help you right now.
④ No, thanks. You can do it.
⑤ It's OK. That's a good idea.

20
① I don't like soup.
② I tasted it earlier.
③ No thanks. I'm full.
④ I'll test you later.
⑤ It's salty but good.

1 다음을 듣고, 남자가 설명하는 그림으로 가장 알맞은 것을 고르시오.

① ② ③ ④ ⑤

M Every computer has one of these. We don't use it _____ _____ _____ _____ or characters. We use it to move the cursor to _____ _____ _____ on a Web page or a document which we are writing. Then we click it to perform some kind of action. We move it _____ _____ _____ of our hand and click it with a finger.

2 대화를 듣고, 여자가 감량한 체중을 고르시오.

① 1 kg ② 2 kg ③ 3 kg
④ 4 kg ⑤ 5 kg

M _____ _____ _____. Are you trying to lose weight?
W Not really. It's just _____ _____ _____. I don't feel like eating.
M But you have lost a few kilograms, right?
W Let's see, I weighed myself this morning and it was 46kg.
M How much did you weigh before the summer began?
W 49kg. So, yes, _____ _____ a few kilograms.

3 대화를 듣고, 여동생의 생일 파티를 계획하고 있는 요일과 날짜를 고르시오.

DECEMBER						
SUN	MON	TUE	WED	THU	FRI	SAT
	1	2	3	4	5	6
7	8	9	10	11	12	13
14	15	16	17	18	19	20
21	22	23	24	25	26	27
28	29	30				

① Friday the 12th
② Saturday the 13th
③ Sunday the 14th
④ Monday the 15th
⑤ Friday the 19th

M When is your sister's birthday?
W On the 15th.
M So you're going to _____ _____ _____ on Monday night.
W No, Monday night is not a good night for a party. We all have to work _____ _____ _____.
M That's right. When will the party _____ _____ for her?
W So the party is on the Friday before her birthday.
M OK. I got it.

4 다음을 듣고, 내일과 모레의 날씨로 바르게 짝지은 것을 고르시오.

① wet – hot
② windy – cloudy
③ stormy – rainy
④ rainy – sunny
⑤ cold – stormy

M Good evening. I'm Mike Miller with tomorrow's weather forecast for ABC News. It's going to _____ _____ tomorrow. A storm will reach the city as you're leaving for work. There will be _____ _____ all day. The storm _____ _____ _____ the city by tomorrow night and the following day will be warm and sunny. _____ _____ _____ _____ .

5 대화를 듣고, 지성이가 학교에 가지 <u>못하는</u> 이유를 고르시오.

① 감기에 걸려서
② 축구 대회에 나가서
③ 병원에 입원해서
④ 배탈이 나서
⑤ 팔이 부러져서

[Telephone rings.]
M Hello.
W Hello. May I speak with Mr. Lee?
M Hello, this is Mr. Lee speaking.
W Hello. I am Jisung's mother. Are you his _____ _____ ?
M Yes, of course, Mrs. Park. We met last year at a parent-teacher meeting. Where is Jisung today?
W Sadly, he is in the hospital. He _____ _____ _____ playing soccer last night.
M I'm very sorry to hear that. I hope he will _____ _____ _____ .
W He will, but he won't be at school for two days.

6 대화를 듣고, 여자가 인터넷 채팅을 하는 이유를 고르시오.

① 영어를 배우려고
② 고민을 상담하려고
③ 많은 친구들을 사귀려고
④ 다른 나라에 대해 배우려고
⑤ 새로운 사람들과 이야기하는 것이 좋아서

M My mom doesn't like it when I _____ _____ _____ _____ with people I don't know.
W You can meet some bad people. I know that.
M So why do you chat _____ _____ with people you don't know?
W I love chatting in English with people _____ _____ _____ .
M So you want to practice your English?
W Not really. I want learn about other countries. I always ask about life in their country.

7 다음을 듣고, 그림의 상황에 가장 어울리는 대화를 고르시오.

① ② ③
④ ⑤

① **M** Is it okay if I go home now?
   W Go ahead.
② **M** Is it okay if I use your cell phone?
   W I'm afraid you can't.
③ **M** _____ _____ _____ _____ I borrow your pen?
   W Of course not.
④ **M** Do you mind if we _____ _____ _____?
   W Certainly not.
⑤ **M** You _____ _____. What's wrong?
   W I'm not feeling well. My stomach hurts.

8 다음을 듣고, 상황에 가장 알맞은 표현을 고르시오.

① Don't worry. I'll do better next time.
② Congratulations! Let's go get ice cream.
③ It was a hard test. It'll be easier next time.
④ Cheer for me loudly when it's my turn.
⑤ You can say that again. They did their best.

M Elizabeth studied hard for the math final test. She studied every night _____ _____ _____. She, however, did very poorly on the test. _____ _____ Elizabeth, but a lot of students did poorly on the test. Her friend, Mike wants to make her _____ _____. In this situation, what would he say to her?

9 대화를 듣고, 두 사람이 대화하는 장소를 고르시오.

① computer store
② library
③ bookstore
④ classroom
⑤ convenience store

M I'm sorry, you can't take that book out.
W Why is that?
M It's a _____ _____. It's only to be used here.
W OK. I didn't know.
M So you _____ _____ these three books?
W Yes, _____ _____ _____ is three weeks right?
M That's right.

10 다음을 듣고, 두 사람의 대화가 <u>어색한</u> 것을 고르시오.

① ② ③
④ ⑤

① **M** Is it OK if I borrow your ruler?

　W Sure. _____ _____ _____.

② **M** I didn't pass the math exam.

　W It was a really hard test. Many people failed.

③ **M** Are you going to the dentist's?

　W No, the doctor's. _____ _____ _____ _____.

　　Not a toothache.

④ **M** Are you older than your sister?

　W Yes, I am. She's only 14. I'm 16.

⑤ **M** Can you sing a song for me?

　W I don't like _____ _____.

11 대화를 듣고, 남자가 지불해야 할 금액을 고르시오.

Pop Concert

(Everyday until July 28th)

Gold Tickets $22
Silver Tickets $17

* $5 off on Monday through Thursday
* $3 off on any holidays

① $15　　② $24　　③ $34
④ $36　　⑤ $51

W May I help you?

M I'd like to buy some tickets _____ _____ _____ _____.

W We have gold tickets and silver tickets. Gold tickets are $22 and silver tickets are $17.

M Are there _____ _____?

W _____ _____ _____ _____. When would you like to see the concert?

M Well, I was thinking Tuesday.

W You can get $5 off for each ticket on Monday through Thursday. And how many of you need the ticket?

M Three, please.

W All right. Are they silver or gold?

M _____ _____ _____, please.

W Sure.

12 다음을 듣고, 무엇에 관한 설명인지 고르시오.

① 어린이들의 교통 사망률
② 학교보호구역 표지판 설치의 중요성
③ 운전면허 시험 요령
④ 고속도로 운전시 주의 사항
⑤ 학교보호구역 내에서의 주의 운전

M Many children are hurt or killed when they are _____ _____ _____. This should not happen. Sometimes children are not careful. But the big problem is that cars are going too fast _____ _____ _____. Please drive carefully and _____ _____ _____ _____ in school zones. Even when you are in hurry, you must drive slowly.

13 대화를 듣고, 두 사람의 관계로 가장 알맞은 것을 고르시오.

① 선생님 – 학생
② 면접관 – 지원자
③ 학생 – 학생
④ 의사 – 환자
⑤ 감독 – 선수

M Final exams are almost over.

W Yeah. _____ _____ _____. But I am happy we will go to high school next year.

M Me too. _____ _____ _____.

W I hope we are in the same class.

M We won't know for a couple of months. But I don't think _____ _____ _____.

W I'll miss all our teachers here. I hope we meet nice teachers.

14 대화를 듣고, 여자가 남자에게 전화 건 목적을 고르시오.

① 집에 오라고 말하려고
② 영화 시간을 물어보려고
③ 고모가 찾는다고 말하려고
④ 늦는다고 말하려고
⑤ 영화 보러 못 간다고 말하려고

[Telephone rings.]

M Hello.

W Hi, dear.

M Oh, Lisa. I just _____ _____ _____ _____.

W Larry, sorry but I'm going to be late.

M Really?

W Yeah. 30 minutes. My aunt came to visit and we started talking.

M OK. I guess we won't have time to eat before the movie.

W I'm sorry, Larry. My aunt _____ _____ for a long time.

15 대화를 듣고, 두 사람이 제일 먼저 할 일로 알맞은 것을 고르시오.

① to buy tickets
② to go to a restaurant
③ to see the concert
④ to drive home
⑤ to pick up the tickets from David

M I'm so hungry.

W Me too. We were _____ _____ _____ _____ for an hour and a half and now it's past dinner time.

M So let's go eat.

W We should buy the concert tickets first. They might _____ _____ _____.

M Didn't I tell you? David gave me these free tickets _____ _____ _____ _____.

W Great, we don't have to buy tickets. Let's go and eat.

M Would you like to eat Korean or Chinese food tonight?

16 다음을 듣고, 표와 일치하지 <u>않는</u> 것을 고르시오.

	Fred (M)	Ted (M)	Jane (F)	Sandra (F)
Age (year)	17	18	16	15
Height (cm)	175	170	172	165
Weight (kg)	75	65	54	49

①   ②   ③
④   ⑤

M ① The girls are younger than the boys.

② Jane is taller than Ted.

③ Sandra is three years older than Ted.

④ Jane _____ _____ _____ Ted.

⑤ Jane is 5kg _____ _____ Sandra.

17 다음을 듣고, 무엇에 관한 내용인지 고르시오.

① 차량 정체
② 황사 현상
③ 지구 온난화
④ 대기 오염
⑤ 에너지 절약

W It's a sunny day, but you can't see very far. You cannot see _____ _____ _____. The air is dirty. It is also making you sick. The pollution in this city is mostly caused by cars. There are too many cars _____ _____ _____. Some car companies are selling cars that make _____ _____ _____ _____. These cars are more expensive, but people must buy them. People must drive cars which make less pollution so we can have clean air.

18 대화를 듣고, 두 사람의 대화 내용과 일치하지 <u>않는</u> 것을 고르시오.

① 슈퍼 주니어 팬클럽을 창단하려고 한다.
② 일주일에 한 번씩 다른 팬들과 만날 것이다.
③ '아이 러브 슈퍼 주니어' 홈페이지를 개설할 것이다.
④ 홈페이지를 통해 팬클럽 활동을 시작할 것이다.
⑤ 두 사람의 이메일 주소를 홈페이지에 남길 것이다.

M Let's start a Super Junior fan club.
W Great idea! We might meet more people _____ _____ _____ of Super Junior.
M We can meet in a cafe _____ _____ _____ and talk about Super Junior.
W Good idea. How do we begin the club? I know, we'll open an 'I love Super Junior' web site.
M That's a good idea. Other fans can leave their e-mail addresses. We'll e-mail them back. _____ _____ _____ to start a club.

19 대화를 듣고, 남자의 마지막 말에 이어질 여자의 응답으로 가장 적절한 것을 고르시오.

① Yes, I'd appreciate it.
② What's wrong with you?
③ I can't help you right now.
④ No, thanks. You can do it.
⑤ It's OK. That's a good idea.

M I'm going to read _____ _____ _____. I'll go to my bedroom if you're going to watch TV.
W I'm going to listen to music.
M OK. Can you _____ _____ _____ so I can read?
W Sure. Hey, it doesn't work! _____ _____?
M Do you want some help?
W _____

20 대화를 듣고, 남자의 마지막 말에 이어질 여자의 응답으로 가장 적절한 것을 고르시오.

① I don't like soup.
② I tasted it earlier.
③ No thanks. I'm full.
④ I'll test you later.
⑤ It's salty but good.

W You never cook. This is a special day.
M Yes, I guess so. Do you want to _____ _____ _____?
W Sure. I'll _____ _____ _____ before dinner.
M _____ _____ _____. I spent two hours to cook this. I hope it is good. What does it taste like?
W _____

1 대화를 듣고, 두 사람이 이야기하고 있는 표지판을 고르시오.

① ②

③ ④

⑤

2 대화를 듣고, 대화가 이루어지는 장소를 고르시오.
① taxi
② train station
③ airport
④ airplane
⑤ lost and found

3 대화를 듣고, 여자가 전화를 건 목적으로 알맞은 것을 고르시오.
① 책을 빌리려고
② 숙제에 대해 물어보려고
③ 수학 공책을 빌리려고
④ 책을 돌려달라고 말하려고
⑤ 내일 만날 약속을 하려고

4 대화를 듣고, 여자가 지금 해야 할 일을 고르시오.
① 풍선 걸기　　　　② 음식 주문하기
③ 케이크 가져오기　④ 손님 모시러 가기
⑤ 케이크 주문하기

5 다음을 듣고, 무엇에 관한 내용인지 고르시오.
① 티켓 환불 안내　　② 새로운 공연 소개
③ 연장 공연 실시　　④ 티켓 구입 안내
⑤ 공연 취소 안내

6 대화를 듣고, 남자와 여자가 학교 축제 때 하려고 하는 것을 고르시오.
① 노래를 한다.
② 춤을 춘다.
③ 대본을 쓰고 감독을 한다.
④ 재미있는 연극을 한다.
⑤ 드라마를 연기한다.

7 대화를 듣고, 남자가 학교에 두고 온 교과서로 알맞은 것을 고르시오.
① Math　　　　　② English
③ History　　　　④ Korean
⑤ Biology

8 다음을 듣고, 예상되는 내일의 날씨를 고르시오.
① sunny　　　　　② cloudy
③ rainy　　　　　④ snowy
⑤ hot and dry

9 다음을 듣고, 남자가 지불해야 할 금액을 고르시오.
① $100　　② $120　　③ $140
④ $150　　⑤ $160

10 다음을 듣고, 두 사람의 대화가 <u>어색한</u> 것을 고르시오.
①　　　②　　　③　　　④　　　⑤

11 대화를 듣고, 남자의 심정으로 알맞은 것을 고르시오.
① surprised
② anticipating
③ worried
④ relieved
⑤ disappointed

12 대화를 듣고, 두 사람의 관계로 적절한 것을 고르시오.

① 약사 – 손님
② 제약회사 사장 – 직원
③ 간호사 – 의사
④ 의사 – 환자
⑤ 제약회사 직원 – 약사

13 다음을 듣고, 그림의 상황에 가장 어울리는 대화를 고르시오.

① ② ③ ④ ⑤

14 대화를 듣고, 남자가 지불해야 할 금액을 고르시오.

① $5   ② $8   ③ $10
④ $16   ⑤ $20

15 다음을 듣고, 내용과 일치하지 <u>않는</u> 것을 고르시오.

① 휴대폰을 꺼야 한다.
② 공연시간은 약 1시간이다.
③ '크리스마스 캐럴'을 공연한다.
④ 공연 중간에 휴식시간이 있다.
⑤ 공연 후에 커피와 쿠키를 제공한다.

16 대화를 듣고, 남자가 여자와 같이 공부하려고 하는 이유를 고르시오.

① 여자를 좋아해서
② 여자가 수학을 잘해서
③ 여자가 사회과학을 잘해서
④ 여자에게 수학 공책을 빌리려고
⑤ 여자에게 사회과학을 가르쳐주려고

17 다음을 듣고, 여자가 만족하지 <u>못하는</u> 것을 고르시오.

① 선생님   ② 식당 음식
③ 기숙사 시설   ④ 기숙사 친구들
⑤ 엄마가 해준 쿠키

[18-19] 대화를 듣고, 여자의 마지막 말에 이어질 남자의 응답으로 가장 적절한 것을 고르시오.

18

① I think I made three or four mistakes.
② I don't know the score of the game.
③ I don't like science very much.
④ Science is very interesting to me.
⑤ $100. That's not too expensive.

19

① You look very smart.
② He isn't in my class.
③ He is from Korea.
④ Hey, look at him.
⑤ He is tall and has dark skin.

20 다음을 듣고, Bill이 할 말로 가장 알맞은 것을 고르시오.

① Are you ready to order?
② Would you like anything else?
③ How would you like your steak?
④ Do you like spaghetti or steak better?
⑤ Do you want to see a menu?

DICTATION • TEST 12

1 대화를 듣고, 두 사람이 이야기하고 있는 표지판을 고르시오.

① **50**
② (children playing sign)
③ (no entry sign)
④ (bump sign)
⑤ (right turn sign)

W Slow down, Harold. You're going too fast.

M It's no problem. The speed limit is 50 along here.

W No, it isn't. Didn't you see that sign back there?

M _____ _____ _____. What sign?

W Harold! Look! All the children are playing outside _____ _____ _____. It must be lunchtime.

M I guess I missed that sign. And that's probably why there are _____ _____ _____ _____.

W Plus, you will have to make a right turn on the next corner. So _____ _____ a little.

M All right. I will.

2 대화를 듣고, 대화가 이루어지는 장소를 고르시오.

① taxi
② train station
③ airport
④ airplane
⑤ lost and found

M Can you _____ _____ _____ on the belt?

W Yes. Here you go.

M That's OK. They are not too heavy. OK. Would you like an aisle or window seat?

W Window seat, please.

M OK. _____ _____ is 1:30 at Gate 35.

W Thank you.

M I hope you have _____ _____ _____.

3 대화를 듣고, 여자가 전화를 건 목적으로 알맞은 것을 고르시오.

① 책을 빌리려고
② 숙제에 대해 물어보려고
③ 수학 공책을 빌리려고
④ 책을 돌려달라고 말하려고
⑤ 내일 만날 약속을 하려고

[Telephone rings.]

M Hi.

W Hi, Bill. It's Susie.

M Hi. Have you finished your math homework?

W Yes, and I was just reading. I finished reading *Another World*.

M Oh, that's by Janet Jones. I have many of her books.

W I know. So I was _____ _____ I could borrow the next book _____ _____ _____, *Another Planet*.

M Sure. I'll bring it to school tomorrow.

4 대화를 듣고, 여자가 지금 해야 할 일을 고르시오.

① 풍선 걸기
② 음식 주문하기
③ 케이크 가져오기
④ 손님 모시러 가기
⑤ 케이크 주문하기

W You _____ _____ all the balloons.

M Yes, do they look nice?

W Yes, they do. And the food is all ready.

M Almost, but I don't want to do anything else until _____ _____ _____ _____.

W And where's the cake? You ordered a special cake from Dobsons' Bakery, didn't you?

M Oh, no! The cake! I forgot to get it. Can you get it?

W Sure. _____ _____ _____.

---

5 다음을 듣고, 무엇에 관한 내용인지 고르시오.

① 티켓 환불 안내
② 새로운 공연 소개
③ 연장 공연 실시
④ 티켓 구입 안내
⑤ 공연 취소 안내

M I'm very sorry, but we _____ _____ _____ the concert. The doctor told Sarah not to sing. If she sings, she may _____ _____ _____ a lot. Sarah will do another concert in a few weeks. You can use your ticket _____ _____ _____. Again we're sorry but the show cannot go on.

---

6 대화를 듣고, 남자와 여자가 학교 축제 때 하려고 하는 것을 고르시오.

① 노래를 한다.
② 춤을 춘다.
③ 대본을 쓰고 감독을 한다.
④ 재미있는 연극을 한다.
⑤ 드라마를 연기한다.

M Did you think what we should do for the school festival?

W Well, Minhye doesn't like to sing. _____ _____ _____. So I don't want to sing a song for the festival.

M How about doing a special dance?

W I want to do some acting. Let's write a funny play and _____ _____ _____ _____.

M Good idea! How about a dramatic play?

W No, it's better _____ _____ _____. We want to have fun.

M OK. I agree. Let's do a funny play.

---

7 대화를 듣고, 남자가 학교에 두고 온 교과서로 알맞은 것을 고르시오.

① Math
② English
③ History
④ Korean
⑤ Biology

W What's wrong, Mike?

M I didn't bring home the proper textbook. _____ _____ _____ my math textbook, but I don't have any math homework tonight.

W Which textbook do you need?

M I have a test on the _____ _____ tomorrow.

W You need your Korean textbook.

M No, Mom, the test is on the Korean War. I need my _____ _____.

W You have to go back to school.

8 다음을 듣고, 예상되는 내일의 날씨를 고르시오.

① sunny
② cloudy
③ rainy
④ snowy
⑤ hot and dry

M Good morning. Here is the weather forecast for the greater _____ _____. It was a windy, rainy night, but the storm is over. It will be cool but clear today. There is _____ _____ _____ _____. Tomorrow, however, the rainy weather will return. So keep an umbrella _____ _____ _____ _____. You'll need it tomorrow.

9 대화를 듣고, 남자가 지불해야 할 금액을 고르시오.

① $100   ② $120   ③ $140
④ $150   ⑤ $160

M How much is a membership?
W $100 a month.
M Does it include the swimming pool?
W No, a fitness club membership which includes the pool is $150 a month.
M Well. I enjoy swimming, but _____ _____ _____. How can I get some discount?
W Sorry, our _____ _____ _____ and we don't offer any discounts.
M OK. I will get the regular membership _____ _____ _____.

10 다음을 듣고, 두 사람의 대화가 어색한 것을 고르시오.

①   ②   ③
④   ⑤

① **M** _____ _____ _____ _____ in a speaking contest.
   W Congratulations. I'm proud of you.
② **M** Is the heater turned on? I'm cold.
   W You'd better go see a doctor this afternoon.
③ **M** How are we going there?
   W I'd like to go there _____ _____. Is it OK?
④ **M** How often do you send e-mail messages?
   W I send e-mails to my friends almost every day.
⑤ **M** Are you hungry?
   W Yes, I am. I haven't eaten _____ _____.

11 대화를 듣고, 남자의 심정으로 알맞은 것을 고르시오.

① surprised
② anticipating
③ worried
④ relieved
⑤ disappointed

M Lisa, _____ _____ _____ _____? I'm looking for you.

W Oh, hi, Jack. I'm looking for you, too.

M By the way, has Deborah _____ _____?

W Oh, she couldn't come. She just phoned and said she was sorry.

M Oh, really? I was _____ _____ _____ meeting her tonight.

W Yeah. I really wanted to introduce her to you. You could become great friends.

M Every time a person arrived at the party, I hoped it was her. It's too bad she won't be coming.

12 대화를 듣고, 두 사람의 관계로 적절한 것을 고르시오.

① 약사 – 손님
② 제약회사 사장 – 직원
③ 간호사 – 의사
④ 의사 – 환자
⑤ 제약회사 직원 – 약사

M You seem to be all better.

W Do I need another prescription for medicine?

M No, I don't think so. _____ _____.

W But it was a bad cold. It started over 10 days ago.

M Well, I examined you and your _____ _____ _____ are fine now. Do you feel better?

W Yes, I do. I don't think I need _____ _____ for medicine. Thank you.

13 다음을 듣고, 그림의 상황에 가장 어울리는 대화를 고르시오.

① ② ③
④ ⑤

① **M** How much is the gift?

  W $35. It was on sale.

② **M** When is your birthday? I will _____ _____ _____.

  W Next Saturday.

③ **M** Here is a little present.

  W Really? _____ _____ _____.

④ **M** I _____ _____ _____ tomorrow.

  W You will do well. Good luck.

⑤ **M** I need a present for my mom.

  W Let's go shopping to the department store.

14 대화를 듣고, 남자가 지불해야 할 금액을 고르시오.

① $5 ② $8 ③ $10
④ $16 ⑤ $20

M How much are these books?

W These children's books are _____ _____. One for $5, two for $8 and three for $10.

M When will the sale be over?

W On the 15th of this month.

M But today is the 14th. I had better buy some today. *[pause]* I'll take these six children's books.

W Oh, _____ _____! You will not _____ _____ them.

15 다음을 듣고, 내용과 일치하지 <u>않는</u> 것을 고르시오.

① 휴대폰을 꺼야 한다.
② 공연시간은 약 1시간이다.
③ '크리스마스 캐럴'을 공연한다.
④ 공연 중간에 휴식시간이 있다.
⑤ 공연 후에 커피와 쿠키를 제공한다.

W Welcome to this year's Christmas festival. *[applause]* This year Clinton School's drama students are _____ _____ _____ a *Christmas Carol* by Charles Dickens. _____ _____ _____ _____ about an hour. There will not be a break during the show. After the show, we invite you to have coffee and cookies with the students. And while I shouldn't have to say this, I will: _____ _____ your cell phones. Thank you. Enjoy the show.

16 대화를 듣고, 남자가 여자와 같이 공부하려고 하는 이유를 고르시오.

① 여자를 좋아해서
② 여자가 수학을 잘해서
③ 여자가 사회과학을 잘해서
④ 여자에게 수학 공책을 빌리려고
⑤ 여자에게 사회과학을 가르쳐주려고

M Are you going to be studying tonight?

W Of course. Finals are _____ _____ soon.

M Would you like to study together?

W Not really. I usually prefer to _____ _____.

M Well, I'll help you with your math homework. You know I'm good at math.

W Hmm... Yes, you could help me.

M And actually, I want you to help me _____ _____ _____. I don't understand so many things in the class.

W OK. Let's help each other.

17 다음을 듣고, 여자가 만족하지 <u>못하는</u> 것을 고르시오.

① 선생님
② 식당 음식
③ 기숙사 시설
④ 기숙사 친구들
⑤ 엄마가 해준 쿠키

W I sleep _____ _____ _____ at my school. It's a boarding school in the countryside. It's a good school and I'm happy except for one thing. _____ _____ _____, every student in the dormitory dislikes the same thing, while the teachers do not. We don't like _____ _____ _____. We want to eat our _____ _____. The food in the cafeteria is not as good as my mother's cooking.

18 대화를 듣고, 여자의 마지막 말에 이어질 남자의 응답으로 가장 적절한 것을 고르시오.

① I think I made three or four mistakes.
② I don't know the score of the game.
③ I don't like science very much.
④ Science is very interesting to me.
⑤ $100. That's not too expensive.

M I'm home, Mom.

W You look tired. How did your exams go, Steven?

M Umm... I don't know well, Mom. I will know _____ _____ _____ after my teacher _____ _____ for the test.

W I guess they weren't so good.

M I did OK, I think.

W What is your score in science likely to be?

M _____

19 대화를 듣고, 여자의 마지막 말에 이어질 남자의 응답으로 가장 적절한 것을 고르시오.

① You look very smart.
② He isn't in my class.
③ He is from Korea.
④ Hey, look at him.
⑤ He is tall and has dark skin.

M Hey, you know Thomas, don't you?

W _____ _____ _____ _____?

M Thomas Jones. He said he knows you.

W I don't remember him.

M He was in your class _____ _____ _____. He sat at the back. In addition, he has always liked you and still does.

W Really? What does he look like?

M _____

20 다음을 듣고, Bill이 할 말로 가장 알맞은 것을 고르시오.

① Are you ready to order?
② Would you like anything else?
③ How would you like your steak?
④ Do you like spaghetti or steak better?
⑤ Do you want to see a menu?

M Bill is a waiter in a restaurant. He is taking the food order for a man and a woman. The woman orders a salad and spaghetti and _____ _____ _____ _____ and a steak. He wants the steak well-done. Bill wants to know if they _____ _____ _____. In this situation, what is he likely to say to them?

WORD AND EXPRESSION REVIEW • TEST 11-12

A Write down the definition of each word or phrase.

1 palm _____

2 pale _____

3 reference book _____

4 loan _____

5 speed limit _____

6 likely _____

7 height _____

8 nearby _____

9 pollution _____

10 depend on _____

11 luggage _____

12 proper _____

13 regular _____

14 recover _____

15 throat _____

16 spoonful _____

17 regret _____

18 applause _____

19 stomachache _____

20 dormitory _____

B Match each word with the right definition.

1 aisle _____

2 seem (to be) _____

3 last _____

4 fixed _____

5 wonder _____

6 hold _____

7 letter _____

8 go on _____

9 examine _____

10 work _____

11 chest _____

12 appreciate _____

13 metropolitan _____

14 board _____

15 take out _____

a 문자, 글자

b (모임 등을) 열다, 개최하다

c (책 등을) 대출하다

d 움직이다, 작동하다

e 고맙게 생각하다, 감사하다

f 주요 도시의

g 통로, 복도

h 타다, 탑승하다, 승차하다

i ~이 아닐까 생각하다, ~인가 하고 생각하다

j 계속하다

k 고정된, 정해진

l ~인 듯하다, ~인 것 같다

m 검사하다, 조사하다

n 가슴

o 계속[지속]하다

C Choose the best answer for the blank.

1 I don't _____ eating these days.

a. want to b. feel like c. seem like

2 _____ be honest with you, I don't like the cafeteria food.

a. In b. For c. To

3 I was looking forward _____ him tonight.

a. to meet b. meeting c. to meeting

4 It depends entirely _____ weather conditions.

a. on b. in c. with

5 You have to _____ a right turn on next corner.

a. have b. make c. get

6 The doctor told me _____ too much.

a. not to eat b. to not eat c. not eating

D Complete the short dialogues.

1 A: Do you _____ if I borrow your pencil?

B: Of course not.

2 A: I've _____ a prize in a speaking contest.

B: Congratulations. I'm proud of you.

3 A: I feel a cold coming on.

B: You'd better go to _____ a doctor this afternoon.

4 A: Summer is coming. I can't wait to go to the beach.

B: That's exactly why I want to _____ my weight.

5 A: Do you walk to school?

B: Yes, I go to school _____ _____ .

1 다음을 듣고, 설명하는 대상으로 알맞은 것을 고르시오.

①   ②

③   ④

⑤

2 대화를 듣고, 여자가 꿈꾸는 장래 희망을 고르시오.

① a conductor
② a pianist
③ a violinist
④ a flutist
⑤ music professor

3 대화를 듣고, 여자가 전화를 건 목적을 고르시오.

① 돌고래 쇼를 예약하려고
② 수영 강습비를 물어보려고
③ 수영 강습료를 납부하려고
④ 아들을 수영 교실에 등록시키려고
⑤ 바빠서 수영을 그만둔다고 말하려고

4 대화를 듣고, 여자가 주말에 가족과 하는 것을 고르시오.

① TV 시청   ② 보드 게임   ③ 외식
④ 영화 보기   ⑤ 화상 통화

5 대화를 듣고, 여자가 하고 있는 것을 고르시오.

① 멀리 떨어져 있는 아들과 전화 통화하고 있다.
② 아들을 공항까지 데려다주고 있다.
③ 방학이라 돌아온 아들을 맞이하고 있다.
④ 학교에 찾아가 아들을 만나고 있다.
⑤ 아들과 함께 학교에서 식사를 하고 있다.

6 다음을 듣고, 남자가 이야기를 하고 있는 대상과 상황으로 짝지어진 것을 고르시오.

① 고3 졸업생 - 대학 합격 축하 인사
② 고3 졸업생 - 졸업 연설
③ 고1 입학생 - 입학 연설
④ 중3 졸업생 - 졸업 연설
⑤ 중3 졸업생 - 고등학교 입시 설명회

7 대화를 듣고, 앞으로 얼마 후에 보이스카우트 여름 대회가 열리는지 고르시오.

① 2주 후   ② 4주 후   ③ 2달 후
④ 7달 후   ⑤ 1년 후

8 다음을 듣고, 날씨가 바르게 연결된 것을 고르시오.

① Today   ② Saturday

③ Sunday   ④ Next Monday

⑤ This Weekend

9 대화를 듣고, 대화가 일어나고 있는 장소로 가장 알맞은 것을 고르시오.

① 옷 수선집   ② 화장품 가게   ③ 세탁소
④ 미용실   ⑤ 헬스클럽

10 다음을 듣고, 두 사람의 대화가 <u>어색한</u> 것을 고르시오.

①   ②   ③   ④   ⑤

11 대화를 듣고, 남자의 심정으로 가장 알맞은 것을 고르시오.

① satisfied   ② sorrowful
③ bored   ④ frustrated
⑤ delighted

12 대화를 듣고, 두 사람의 관계로 가장 알맞은 것을 고르시오.

① 손님 – 요리사   ② 손님 – 식당 종업원
③ 식당 종업원 – 요리사   ④ 손님 – 정육점 주인
⑤ 야채가게 주인 – 정육점 주인

13 다음을 듣고, 도표의 내용과 <u>다른</u> 것을 고르시오.

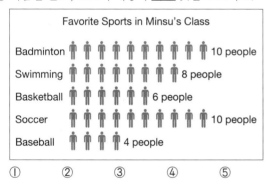

Favorite Sports in Minsu's Class

Badminton   10 people
Swimming   8 people
Basketball   6 people
Soccer   10 people
Baseball   4 people

①   ②   ③   ④   ⑤

14 다음을 듣고, 내용과 일치하지 <u>않는</u> 것을 고르시오.

① 말하는 사람은 교감 선생님이다.
② 어제 한 여학생이 떠밀려서 넘어졌다.
③ 식당으로 뛰어가는 학생은 벌을 받게 된다.
④ 어제 한 여학생이 다리를 심하게 다쳤다.
⑤ 뛰는 학생은 방과 후에 1시간 동안 남아 있어야 한다.

15 대화를 듣고, 아들이 신문을 찾는 이유를 고르시오.

① 뉴스에 관심을 갖게 되어서
② 학교 과제 때문에
③ 환경문제에 관심이 생겨서
④ 신문기자가 꿈이라서
⑤ 학교신문에 참고하려고

16 다음을 듣고, 내용과 일치하는 것을 고르시오.

① 상대방이 먼저 반칙을 했다.
② 심판은 상대선수가 David을 발로 차는 걸 보았다.
③ David의 파울로 상대팀이 득점했다.
④ David은 아주 침착하게 경기를 하고 있다.
⑤ 감독은 David의 득점을 칭찬하고 있다.

17 대화를 듣고, 이어지는 질문에 가장 알맞은 답을 고르시오.

① 돈을 빌려가서 갚지 않는 것
② 펜이나 공책을 빌려주지 않는 것
③ 싸우고 나서 먼저 사과하지 않는 것
④ 물어보지도 않고 물건을 빌려가는 것
⑤ 아무리 부탁해도 숙제를 도와주지 않는 것

18 다음을 듣고, 남자가 주장하는 내용을 고르시오.

① 길에서 담배 피우는 것을 법으로 금지시켜야 한다.
② 모든 건물을 금연으로 만들어야 한다.
③ 십대들에게 담배를 팔면, 벌금을 부과해야 한다.
④ 십대 흡연자들을 처벌해야 한다.
⑤ 정부는 담뱃값을 인상해야 한다.

[19-20] 대화를 듣고, 여자의 마지막 말에 대한 남자의 응답으로 가장 적절한 것을 고르시오.

19

① That's great you're accepted.
② Don't worry. You did your best.
③ Hurry open it! I can't wait.
④ Congratulations! You love science.
⑤ I'll never forget. Let's visit the school someday.

20

① I disagree.
② So do I.
③ Me neither.
④ So am I.
⑤ Neither do I.

T E S T   13

DICTATION • TEST 13

1 다음을 듣고, 설명하는 대상으로 알맞은 것을 고르시오.

① ② ③ ④ ⑤

W This is a very popular fruit. It doesn't grow on tall trees. It grows on plants which are very low _____ _____ _____. This fruit isn't round like other fruits. As it grows, it is mostly triangle-shaped. And neither do we _____ _____ _____ _____ or peel before we eat it.

---

2 대화를 듣고, 여자가 꿈꾸는 장래 희망을 고르시오.

① a conductor
② a pianist
③ a violinist
④ a flutist
⑤ music professor

M What instrument can you play? I heard you like playing the violin.

W I learned to play the violin for one year, but I didn't like it. It was _____ _____ _____ _____. These days, I learn to play the piano.

M Do you enjoy playing it?

W Yes, I practice 3 hours a day.

M 3 hours a day?

W Yes, I love it. _____ _____ _____ _____, the first thing I do is playing the piano.

M You must be really good.

W My teacher said I should go and study at a music school in Paris.

M Wow!

W I hope I can be _____ _____ _____ and play in an orchestra.

---

3 대화를 듣고, 여자가 전화를 건 목적을 고르시오.

① 돌고래 쇼를 예약하려고
② 수영 강습비를 물어보려고
③ 수영 강습료를 납부하려고
④ 아들을 수영 교실에 등록시키려고
⑤ 바빠서 수영을 그만둔다고 말하려고

[Telephone rings.]

M Hello. Olympic Swimming Center.

W Hello. I'd like my son to join the little dolphin's swimming class.

M The one on Tuesday and Thursday or Wednesday and Friday.

W _____ _____ are at 4:30, right?

M Yes, they are.

W He's busy on Wednesday, so I'd like him to join the Tuesday and Thursday class.

M What's your son's name?

W Matthew Ray.

M OK, Mrs. Ray. I'll _____ _____ _____. On Tuesday you can _____ _____ _____.

W Thank you.

4 대화를 듣고, 여자가 주말에 가족과 하는 것을 고르시오.

① TV 시청
② 보드 게임
③ 외식
④ 영화 보기
⑤ 화상 통화

M What did you do last weekend?

W My family usually spends Saturday together.

M Then, did you watch the movie on TV last Saturday with your family?

W No, I didn't.

M Did you _____ _____?

W No, we stayed home. We like to _____ _____ _____ on weekends. My favorite is *Monopoly*. I love to _____ _____ _____.

M Sounds good.

---

5 대화를 듣고, 여자가 하고 있는 것을 고르시오.

① 멀리 떨어져 있는 아들과 전화 통화하고 있다.
② 아들을 공항까지 데려다주고 있다.
③ 방학이라 돌아온 아들을 맞이하고 있다.
④ 학교에 찾아가 아들을 만나고 있다.
⑤ 아들과 함께 학교에서 식사를 하고 있다.

W Steve! Steve! _____ _____!

M Hi, Mom. It's great to see you.

W Oh, I missed you! [pause] Steve, you look thin. Are you eating at university?

M Yes, I am, Mom.

W You have to _____ _____. You know? But, oh, I'm so happy to see you. _____ _____ _____ _____ since Christmas.

M Well, I'll be here all summer vacation, Mom. Thanks for picking me up at the airport.

---

6 다음을 듣고, 남자가 이야기를 하고 있는 대상과 상황으로 짝지어진 것을 고르시오.

① 고3 졸업생 – 대학 합격 축하 인사
② 고3 졸업생 – 졸업 연설
③ 고1 입학생 – 입학 연설
④ 중3 졸업생 – 졸업 연설
⑤ 중3 졸업생 – 고등학교 입시 설명회

M Congratulations! You did it. Soon you'll _____ _____ _____ _____. You're going on to bigger and better things. _____ _____ _____ _____ all of you. You'll be first year high school students soon. But school doesn't begin until March, so you're still my students. And I want to tell you that I'll miss you a lot when the next school year begins. You're a special group of third graders and I'll miss seeing you _____ _____ _____ next year. Good luck!

7 대화를 듣고, 앞으로 얼마 후에 보이스카우트 여름 대회가 열리는지 고르시오.

① 2주 후
② 4주 후
③ 2달 후
④ 7달 후
⑤ 1년 후

W Your Boy Scout Meeting is every four weeks, isn't it?

M No. We have a meeting every two weeks. Next meeting will be held on May 20th.

W That's next week. You guys are meeting _____ _____. Are you having fun at Boy Scouts?

M Of course. And our big meeting in the summer will be fun, too. It's _____ _____ _____ _____ of July. We'll do all kinds of summer sports and activities.

W I thought it would be your first year to go to the summer meeting.

M No, this is _____ _____ _____. And I can't wait to be in the summer meeting.

W Summer will come soon. It is _____ _____ _____ from now.

M Right. And the regular meetings every other week are fun, too.

8 다음을 듣고, 날씨가 바르게 연결된 것을 고르시오.

① Today
② Saturday
③ Sunday
④ Next Monday
⑤ This Weekend

W And now _____ _____ _____ weather forecast. Next Monday is a holiday, so we all want to know the long-term weather forecast. We all want the warm, sunny weather we had today to continue through the weekend. But _____ _____ _____. It will rain all day on Saturday and Sunday. Next Monday, the rain will stop and the _____ _____ _____, but it may be too late for many people to enjoy their long-weekend.

9 대화를 듣고, 대화가 일어나고 있는 장소로 가장 알맞은 것을 고르시오.

① 옷 수선집
② 화장품 가게
③ 세탁소
④ 미용실
⑤ 헬스클럽

W How would you like it cut this time?

M I want to change my style.

W _____ _____ _____ a very short hairstyle? Perhaps one or two centimeters long.

M That's a good idea. I was thinking that, too.

W You can use lots of gel and _____ _____ _____ _____.

M It's very fashionable. It will _____ _____ _____ my face.

W Yes, it will.

10 다음을 듣고, 두 사람의 대화가 <u>어색한</u> 것을 고르시오.

① ② ③
④ ⑤

① **W** I've been looking for you, John.

   M I've been studying in my room, Mom.

② **W** My mother has four brothers and three sisters.

   M Wow, you must _____ _____ _____.

③ **W** How much did you pay for the shirt?

   M $25. I saved 10%.

④ **W** Does your father smoke?

   M No, he doesn't. _____ _____ a year ago.

⑤ **W** I did better than I thought I would do.

   M _____ _____ _____. You'll do better next time.

---

11 대화를 듣고, 남자의 심정으로 가장 알맞은 것을 고르시오.

① satisfied
② sorrowful
③ bored
④ frustrated
⑤ delighted

W Is the game over?

M Yes, it ended a few minutes ago.

W Well, did your team win the game?

M No, but they played well. They did _____ _____ _____ _____.

W They were playing Brazil, the World Champions?

M That's right. And they only lost _____ _____ _____. So while I am not happy, I am not sad either. They might have lost by many goals.

---

12 대화를 듣고, 두 사람의 관계로 가장 알맞은 것을 고르시오.

① 손님 – 요리사
② 손님 – 식당 종업원
③ 식당 종업원 – 요리사
④ 손님 – 정육점 주인
⑤ 야채가게 주인 – 정육점 주인

W I'm sorry, but the woman at table 5 says she wants her steak cooked more.

M She wants her steak _____ _____?

W Yes, she ordered it medium. But she says it's rare.

M No problem. I will cook it for a few more minutes. Then you can _____ _____ _____ to her.

W Thanks. I will.

M I'll put some more vegetables _____ _____ _____, too.

13 다음을 듣고, 도표의 내용과 <u>다른</u> 것을 고르시오.

Favorite Sports in Minsu's Class		
Badminton	🧍🧍🧍🧍🧍🧍🧍🧍🧍🧍	10 people
Swimming	🧍🧍🧍🧍🧍🧍🧍🧍	8 people
Basketball	🧍🧍🧍🧍🧍🧍	6 people
Soccer	🧍🧍🧍🧍🧍🧍🧍🧍🧍🧍	10 people
Baseball	🧍🧍🧍🧍	4 people

①   ②   ③
④   ⑤

W ① Badminton is _____ _____ _____ soccer.
② Swimming is more popular than basketball.
③ _____ _____ as popular as basketball.
④ Soccer and badminton aren't _____ _____ _____
_____.
⑤ Basketball is more popular than baseball.

---

14 다음을 듣고, 내용과 일치하지 <u>않는</u> 것을 고르시오.

① 말하는 사람은 교감 선생님이다.
② 어제 한 여학생이 떠밀려서 넘어졌다.
③ 식당으로 뛰어가는 학생은 벌을 받게 된다.
④ 어제 한 여학생이 다리를 심하게 다쳤다.
⑤ 뛰는 학생은 방과 후에 1시간 동안 남아 있어야 한다.

M Attention! This is the vice-principal speaking. Students, you must not run when the school lunch bell rings. Yesterday one student _____ _____ _____ _____. She wasn't pushed. She fell because she was running too fast. Today I will stand _____ _____ _____. Any student who runs to the cafeteria _____ _____ _____. He or she will have to stay for one hour after school. Walk, do not run, to the cafeteria. Thank you.

---

15 대화를 듣고, 아들이 신문을 찾는 이유를 고르시오.

① 뉴스에 관심을 갖게 되어서
② 학교 과제 때문에
③ 환경문제에 관심이 생겨서
④ 신문기자가 꿈이라서
⑤ 학교신문에 참고하려고

M Where is the morning newspaper, Mom?
W Wow! It's great you're becoming interested in the news.
M Umm... I have to _____ _____ _____ of newspaper stories on the environment for my social science class.
W So you're only reading the paper because of a school project.
M That's right.
W I hope _____ _____ _____ _____ after the project is finished.
M Yes, I think I will. I've become interested in many things.

---

16 다음을 듣고, 내용과 일치하는 것을 고르시오.

① 상대방이 먼저 반칙을 했다.
② 심판은 상대선수가 David을 발로 차는 걸 보았다.
③ David의 파울로 상대팀이 득점했다.
④ David은 아주 침착하게 경기를 하고 있다.
⑤ 감독은 David의 득점을 칭찬하고 있다.

M David! Why did you do that? You can't kick another player! I don't care if he kicked you first! The referee saw you kick him. You fouled him and they _____ _____ _____ _____. They scored. You must _____ _____ in big games. You can't get too excited and _____ _____ _____ when you're angry. I'll take you out of the game if you do it one more time.

17 대화를 듣고, 이어지는 질문에 가장 알맞은 답을 고르시오.

① 돈을 빌려가서 갚지 않는 것
② 펜이나 공책을 빌려주지 않는 것
③ 싸우고 나서 먼저 사과하지 않는 것
④ 물어보지도 않고 물건을 빌려가는 것
⑤ 아무리 부탁해도 숙제를 도와주지 않는 것

M My sister is really nice. She often helps me with my homework.
W Do you _____ _____ _____?
M Yes, we fight. I get angry when she borrows things without asking.
W What does she borrow?
M Sometimes a pen or a book. Then I can't find it because _____
_____ _____ _____.
W That would make me angry, too.
Q What makes him angry about his sister?

18 다음을 듣고, 남자가 주장하는 내용을 고르시오.

① 길에서 담배 피우는 것을 법으로 금지시켜야 한다.
② 모든 건물을 금연으로 만들어야 한다.
③ 십대들에게 담배를 팔면, 벌금을 부과해야 한다.
④ 십대 흡연자들을 처벌해야 한다.
⑤ 정부는 담뱃값을 인상해야 한다.

M Many teenagers smoke and it is a big problem in our society. It is hard to stop _____ _____ _____ _____. So we must stop teenagers from beginning to smoke. Maybe the price of cigarettes is too low. The government must _____ _____ _____. Teens don't have a lot of money, so it's likely they won't be able to smoke.

19 다음을 듣고, 남자가 주장하는 내용을 고르시오.

① That's great you're accepted.
② Don't worry. You did your best.
③ Hurry open it! I can't wait.
④ Congratulations! You love science.
⑤ I'll never forget. Let's visit the school someday.

M Here is a letter for you. Is it _____ _____ _____ we have waited for?
W Yes, it is. It's from the Science High School.
M Would you open it now? Did _____ _____ _____ _____?
W I'll open it. Aw, no! Dad, it's not good news. What should I do?
M _____

20 다음을 듣고, 남자가 주장하는 내용을 고르시오.

① I disagree.
② So do I.
③ Me neither.
④ So am I.
⑤ Neither do I.

W Let's go to Europe for our _____ _____.
M OK. That would be great.
W Let's see all the big, great cities of Europe. I want to _____ _____ _____ and the history.
M Oh, I'd love to do that. _____ _____ _____ _____ in this small town. There are no cultural activities here.
W I agree. I want to visit the great museums of London and Paris.
M _____

1 대화를 듣고, 여자가 이번 여름에 할 일을 고르시오.

①  ②

③  ④

⑤

2 대화를 듣고, 콘서트가 끝난 시각을 고르시오.

① 9:15　　② 9:35　　③ 9:50
④ 10:00　　⑤ 10:15

3 대화를 듣고, 여자가 가고자 하는 길을 고르시오.

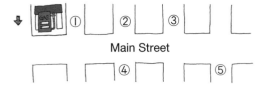

Main Street

4 대화를 듣고, 남자가 오늘 할 일을 고르시오.

① 여자친구와 영화를 보러 간다.
② 여자와 영화배우를 만나러 간다.
③ Susie에게 전화를 건다.
④ 수업을 들으러 간다.
⑤ 영화티켓을 사러 간다.

5 대화를 듣고, 두 사람이 한 일과 그 이유로 알맞게 짝지어진 것을 고르시오.

① 저녁 식사 준비 – 부모님이 직장에서 늦게 오시기 때문에
② 밀린 빨래하기 – 부모님이 여행 가고 안 계셔서
③ 파티 준비하기 – 엄마의 생신을 축하해 드리려고
④ 저녁 설거지하기 – 부모님에게 용돈을 받으려고
⑤ 집과 자동차 청소 – 어버이날에 부모님을 놀라게 해드리려고

6 대화를 듣고, 두 사람의 심정으로 가장 알맞은 것을 고르시오.

① bored　　② joyful　　③ sad
④ annoyed　　⑤ tired

7 대화를 듣고, 남자가 여자에게 전화를 건 목적으로 알맞은 것을 고르시오.

① 차를 빼달라고
② 10분만 기다려 달라고
③ 차를 주차시켜야 한다고
④ 차를 찾았다고 알려주려고
⑤ 차 사고가 났다고 말하려고

8 다음 자동응답기의 내용을 듣고, 질문에 답하시오.

① 1　　② 2　　③ 3　　④ 4　　⑤ 5

9 대화를 듣고, 두 사람의 관계로 알맞은 것을 고르시오.

① bank teller　..... customer
② bus driver　..... passenger
③ cashier　　..... customer
④ pilot　　　..... flight attendant
⑤ taxi driver　..... passenger

10 다음을 듣고, 무엇에 관한 내용인지 고르시오.

① 새 자동차 구입 요령
② 시험 준비 요령
③ 퀴즈 게임 설명
④ 기말고사 예상문제 설명
⑤ 자동차 경품 행사 안내

11 대화를 듣고, 내용과 일치하지 <u>않는</u> 것을 고르시오.

① Jennifer는 빨래를 할 것이다.
② Jennifer는 저녁식사를 도울 것이다.
③ 아빠는 고기를 사러 갈 것이다.
④ 엄마는 아파서 누워계신다.
⑤ Jennifer는 컴퓨터를 하고 있었다.

12 다음을 듣고, 그림의 상황에 가장 어울리는 대화를 고르시오.

① ② ③ ④ ⑤

13 대화를 듣고, 여자의 직업으로 알맞은 것을 고르시오.
① waitress   ② bus driver
③ pilot   ④ counselor
⑤ flight attendant

14 대화를 듣고, 나머지 컴퓨터 한 대가 있는 곳이 어디인지 고르시오.
① 남동생 방   ② 남자의 방
③ 부모님 방   ④ 거실
⑤ 베란다

15 다음을 듣고, 내용과 어울리는 속담을 고르시오.
① Ignorance is bliss.
② Many drops make a shower.
③ Experience is the best teacher.
④ Necessity is the mother of invention.
⑤ Strike while the iron is hot.

16 대화를 듣고, 남자가 지금 무엇을 하고 있는지 고르시오.
① 컴퓨터 바이러스 백신을 깔고 있다.
② 새로 구입한 하드 드라이브를 설치하고 있다.
③ 컴퓨터에 무슨 문제가 있는지 확인하고 있다.
④ 해킹방지 프로그램을 깔고 있다.
⑤ 고장난 컴퓨터를 수리하고 있다.

[17-18] 다음을 듣고, 이어지는 질문에 알맞은 답을 고르시오.

17
① math   ② science
③ history   ④ social science
⑤ English

18
① 공부를 더 잘할 수 있어서
② 선생님들이 너무 좋아서
③ 스트레스가 별로 없어서
④ 친한 친구들이 있어서
⑤ 곧 있으면 대학에 갈 수 있어서

[19-20] 대화를 듣고, 여자의 마지막 말에 이어질 남자의 응답으로 가장 적절한 것을 고르시오.

19
① She never asks me to.
② She has a good job.
③ I usually do the chores.
④ I clean the living room.
⑤ Your husband is kind.

20
① Thank you for helping me.
② Yes, you can't miss it.
③ No, turn around and walk back.
④ Yes, I go to Munhwa University.
⑤ No, you've gone too far.

T E S T **14**

DICTATION • TEST 14

1 대화를 듣고, 여자가 이번 여름에 할 일을 고르시오.

① ② ③ ④ ⑤

M What are you doing this summer, Mina?

W I'm going to do some volunteer work.

M Oh, really? Are you going to _____ _____ _____ old people, or take care of poor children?

W No, I'm not. I've volunteered to work on a farm.

M That should be _____ _____ _____ .

W Yes, it should. And there are many old farmers who really need help _____ _____ _____ .

---

2 대화를 듣고, 콘서트가 끝난 시각을 고르시오.

① 9:15
② 9:35
③ 9:50
④ 10:00
⑤ 10:15

M Wow! _____ _____ _____ _____ outside the coffee shop.

W And it's 10 before 10 at night. Strange!

M Are they selling coffee at a cheap price?

W I don't see any signs.

M Oh, I know. The music concert at the theater _____ _____ _____ just ended 15 minutes ago.

W Yes, I can see people _____ _____ _____ and walking over here.

---

3 대화를 듣고, 여자가 가고자 하는 길을 고르시오.

① ② ③
Main Street
④ ⑤

M That'll be $50 for the gas.

W _____ _____ _____ . And I wonder if you could help me. What is the quickest way to get on the Golden Expressway?

M Let's see. _____ _____ _____ Arch Road is the quickest. Leave the gas station and turn left onto Main Street.

W Isn't Arch Road the second street?

M No, it isn't. It's the third street.

W And then I should turn left to _____ _____ _____ _____ , right?

M That's right.

4 대화를 듣고, 남자가 오늘 할 일을 고르시오.

① 여자친구와 영화를 보러 간다.
② 여자와 영화배우를 만나러 간다.
③ Susie에게 전화를 건다.
④ 수업을 들으러 간다.
⑤ 영화티켓을 사러 간다.

M I'm going to take Susie to see Brad Pitt's new movie this weekend.

W Susie? Did you ask her?

M _____ _____. But I know she will say yes.

W Bill, I don't think she likes you. I'm sorry to tell you.

M Really? She doesn't like me. But _____ _____ _____ the tickets for the movie.

W Why did you buy the tickets without asking her first? You should have asked her first. _____ _____ _____ _____ her right now?

M Oh, no. I will ask her when I meet her in the class this afternoon.

5 대화를 듣고, 두 사람이 한 일과 그 이유로 알맞게 짝지어진 것을 고르시오.

① 저녁 식사 준비 – 부모님이 직장에서 늦게 오시기 때문에
② 밀린 빨래하기 – 부모님이 여행 가고 안 계셔서
③ 파티 준비하기 – 엄마의 생신을 축하해 드리려고
④ 저녁 설거지하기 – 부모님에게 용돈을 받으려고
⑤ 집과 자동차 청소 – 어버이날에 부모님을 놀라게 해드리려고

M I finished washing and cleaning the inside of Dad's car.

W And I _____ _____ _____ and cleaned the kitchen really well.

M When they come home from work, they _____ _____ _____. What else can we do for them today?

W Washing the dishes after dinner.

M That is something _____ _____ _____. On Parents' Day we have to do special things that we don't do every day.

W You're right. Hmm... Let me think.

6 대화를 듣고, 두 사람의 심정으로 가장 알맞은 것을 고르시오.

① bored
② joyful
③ sad
④ annoyed
⑤ tired

M Rover was a happy, _____ _____.

W He always made us smile.

M Especially when he _____ _____ _____.

W I'm really going to miss him. I can't believe he got hit by a car.

M Yeah. I cried for an hour when I first _____ _____ _____. I don't feel like having another dog for some time.

7 대화를 듣고, 남자가 여자에게 전화를 건 목적으로 알맞은 것을 고르시오.

① 차를 빼달라고
② 10분만 기다려 달라고
③ 차를 주차시켜야 한다고
④ 차를 찾았다고 알려주려고
⑤ 차 사고가 났다고 말하려고

[Cell phone rings.]

W Hello.

M Hi. Are you _____ _____ _____ a white Hyundai Sonata?

W Yes, I am.

M And you parked in front of the RT apartment building, didn't you?

W Yes, I did. What's wrong?

M Well, your car _____ _____ _____ _____. I want to get out.

W Oh, I'm sorry. I stopped for 10 minutes _____ _____ _____ _____ at a friend's apartment.

M Ma'am, I've already been waiting 10 minutes.

W I'll be right there.

8 다음 자동응답기의 내용을 듣고, 질문에 답하시오.

① 1　　② 2　　③ 3
④ 4　　⑤ 5

M Thank you for calling Whistle Ski Mountain. Press 1 to learn what the weather is like at the top of the mountain. Press 2 to learn about ticket prices for children, adult and _____ _____ _____. Press 3 to talk to the ski _____ _____ _____ _____. Press 4 to learn about skiing lessons. And press 5 to talk to our staff.

Q What number do you press to learn about the price of renting skis?

9 대화를 듣고, 두 사람의 관계로 알맞은 것을 고르시오.

① bank teller ..... customer
② bus driver ..... passenger
③ cashier ..... customer
④ pilot ..... flight attendant
⑤ taxi driver ..... passenger

W I want to go to First Street. How much is the fare?

M It's $1.25, ma'am.

W OK. [pause] Oh, no. I only have a $10 bill.

M I'm sorry, ma'am, that bill is too large. Please don't put it _____ _____ _____ _____.

W But what can I do?

M You really should _____ _____ _____ _____, ma'am. It'll save you a lot of trouble. Please ask if anyone can _____ _____ _____ for that $10.

10 다음을 듣고, 무엇에 관한 내용인지 고르시오.

① 새 자동차 구입 요령
② 시험 준비 요령
③ 퀴즈 게임 설명
④ 기말고사 예상문제 설명
⑤ 자동차 경품 행사 안내

M OK. Clara, welcome to the winner's bonus round of 'Question, Question.' You'll have one minute to answer 10 questions. The first few questions are easy. Then _____ _____ _____ _____. The final question is very difficult. You must answer all ten questions correctly in order to win the new car. If you make one mistake, _____ _____ _____ is over. And you don't get to _____ _____ in a new car. Good luck.

11 대화를 듣고, 내용과 일치하지 않는 것을 고르시오.

① Jennifer는 빨래를 할 것이다.
② Jennifer는 저녁식사를 도울 것이다.
③ 아빠는 고기를 사러 갈 것이다.
④ 엄마는 아파서 누워계신다.
⑤ Jennifer는 컴퓨터를 하고 있었다.

M Jennifer, Mom and I need your help.
W Washing the dishes?
M No, some clothes were washed. They need to _____ _____ _____. Mom is sick. She went to _____ _____.
W OK. I'll do it. I'll just turn off my computer first.
M I'm going to go buy some meat. Can you cook dinner with me?
W Sure. _____ _____ _____ Mom first.

12 다음을 듣고, 그림의 상황에 가장 어울리는 대화를 고르시오.

① ② ③
④ ⑤

① **W** I'm sorry. I'm a few minutes late.
   M _____ _____. Don't worry about it.
② **W** How can I get to the Central Park?
   M Go straight two blocks and turn right. You will see it on your left.
③ **W** Don't throw your garbage on the street.
   M I'm sorry. I'll pick it up. Where is _____ _____ _____?
④ **W** It's time to go to bed.
   M Really? Is it late? I'm not sleepy.
⑤ **W** I am very hungry.
   M Would you like _____ _____ _____ _____?

13 대화를 듣고, 여자의 직업으로 알맞은 것을 고르시오.

① waitress
② bus driver
③ pilot
④ counselor
⑤ flight attendant

W Excuse me, is your _____ _____ _____?

M Yes, it is. How long will it take to get to Vancouver?

W Three hours, sir. The scheduled _____ _____ is 8 p.m.

M Will you be serving dinner _____ _____ _____?

W Yes, we will. About an hour after we take off.

M OK. Thank you.

W Have a nice flight.

14 대화를 듣고, 나머지 컴퓨터 한 대가 있는 곳이 어디인지 고르시오.

① 남동생 방
② 남자의 방
③ 부모님 방
④ 거실
⑤ 베란다

M How many computers do you have in your house?

W _____ _____ _____. One is in my bedroom.

M I guess the other is in your brother's bedroom.

W No, he was playing too many computer games, so my mom and dad moved it to the living room first. But _____ _____ _____ _____ to their bedroom.

M Do they use it?

W Yeah. Dad likes to surf the Net _____ _____ _____.

15 다음을 듣고, 내용과 어울리는 속담을 고르시오.

① Ignorance is bliss.
② Many drops make a shower.
③ Experience is the best teacher.
④ Necessity is the mother of invention.
⑤ Strike while the iron is hot.

W Before computers, people used typewriters. On typewriters mistakes could not be easily corrected. The page was typed again. Bessie Nesmith typed a lot and she was not happy. When she made a mistake, she had to type the whole page again. So _____ _____ 'Mistake Out' in 1956. 'Mistake Out' was _____ _____. People painted over their mistakes. Then _____ _____ _____. 'Mistake Out' saved Bessie a lot of time.

16 대화를 듣고, 남자가 지금 무엇을 하고 있는지 고르시오.

① 컴퓨터 바이러스 백신을 깔고 있다.
② 새로 구입한 하드 드라이브를 설치하고 있다.
③ 컴퓨터에 무슨 문제가 있는지 확인하고 있다.
④ 해킹방지 프로그램을 깔고 있다.
⑤ 고장난 컴퓨터를 수리하고 있다.

M I don't think you have a computer virus.

W Really? Is the problem something else?

M I think your hard drive is broken. Sometimes a hard drive _____ _____ _____. Is it old?

W 9 years. But I have never had a problem with it before.

M Hmm... I really think you need _____ _____ _____ _____.

W It sounds like something was broken when _____ _____ _____ _____ this morning. Do I really need a new one?

17 다음을 듣고, 이어지는 질문에 알맞은 답을 고르시오.

① math
② science
③ history
④ social science
⑤ English

M I am good at math, but I'm not good at history. I spent Saturday and Sunday _____ _____ _____ _____ . My mom said I should study history harder and spend more time for it. But I didn't. I studied math _____ _____ _____ . Why? Because I like it. And I studied history for a short time. I studied science and social science for a short time, too.

Q Which subject did he _____ _____ _____ _____ studying?

18 다음을 듣고, 이어지는 질문에 알맞은 답을 고르시오.

① 공부를 더 잘할 수 있어서
② 선생님들이 너무 좋아서
③ 스트레스가 별로 없어서
④ 친한 친구들이 있어서
⑤ 곧 있으면 대학에 갈 수 있어서

M My sister is in high school. And she said _____ _____ _____ _____ . She said she loves being a high school student. Of course she has a lot of work to do and she has _____ _____ _____ . She is also worried about her future. But she loves high school because she loves her friends. She is very close to her friends. They study together all day and all night. And _____ _____ _____ _____ really well. I guess it is her friends that make her happy.

Q Why does she like high school?

19 대화를 듣고, 여자의 마지막 말에 이어질 남자의 응답으로 가장 적절한 것을 고르시오.

① She never asks me to.
② She has a good job.
③ I usually do the chores.
④ I clean the living room.
⑤ Your husband is kind.

W My husband _____ _____ _____ _____ .
M What does he do for you?
W He vacuums once a week and he cooks a few times a week.
M _____ _____ _____ . I never help my wife at home.
W Why don't you help her? She will be really happy.
M _____

20 대화를 듣고, 여자의 마지막 말에 이어질 남자의 응답으로 가장 적절한 것을 고르시오.

① Thank you for helping me.
② Yes, you can't miss it.
③ No, turn around and walk back.
④ Yes, I go to Munhwa University.
⑤ No, you've gone too far.

W Excuse me, where is Munhwa University?
M Oh, just walk straight down this road.
W _____ _____ _____ this road.
M It takes about 6 or 7 minutes. Then you come to _____ _____ . You'll be able to easily see the entrance to the university.
W I got it. At the crossroads I can easily _____ _____ _____ .
M _____

WORD AND EXPRESSION REVIEW • TEST 13-14

A Write down the definition of each word or phrase.

1 plant

2 peel

3 fee

4 hallway

5 outer

6 quit

7 plate

8 cafeteria

9 punish

10 environment

11 anniversary

12 disagree

13 take care of

14 vacuum

15 rate

16 transit

17 fasten

18 invent

19 break down

20 chores

B Match each word with the right definition.

1 lie down ｜ _____

2 repair ｜ _____

3 correct ｜ _____

4 entrance ｜ _____

5 hang up ｜ _____

6 fare ｜ _____

7 normally ｜ _____

8 drop off ｜ _____

9 continue ｜ _____

10 gas station ｜ _____

11 vegetable ｜ _____

12 miss ｜ _____

13 increase ｜ _____

14 block ｜ _____

15 put down ｜ _____

a 기입하다, 적다

b ~을 놓치다, ~하지 못하다

c 계속하다, 지속되다

d 야채, 채소

e 늘리다, 증가시키다

f 주유소

g 보통, 통상적으로

h 막다, 방해하다

i ~을 도중에 내려놓다

j 수선(하다), 수리(하다)

k 운임, 요금, 통행료

l ~을 걸다, 매달다

m 눕다, 쉬다

n 고치다, 바로잡다, 수정하다

o 입장, 입구

Choose the best answer for the blank.

1 I'm so proud _____ you.

    a. on   b. of   c. with

2 We have a regular meeting every _____ week.

    a. two   b. another   c. other

3 I have to read the paper _____ a school project.

    a. because   b. because of   c. as

4 We must stop teenagers _____ beginning to smoke.

    a. from   b. of   c. by

5 Are they selling coffee _____ a cheap price?

    a. at   b. for   c. by

6 My father quit _____ two years ago.

    a. smoke   b. to smoke   c. smoking

D Complete the short dialogues.

1 A: I don't want to go there.

    B: Me _____.

2 A: Let's go to the cinema tonight. I bought the ticket for you.

    B: Really? I have to work late today. You _____ have asked me first.

3 A: How can I win the new car?

    B: You must answer all the questions _____ _____ to win the new car.

4 A: There are two computers in my house. One is in my bedroom.

    B: I guess _____ _____ is in your brother's bedroom.

5 A: Here is a letter for you.

    B: Really? It is the _____ letter that I have waited for.

1 다음을 듣고, 남자가 설명하는 그림으로 가장 알맞은 것을 고르시오.

①
②
③
④
⑤

2 대화를 듣고, 여자의 생일을 고르시오.

① April 14th   ② April 15th
③ April 16th   ④ May 14th
⑤ May 15th

3 대화를 듣고, 두 사람이 언제 만나기로 했는지를 고르시오.

① Tuesday afternoon
② Tuesday evening
③ Wednesday afternoon
④ Wednesday evening
⑤ Thursday afternoon

4 다음을 듣고, 날씨에 대한 설명으로 옳지 <u>않은</u> 것을 고르시오.

① 내일은 폭설이 내린다.
② 오늘은 내일보다 더 춥다.
③ 오늘은 매우 춥지만, 화창하다.
④ 내일의 기온은 영하 2-3도이다.
⑤ 오늘은 영하 10도로 떨어진다.

5 대화를 듣고, 여자가 차를 판 이유를 고르시오.

① 수리비가 너무 많이 들어서
② 고장이 나서
③ 기름값이 너무 비싸서
④ 더 좋은 차를 구입하려고
⑤ 좋은 가격에 팔 수 있어서

6 대화를 듣고, 여자가 버스 대신 지하철을 타는 이유를 고르시오.

① 교통 정체를 피할 수 있어서
② 자리에 앉을 수 있어서
③ 요금이 더 저렴해서
④ 더 빨리 출근할 수 있어서
⑤ 책을 읽을 수 있어서

7 다음을 듣고, 그림의 상황에 가장 어울리는 대화를 고르시오.

①   ②   ③   ④   ⑤

8 대화를 듣고, 상황에 가장 알맞은 표현을 고르시오.

① Is this seat taken?
② May I join your group?
③ Could you sit over there?
④ Have the concert already started?
⑤ How much did you enjoy this concert?

9 대화를 듣고, 두 사람이 대화하는 장소를 고르시오.

① gas station   ② jail
③ bank   ④ subway station
⑤ police station

10 다음을 듣고, 두 사람의 대화가 <u>어색한</u> 것을 고르시오.

①   ②   ③   ④   ⑤

11 대화를 듣고, 남자가 팁으로 지불할 금액을 고르시오.

① $2   ② $3   ③ $3.5   ④ $4   ⑤ $4.5

12 다음을 듣고, 무엇에 관한 설명인지 고르시오.

① 학교 폭력   ② 교내 봉사
③ 교우 관계 조사   ④ 반 대항 체육대회
⑤ 분실물 센터 설치

13 대화를 듣고, 두 사람의 관계로 가장 알맞은 것을 고르시오.

① doctor   ..... patient
② grandmother ..... grandson
③ doctor   ..... nurse
④ husband   ..... wife
⑤ mother   ..... son

14 대화를 듣고, 남자가 찾고 있는 것을 고르시오.

① pencil   ② schoolbag
③ book   ④ eraser
⑤ notebook

15 대화를 듣고, 여자가 희망하는 미래의 직업을 고르시오.

① singer
② dancer
③ fashion designer
④ movie star
⑤ fashion model

16 다음을 듣고, 그림과 일치하지 <u>않는</u> 것을 고르시오.

①   ②   ③   ④   ⑤

17 대화를 듣고, 무엇에 관한 내용인지 고르시오.

① 어떤 장르의 영화를 좋아하는지
② 그 영화가 좋았는지 나빴는지
③ 어떤 영화배우를 가장 좋아하는지
④ 사람들이 왜 그 영화를 싫어하는지
⑤ 누가 올해 아카데미 남우주연상을 받을지

18 대화를 듣고, 내용과 일치하는 것을 고르시오.

① 내일은 한라산과 해변에 간다.
② 오늘은 녹차밭과 한라산을 간다.
③ 오늘은 해변에 가서 신선한 생선을 먹는다.
④ 오늘은 녹차밭에 갔다가 오렌지농장에 간다.
⑤ 내일은 신선한 생선을 먹고 나서, 한라산에 간다.

[19-20] 대화를 듣고, 남자의 마지막 말에 이어질 여자의 응답으로 가장 적절한 것을 고르시오.

19

① No thanks. It's OK.
② Put mine in your bag.
③ Tomorrow it will be sunny.
④ Thanks. I really appreciate it.
⑤ It's OK. We can share mine.

20

① Do you like it?
② How much is it?
③ Where is Thailand?
④ What color is it?
⑤ Can I go with you?

1 다음을 듣고, 남자가 설명하는 그림으로 가장 알맞은 것을 고르시오.

① ② ③ ④ ⑤

M This is used to tell _____ _____ _____ _____. It was the first device invented by ancient people to do so. There are many types, but the most basic type works like this. The sun _____ _____ _____ on a surface on which the hours of the day are marked. The shadow tells us what time it is. And the biggest problem is that they can't be used to tell the time _____ _____ _____ _____ _____.

2 대화를 듣고, 여자의 생일을 고르시오.

① April 14th
② April 15th
③ April 16th
④ May 14th
⑤ May 15th

M _____! Happy Birthday!
W Thank you. But my birthday _____ _____ _____.
M Really? I thought your birthday was April 15th.
W It is. And that's tomorrow.
M So that means today is the 14th.
W Yes, it is.

3 대화를 듣고, 두 사람이 언제 만나기로 했는지를 고르시오.

① Tuesday afternoon
② Tuesday evening
③ Wednesday afternoon
④ Wednesday evening
⑤ Thursday afternoon

M Sujin, we must _____ _____ _____ _____ our science project. Today is Tuesday. We must meet today or tomorrow. _____ _____ _____ _____ on Thursday.
W How about this afternoon?
M I have a piano lesson today.
W But I have a swimming lesson tomorrow afternoon.
M _____ _____ _____ on Wednesday, either. Then let's meet today after dinner.
W Good idea.

4 다음을 듣고, 날씨에 대한 설명으로 옳지 **않은** 것을 고르시오.

① 내일은 폭설이 내린다.
② 오늘은 내일보다 더 춥다.
③ 오늘은 매우 춥지만, 화창하다.
④ 내일의 기온은 영하 2~3도이다.
⑤ 오늘은 영하 10도로 떨어진다.

W Good morning. Rise and shine. _____ _____ _____ _____. And remember to dress warmly today as the temperature will _____ _____ _____ _____. The skies will be clear and sunny, but the temperature will be really low. Don't worry _____ _____ _____ _____ for long. Tomorrow there will be light snow. And it should be only minus 2 or 3.

---

5 대화를 듣고, 여자가 차를 판 이유를 고르시오.

① 수리비가 너무 많이 들어서
② 고장이 나서
③ 기름값이 너무 비싸서
④ 더 좋은 차를 구입하려고
⑤ 좋은 가격에 팔 수 있어서

M Suzanne, are you taking a bus, too?
W Yes, I am.
M I thought you had a car. Is your car _____ _____?
W No, it's not broken. _____ _____ _____.
M Why is that?
W _____ _____ _____ _____ _____. It's too expensive to drive.
M Well, taking a bus is _____ _____.

---

6 대화를 듣고, 여자가 버스 대신 지하철을 타는 이유를 고르시오.

① 교통 정체를 피할 수 있어서
② 자리에 앉을 수 있어서
③ 요금이 더 저렴해서
④ 더 빨리 출근할 수 있어서
⑤ 책을 읽을 수 있어서

W It takes me an hour to get to work by subway.
M That's a long time.
W I have to _____ _____.
M I am sure you can get to work more quickly if you take a bus.
W I could. But whenever I take a bus, I can't find a seat.
M Oh, I hate _____ _____ _____ _____, too.
W That's why I take a subway. I always _____ _____ _____.

---

7 다음을 듣고, 그림의 상황에 가장 어울리는 대화를 고르시오.

① ② ③
④ ⑤

① **M** _____ _____ _____ _____. I have to go now.
   W Sure. Wait! Didn't you forget something?
② **M** Anna, you're not ready yet! I'm sure we'll be late.
   W I'm sorry. I'll get ready in 5 minutes.
③ **M** Good evening, ma'am. How may I help you?
   W Well, I'm looking for a pair of shoes.
④ **M** _____ _____ _____ _____ in the play.
   W Thank you. Did you really like it?
⑤ **M** Welcome to the our shop. How may I help you?
   W Well, what are _____ _____ _____ _____ the lockers?

8 다음을 듣고, 상황에 가장 알맞은 표현을 고르시오.

① Is this seat taken?
② May I join your group?
③ Could you sit over there?
④ Have the concert already started?
⑤ How much did you enjoy this concert?

M You go to _____ _____ _____ in the park. There are many people who are watching the free concert. You look for an empty seat. There is one empty seat on _____ _____ _____ _____ _____. You, however, are not sure the seat is free. In this situation, what would you ask the man sitting in the seat _____ _____ _____ _____ _____?

9 대화를 듣고, 두 사람이 대화하는 장소를 고르시오.

① gas station
② jail
③ bank
④ subway station
⑤ police station

M Thanks for coming here.
W It's OK. I want the criminal _____ _____ _____ _____ _____.
M Please look at these pictures. Look for a picture of the man _____ _____ _____ _____. *[pause]*
W This man! He took my purse _____ _____ _____.
M Are you sure?
W I'm sure he stole my purse.

10 다음을 듣고, 두 사람의 대화가 <u>어색한</u> 것을 고르시오.

① ② ③
④ ⑤

① **M** Shall we go shopping this weekend?
　W Sorry, I'm busy. I have to visit my grandmother.
② **M** The classroom is really dirty.
　W Let's _____ _____ _____ _____.
③ **M** Here's $10.
　W And _____ _____ _____. Your order will be ready in one minute.
④ **M** Excuse me, can I have the bill?
　W Yes, is there _____ _____ _____ with your order?
⑤ **M** Excuse me, can you tell me how to get to Lake Park?
　W Walk straight for 10 minutes.

11 대화를 듣고, 남자가 팁으로 지불할 금액을 고르시오.

① $2 ② $3 ③ $3.5
④ $4 ⑤ $4.5

M How much _____ _____ _____ the waitress?

W Let's see, the bill is $20. And the service was not bad.

M Should I leave a 20% tip?

W The service was okay, _____ _____ _____. Leave a 10% tip.

M Oh, _____ _____. Why don't I just leave 15%?

---

12 다음을 듣고, 무엇에 관한 설명인지 고르시오.

① 학교 폭력
② 교내 봉사
③ 교우 관계 조사
④ 반 대항 체육대회
⑤ 분실물 센터 설치

M Some students take things from other students. Some students take other students' money. And _____ _____ _____ _____ in the school yard. It is a problem that _____ _____. But together we can _____ _____ _____. Please tell your teacher about problems you have with other students.

---

13 대화를 듣고, 두 사람의 관계로 가장 알맞은 것을 고르시오.

① doctor ..... patient
② grandmother ..... grandson
③ doctor ..... nurse
④ husband ..... wife
⑤ mother ..... son

W I was just talking to my mother _____ _____ _____.

M Is she feeling better?

W A little. But I want our family to visit her in the hospital today.

M I already told the children that we would visit grandma today.

W After she leaves the hospital, she wants to _____ _____ _____ with us. Is that OK?

M Of course. I'll do my best to _____ _____ _____ _____.

---

14 대화를 듣고, 남자가 찾고 있는 것을 고르시오.

① pencil
② schoolbag
③ book
④ eraser
⑤ notebook

W Are you looking for a pencil, Mark?

M No, I'm not. I've got a pencil right here. I'm looking for my eraser. I bought a new one _____ _____ _____ _____ and now I can't find it.

W You should look in your schoolbag.

M _____ _____ _____ _____.

W There it is! Under those books. You have to be more careful, Mark.

M I know. I need to _____ _____ _____.

15 대화를 듣고, 여자가 희망하는 미래의 직업을 고르시오.

① singer
② dancer
③ fashion designer
④ movie star
⑤ fashion model

M Lisa, did you buy some new clothes?

W No, I made changes to an old shirt and a skirt.

M _____ _____ _____.

W Yes, I can. And I love it.

M Well, that shirt looks really nice. It's tight _____ _____ _____.

W And the skirt?

M It's _____ _____.

W Thanks. I hope this is my job in the future.

---

16 다음을 듣고, 그림과 일치하지 <u>않는</u> 것을 고르시오.

① ② ③
④ ⑤

M ① Little Italy is between Soho and Lower East Side.

② Tribeca is _____ _____ _____ and north of Financial District.

③ Chinatown is between Financial District and Tribeca.

④ _____ _____ is between Chinatown and East Village.

⑤ Greenwich Village is _____ _____ _____ _____.

---

17 대화를 듣고, 무엇에 관한 내용인지 고르시오.

① 어떤 장르의 영화를 좋아하는지
② 그 영화가 좋았는지 나빴는지
③ 어떤 영화배우를 가장 좋아하는지
④ 사람들이 왜 그 영화를 싫어하는지
⑤ 누가 올해 아카데미 남우주연상을 받을지

M I don't think the story is very interesting. And _____ _____ _____ _____ in the movie.

W I think the story was okay, though.

M Well, did you like the movie?

W Yes, I did. It's one of the best I've seen this year.

M Not me. _____ _____ _____.

W Well, you _____ _____ _____ next time then.

18 대화를 듣고, 내용과 일치하는 것을 고르시오.

① 내일은 한라산과 해변에 간다.
② 오늘은 녹차밭과 한라산을 간다.
③ 오늘은 해변에 가서 신선한 생선을 먹는다.
④ 오늘은 녹차밭에 갔다가 오렌지농장에 간다.
⑤ 내일은 신선한 생선을 먹고 나서, 한라산에 간다.

M What's _____ _____ _____ like?
W Well, on Saturday we will visit an orange farm. After the orange farm, we'll visit a green tea farm and a museum.
M Oh, _____ _____ _____ _____.
W And tomorrow, we will go to Mt. Halla. Then we'll visit a few beaches and _____ _____ _____ _____.
M I can't wait. I hope it's delicious.

19 대화를 듣고, 남자의 마지막 말에 이어질 여자의 응답으로 가장 적절한 것을 고르시오.

① No thanks. It's OK.
② Put mine in your bag.
③ Tomorrow it will be sunny.
④ Thanks. I really appreciate it.
⑤ It's OK. We can share mine.

M It's raining.
W I _____ _____ _____ an umbrella. Do you have one?
M I think so. _____ _____ _____ my bag. I think I put one in my backpack this morning.
W _____ _____ _____ while you look.
M Oh, I forgot to put one in.
W _____

20 대화를 듣고, 남자의 마지막 말에 이어질 여자의 응답으로 가장 적절한 것을 고르시오.

① Do you like it?
② How much is it?
③ Where is Thailand?
④ What color is it?
⑤ Can I go with you?

W I had a good vacation. I stayed in Thailand for a month.
M That's great. _____ _____ _____ _____.
W I am. _____ _____ _____ _____ a present. Here it is.
M Oh, thank you. Let me _____ _____ _____. *[pause]* Oh? A T-shirt from Thailand.
W _____

T E S T 15

1 대화를 듣고, 남자가 연주하는 악기를 고르시오.

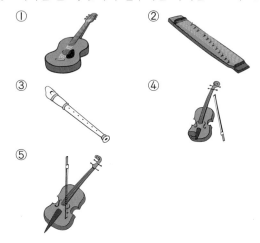

① ② ③ ④ ⑤

2 대화를 듣고, 여자가 오늘 오후에 한 일을 고르시오.
① 공부
② 연극 예행 연습
③ 교실 청소
④ 쇼핑
⑤ 테니스 시합

3 대화를 듣고, 남자가 여자에게 전화한 목적을 고르시오.
① 노래 대회에 나가달라고
② 내일 밤 파티가 취소됐다고
③ 내일 간식을 가져오라고
④ 게임기를 파티에 가져오라고
⑤ 파티 준비가 잘 되는지 물어보려고

4 대화를 듣고, 여자가 공책을 빌리는 이유를 고르시오.
① 공책을 잃어버려서
② 선생님이 가져오라고 시켜서
③ 남자가 반에서 노트 필기를 제일 잘해서
④ 아파서 필기를 하지 못해서
⑤ 숙제를 하는 데 도움을 받으려고

5 다음을 듣고, 무엇에 관한 설명인지 고르시오.

① ② ③ ④ ⑤

6 대화를 듣고, 두 사람이 대화하는 장소를 고르시오.
① hospital ② taxi
③ bus ④ police station
⑤ subway station

7 대화를 듣고, 남자가 마시고 싶어 하는 음료를 고르시오.
① water ② milk
③ cola ④ coffee
⑤ orange juice

8 대화를 듣고, 여자가 지불해야 할 금액을 고르시오.
① $7 ② $8 ③ $9 ④ $10 ⑤ $11

9 다음을 듣고, 무엇에 관한 내용인지 고르시오.
① 매니저 구인 광고 ② 새 음반 발표
③ 수상 소감 발표 ④ 수상 후보 소개
⑤ 매니저 소개

10 대화를 듣고, 두 사람의 관계로 가장 알맞은 것을 고르시오.
① 학생 – 학생 ② 선생님 – 학부모
③ 선생님 – 선생님 ④ 선생님 – 학생
⑤ 학부모 – 학부모

11 대화를 듣고, 상황에 어울리는 속담을 고르시오.

① It's a piece of cake.
② Beauty is in the eye of the beholder.
③ Honesty is the best policy.
④ Easy come, easy go.
⑤ A stitch in time saves nine.

12 다음을 듣고, 이 상황에서 Frank가 할 수 있는 질문으로 적절한 것을 고르시오.

① Excuse me, can I park here?
② Excuse me, is there a zoo in Central Park?
③ Excuse me, how much is a ticket for the zoo?
④ Excuse me, how can I get to the zoo?
⑤ Excuse me, where is Central Park subway station?

13 다음은 어떤 설문지의 결과입니다. 도표의 내용과 다른 것을 고르시오.

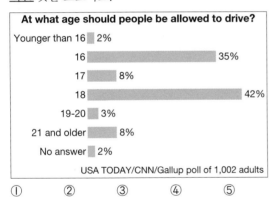

At what age should people be allowed to drive?

Younger than 16	2%
16	35%
17	8%
18	42%
19-20	3%
21 and older	8%
No answer	2%

USA TODAY/CNN/Gallup poll of 1,002 adults

①　　②　　③　　④　　⑤

14 대화를 듣고, 남자가 목적지까지 몇 정거장을 더 가야 하는지 고르시오.

① 3　　② 4　　③ 5　　④ 6　　⑤ 7

15 다음을 듣고, 내용과 일치하는 것을 고르시오.

① 낚시를 해도 된다.
② 해변에 사람들이 별로 없다.
③ 쓰레기는 집으로 다 가져가야 한다.
④ 표시된 구역 안에서만 수영해야 한다.
⑤ 규칙을 안 지키면 벌금을 내야 한다.

16 대화를 듣고, 두 사람이 지금 먼저 해야 할 일을 고르시오.

① to go to a beach
② to have dinner in a hotel
③ to wear shorts
④ to unpack their bags
⑤ to make a hotel reservation

17 대화를 듣고, 남자가 하는 말의 의도를 고르시오.

① 칭찬　　② 불만　　③ 격려
④ 사과　　⑤ 걱정

18 대화를 듣고, 남자의 심정으로 알맞은 것을 고르시오.

① confused　　② bored
③ satisfied　　④ worried
⑤ upset

[19-20] 대화를 듣고, 마지막 말에 이어질 응답으로 가장 적절한 것을 고르시오.

19

① Not as bad as yesterday.
② I think you're right.
③ Yes, I've done it.
④ Thanks a lot for the notes.
⑤ I hope you're fine, too.

20

① I forgot to give it to you.
② I like him very much.
③ I will go to the bank today.
④ Then I will ask him today.
⑤ Here's the money I borrowed.

1 대화를 듣고, 남자가 연주하는 악기를 고르시오.

① (이미지: 기타)
② (이미지: 가야금)
③ (이미지: 리코더)
④ (이미지: 바이올린)
⑤ (이미지: 해금)

M Hey, I can _____ _____ _____. Try and guess which instrument I play.

W Well, is it an instrument you play _____ _____ _____?

M Yes, it is. You use your hands, but not your mouth.

W Does it _____ _____?

M Yes, it does. And it's smaller than a guitar and you play it with a long stick _____ _____ _____.

2 대화를 듣고, 여자가 오늘 오후에 한 일을 고르시오.

① 공부
② 연극 예행 연습
③ 교실 청소
④ 쇼핑
⑤ 테니스 시합

W I'm home. I'm too late. Where is Mom?

M Mom went to shopping. Why did you stay at school _____ _____ this afternoon? Were you studying? Or cleaning the classroom?

W _____ _____ _____ for our school play next week. Mr. Jones, the teacher _____ _____ _____ _____ _____ told us to practice.

M I was waiting for you to come home and play tennis with me.

3 대화를 듣고, 남자가 여자에게 전화한 목적을 고르시오.

① 노래 대회에 나가달라고
② 내일 밤 파티가 취소됐다고
③ 내일 간식을 가져오라고
④ 게임기를 파티에 가져오라고
⑤ 파티 준비가 잘 되는지 물어보려고

[Telephone rings.]

W Hello.

M Hi, Barbara. This is Harry.

W Hi, Harry. Are you _____ _____ _____ Bob's birthday party tomorrow night?

M Yes, I am.

W Good. I'm looking forward to it. Your parties _____ _____.

M Thanks. We're going to play some games and _____ _____ _____ _____. But I phoned because I want you to bring some snacks tomorrow?

W Sure. What kind of snacks do I need to bring?

M _____ _____ _____ _____.

W OK. See you tomorrow.

4 대화를 듣고, 여자가 공책을 빌리는 이유를 고르시오.

① 공책을 잃어버려서
② 선생님이 가져오라고 시켜서
③ 남자가 반에서 노트 필기를 제일 잘해서
④ 아파서 필기를 하지 못해서
⑤ 숙제를 하는 데 도움을 받으려고

W Namsu, _____ _____ _____ some of your class notes?

M Borrow my class notes?

W Yes, will that be OK? I want to know what the teacher said.

M What happened to your notes? Did you _____ _____ _____?

W No, I couldn't _____ _____ _____ because I was sick last Thursday and Friday.

M Oh, that's right. Which class notes do you need?

---

5 다음을 듣고, 무엇에 관한 설명인지 고르시오.

①
②
③
④
⑤

M When we don't use this, it is small. When we use it, it is very large. This is usually _____ _____ _____. But when we are lost we need it. So _____ _____ _____ and it can be as big as _____ _____ _____. We use it not only when we are lost but also when we don't know how to get somewhere. It can _____ _____ _____ _____ of a city on it.

---

6 대화를 듣고, 두 사람이 대화하는 장소를 고르시오.

① hospital
② taxi
③ bus
④ police station
⑤ subway station

M _____ _____, ma'am?

W Hightop Medical Building on Fifth Street. Near the Fifth Street subway station.

M OK. I know where it is.

W _____ _____ _____ my doctor's appointment. I hope you can drive fast.

M I'll drive _____ _____ _____ _____.

W Thanks. How long do you think will it take?

7 대화를 듣고, 남자가 마시고 싶어 하는 음료를 고르시오.

① water
② milk
③ cola
④ coffee
⑤ orange juice

W Welcome to BigTop Industries, Mr. Johnson. Please _____ _____ _____.

M Thank you. Please call me Paul.

W OK. Paul, I'm Elizabeth and _____ _____ _____ of your co-workers.

M It's nice to meet you.

W It's nice to meet you, too. Mr. Smith, our manager will be here _____ _____ _____. While we wait, do you want some coffee?

M Water would be fine. I've already had coffee.

W Then, should I get you green tea or juice instead of water?

M Thanks, but _____ _____ _____ _____.

W OK. One moment, please. I'll be right back.

8 대화를 듣고, 여자가 지불해야 할 금액을 고르시오.

① $7
② $8
③ $9
④ $10
⑤ $11

M Look! The Laughing Walnut's new album is _____ _____.

W It's $10 on sale.

M Do you _____ _____ _____ _____ at this store?

W Yes, I do.

M Then you can get 10% _____ _____ _____ _____. But I have a VIP membership card. You can get another 10% off with this.

W Oh, thanks. I will buy it, then.

9 다음을 듣고, 무엇에 관한 내용인지 고르시오.

① 매니저 구인 광고
② 새 음반 발표
③ 수상 소감 발표
④ 수상 후보 소개
⑤ 매니저 소개

W I'm very happy to _____ _____ _____ for Song of the Year. I'd like to thank my manager. He works hard for me. First, I didn't want to _____ _____ _____ that won me this award. But he told me it would be very popular. I did _____ _____ _____. And now I have this award. Thank you, everyone.

10 대화를 듣고, 두 사람의 관계로 가장 알맞은 것을 고르시오.

① 학생 – 학생
② 선생님 – 학부모
③ 선생님 – 선생님
④ 선생님 – 학생
⑤ 학부모 – 학부모

M _____ _____ _____. It's time to get to class.

W Which class are you going to teach now?

M Class 5. What do you think about the students?

W Oh, they are very _____ _____ _____. They study hard.

M And _____ _____ are you going to?

W Class 7. I taught class 5 last time. I hope you have a good class.

11 대화를 듣고, 상황에 어울리는 속담을 고르시오.

① It's a piece of cake.
② Beauty is in the eye of the beholder.
③ Honesty is the best policy.
④ Easy come, easy go.
⑤ A stitch in time saves nine.

W I need to buy a notebook. I want this notebook with the big, green monster on it.

M There are many other notebooks _____ _____ _____ characters on them. I will buy you this one _____ _____.

W This monster is cute.

M It's got a really _____ _____. And really big ears. It's not cute.

W Well, _____ _____ _____ _____ of this character. I'd like to hold him at night.

M Oh, come on.

12 다음을 듣고, 이 상황에서 Frank가 할 수 있는 질문으로 적절한 것을 고르시오.

① Excuse me, can I park here?
② Excuse me, is there a zoo in Central Park?
③ Excuse me, how much is a ticket for the zoo?
④ Excuse me, how can I get to the zoo?
⑤ Excuse me, where is Central Park subway station?

M Frank wants to go to the zoo. There is a zoo in Central Park, so Frank _____ _____ _____ to Central Park station. As he _____ _____ _____, he doesn't see any signs for the zoo. He doesn't really know _____ _____ _____ _____. In this situation, what would Frank ask someone?

13 다음은 어떤 설문지의 결과입니다. 도표의 내용과 <u>다른</u> 것을 고르시오.

At what age should people be allowed to drive?

Younger than 16 ▎2%
16 ████████ 35%
17 ███ 8%
18 █████████ 42%
19–20 ▎3%
21 and older ███ 8%
No answer ▎2%

USA TODAY/CNN/Gallup poll of 1,002 adults

① ② ③
④ ⑤

W ① 8% of people think _____ _____ _____ should be 17.

② Only 8% of people think the driving age should be 21 _____ _____.

③ Less than 10% of the people chose 17 for the driving age.

④ Most of the people think the driving age should be _____ _____ _____.

⑤ 35% of people think the driving age should be 16.

14 대화를 듣고, 남자가 목적지까지 몇 정거장을 더 가야 하는지 고르시오.

① 3
② 4
③ 5
④ 6
⑤ 7

M Excuse me, _____ _____ _____ are there before West Station?

W _____ _____. We are at Midwest Station. From Midwest Station, it's one, two, three, four, five, six. Yes, six stops.

M Are you sure we are _____ _____ _____? I think we are at Park Station.

W Oh, I'm sorry, you're right. We are at Park Station. Midwest Station was the station _____ _____ _____.

15 다음을 듣고, 내용과 일치하는 것을 고르시오.

① 낚시를 해도 된다.
② 해변에 사람들이 별로 없다.
③ 쓰레기는 집으로 다 가져가야 한다.
④ 표시된 구역 안에서만 수영해야 한다.
⑤ 규칙을 안 지키면 벌금을 내야 한다.

M Attention, everyone! The beach is crowded today. So you must _____ _____ _____ carefully. Please put all your garbage in the garbage cans. Do not leave it _____ _____ _____. Secondly, please swim _____ _____ _____ _____ for swimming. Do not swim outside the marked area. And finally, _____ _____ on this beach.

16 대화를 듣고, 두 사람이 지금 먼저 해야 할 일을 고르시오.

① to go to a beach
② to have dinner in a hotel
③ to wear shorts
④ to unpack their bags
⑤ to make a hotel reservation

W The hotel is very nice.

M Yes, it is. I'm sure _____ _____ _____ _____ in one of the restaurants here.

W Yes, we can.

M Let's go to the beach _____ _____. I want to see what the beach is like.

W Harry, _____ _____ our bags and put everything _____ _____ _____ first.

M OK. I guess I need to _____ _____ _____ after that.

17 대화를 듣고, 남자가 하는 말의 의도를 고르시오.

① 칭찬
② 불만
③ 격려
④ 사과
⑤ 걱정

M Good morning. Are you going to work?

W Yes, I am. Good morning, Mr. Jones.

M Cecilia, I have _____ _____ _____ _____. Do you like music?

W Yes, I do. Most young people like music.

M Well, I am sure you like hip hop music. I can hear it _____ _____ _____ _____ in your apartment.

W Oh, I'm sorry. I didn't know _____ _____ _____.

M It does. It is too loud most of the time. Would you _____ _____ _____?

---

18 대화를 듣고, 남자의 심정으로 알맞은 것을 고르시오.

① confused
② bored
③ satisfied
④ worried
⑤ upset

W John, I'm home.

M Hi, Mom.

W Did you have the sandwich I made for you?

M Yes. But I ate a little _____ _____ _____ _____.

W What were you doing _____ _____ _____ _____?

M Nothing. I was watching TV. But there's nothing on TV. I wanted to play with Mike, but his parents took him _____ _____ _____ this weekend.

W I guess you should study for the test.

M Right. But it's no fun to stay home _____ _____ _____.

---

19 대화를 듣고, 마지막 말에 이어질 응답으로 가장 적절한 것을 고르시오.

① Not as bad as yesterday.
② I think you're right.
③ Yes, I've done it.
④ Thanks a lot for the notes.
⑤ I hope you're fine, too.

M Hi, Jenny.

W Hi, Bill. What did you study _____ _____ _____ yesterday?

M What do you mean? Weren't you in the class?

W _____ _____ _____ yesterday because I was sick.

M What happened?

W _____ _____. I just had a bad cold.

M Are you feeling better today?

W _____

---

20 대화를 듣고, 마지막 말에 이어질 응답으로 가장 적절한 것을 고르시오.

① I forgot to give it to you.
② I like him very much.
③ I will go to the bank today.
④ Then I will ask him today.
⑤ Here's the money I borrowed.

M Do you know Fred? What is he like?

W I like him. He is _____ _____ _____.

M But you know what? He _____ _____ from me last week. And he hasn't given it back yet.

W He is not such a bad person. _____ _____ _____.

M _____

A Write down the definition of each word or phrase.

1	ancient	11	financial
2	device	12	share
3	shadow	13	well rested
4	surface	14	string
5	temperature	15	fold up
6	transfer	16	locate
7	empty	17	industry
8	criminal	18	co-worker
9	the other day	19	polite
10	sew	20	bother

B Match each word with the right definition.

1	bow		a	만기인, ~하기로 되어 있는
2	allow		b	요금, 비용, 경비
3	absent		c	줄, 열
4	have got		d	감옥에 넣다, 수감하다
5	unpack		e	사소한, 작은
6	unfold		f	보는 사람, 구경꾼
7	award		g	~을 고맙게 생각하다, 감사하다
8	row		h	활
9	crowded		i	소유하다, 가지고 있다
10	appreciate		j	펴다, 펼치다
11	slight		k	상, 상금
12	due		l	~을 허락[허가]하다
13	put in jail		m	붐비는, 혼잡한, 만원인
14	beholder		n	짐을 풀다
15	charge		o	결석의, 부재의

C Choose the best answer for the blank.

1 Can I borrow your note? I couldn't _____ any notes because I was sick.

a. get　　　　　　　b. take　　　　　　　c. leave

2 I'll meet you sometime between two _____ three o'clock.

a. to　　　　　　　b. by　　　　　　　c. and

3 I'm looking for a pair of _____.

a. shoes　　　　　　b. skirts　　　　　　c. sweaters

4 I was waiting _____ come home and play tennis with me.

a. for you to　　　　b. of you for　　　　c. to you for

5 I'm in _____ of a second-grade class.

a. teaching　　　　b. care　　　　　c. charge

6 I'll drive as fast _____.

a. possible　　　　b. as possible　　　　c. as possibly

D Complete the short dialogues.

1 A: Rise and _____. It's time to get up.

B: Oh, no. I need more sleep.

2 A: Where _____, ma'am?

B: ABC Building on Fifth Street.

3 A: Do you walk to work these days?

B: Yes, it is not only economical _____ _____ good for my health.

4 A: I hate standing on a bus.

B: That's why I take a subway. I always get a _____.

5 A: I want to know what the weather is _____.

B: It's cloudy and windy.

1 다음을 듣고, 설명하는 대상으로 알맞은 것을 고르시오.

① 　②

③ 　④

⑤

2 대화를 듣고, 두 사람의 관계로 가장 알맞은 것을 고르시오.

① dad ····· daughter
② friend ····· friend
③ teacher ····· student
④ scientist ····· student
⑤ teacher ····· teacher

3 대화를 듣고, 남자가 전화를 건 목적으로 알맞은 것을 고르시오.

① 호텔방을 예약하려고
② 결혼식에 참가해 달라고
③ 전화번호를 알려 주려고
④ 식당을 예약하려고
⑤ 예약을 변경하려고

4 대화를 듣고, 두 사람이 할 일을 고르시오.

① 노래방 가기　　② 영화 보러 가기
③ 콘서트 보러 가기　④ 맛있는 거 먹으러 가기
⑤ 시험 공부하기

5 다음을 듣고, this country가 가리키는 나라를 고르시오.

① Finland　② Ireland　③ Iceland
④ Japan　⑤ Tuvalu

6 대화를 듣고, 여자가 남자에게 부탁하는 물건과 장소로 알맞게 짝지어진 것을 고르시오.

① 만화책 — 도서 대여점　② DVD — 비디오 가게
③ 책 — 도서관　　　　④ DVD — 도서관
⑤ 책 — 지하철 역

7 대화를 듣고, 의사가 말한 남자가 입원해 있을 기간을 고르시오.

① 1 day　② 1 week　③ 2 weeks
④ 2 months　⑤ 3 months

8 다음을 듣고, 내용이 순서대로 나열된 것을 고르시오.

(A) 　　(B)

(C)

① (A)-(B)-(C)　② (A)-(C)-(B)　③ (B)-(C)-(A)
④ (C)-(B)-(A)　⑤ (C)-(A)-(B)

9 대화를 듣고, 대화가 일어나고 있는 장소로 가장 알맞은 것을 고르시오.

① hospital　② hotel　③ airport
④ pharmacy　⑤ restaurant

10 다음을 듣고, 두 사람의 대화가 <u>어색한</u> 것을 고르시오.

①　　②　　③　　④　　⑤

11 대화를 듣고, 남자의 심정으로 가장 알맞은 것을 고르시오.

① proud　② surprised　③ frustrated
④ relieved　⑤ thankful

12 대화를 듣고, 두 사람의 관계로 가장 알맞은 것을 고르시오.

① waiter ····· customer
② customer ····· customer
③ cook ····· waitress
④ customer ····· cook
⑤ waiter ····· waitress

13 다음을 듣고, 버스가 정차해 있을 시간을 고르시오.

① 20분 ② 30분 ③ 1시간 10분
④ 1시간 40분 ⑤ 2시간

14 다음을 듣고, 내용과 일치하는 것을 고르시오.

① 과식은 몸에 좋지 않다.
② 다이어트는 건강에 해롭다.
③ 가장 좋은 다이어트는 운동이다.
④ 적게 먹으면 지방이 연소된다.
⑤ 적게 먹고 운동을 해야 살이 빠진다.

15 대화를 듣고, 남자가 햄버거 가게에서 하는 일을 고르시오.

① to cook the hamburgers
② to clean tables
③ to work as a cashier
④ to take an order
⑤ to do the dishes

16 대화를 듣고, 이어지는 질문에 가장 알맞은 답을 고르시오.

① 사고로 재활치료 중이기 때문에
② 오늘 컨디션이 좋지 않아서
③ 다른 선수가 다리를 발로 차서
④ 교통 사고의 후유증 때문에
⑤ 상대팀의 수비에 막혀서

[17-19] 대화를 듣고, 남자의 마지막 말에 이어질 여자의 응답으로 가장 적절한 것을 고르시오.

17

① No, I'm an only child.
② That is really interesting.
③ Yes, I have two brothers.
④ Of course I do. Maybe 30.
⑤ No, he doesn't have any.

18

① How about a dentist?
② I'd like to be an animator.
③ Why don't you try to be a doctor?
④ I agree. I will success as a businessman.
⑤ I think a lawyer could help the poor.

19

① Let's go have coffee together.
② My school is right near here.
③ I'm an elementary school teacher.
④ We are 25 years old.
⑤ I haven't gotten married yet.

20 다음을 듣고, 상황에 가장 어울리는 표현을 고르시오.

① Bye. I can't wait to get there.
② Vacations are never long enough.
③ I'm sorry not to have written you back.
④ I'll miss you while you're gone.
⑤ How can I get to your place?

TEST 17

DICTATION • TEST 17

1 다음을 듣고, 설명하는 대상으로 알맞은 것을 고르시오.

① ② ③ ④ ⑤

M This can fly through the air. It is a 20th century invention which was not produced _____ _____ _____ until 1942. Only a few passengers can ride in it. It is quite small. It flies because _____, _____ _____ on top of it move very fast. _____ _____ _____ _____ when it leaves the ground. It does not need a runway to take off. So it is often used in busy areas where _____ _____ _____ _____.

2 대화를 듣고, 두 사람의 관계로 가장 알맞은 것을 고르시오.
① dad ····· daughter
② friend ····· friend
③ teacher ····· student
④ scientist ····· student
⑤ teacher ····· teacher

M Have you finished _____ _____?
W I tried, but it was too hard.
M Can I see your notebook, then?
W Yes, here it is. I tried to solve these two math problems last night, but I couldn't. Would you explain _____ _____ _____ these?
M Hmm... I put the questions _____ _____ _____ now. Is there anyone who can solve these questions? Well, Susan, can you do it?

3 대화를 듣고, 남자가 전화를 건 목적으로 알맞은 것을 고르시오.
① 호텔방을 예약하려고
② 결혼식에 참가해 달라고
③ 전화번호를 알려 주려고
④ 식당을 예약하려고
⑤ 예약을 변경하려고

[Telephone rings.]
W Hello. Best Eastern Inn.
M Hello. Do you have _____ _____ _____ next weekend?
W Yes, we do. Would you like a double?
M Yes, my wife and I will be going to a _____ _____ _____ _____.
W _____ _____ _____ will you need it for?
M Just one. Saturday night. The name is Paulson. Paul Paulson.
W OK, sir. I'll just need your phone number to _____ _____ _____.

4 대화를 듣고, 두 사람이 할 일을 고르시오.

① 노래방 가기
② 영화 보러 가기
③ 콘서트 보러 가기
④ 맛있는 거 먹으러 가기
⑤ 시험 공부하기

W _____ _____ _____ _____. Wow!

M Let's go to a singing room and celebrate.

W I like to sing, but I don't want to do that now. I'd like to _____ _____ _____ _____.

M What do you want to do?

W Just watch a movie. I really want to see *Singing All Night*.

M Oh, Theresa Jones is in that. I've heard _____ _____ _____ _____. I'd love to see it, too. Let's go.

5 다음을 듣고, this country가 가리키는 나라를 고르시오.

① Finland
② Ireland
③ Iceland
④ Japan
⑤ Tuvalu

M This country is _____ _____. The island is quite large, but only 300,000 people live on it. There are _____ _____ _____ on the island. It has a well-developed social system. There are few social and _____ _____ between the people. Its name makes it sound like it's a really, really cold country. But it isn't _____ _____ _____ its name sounds. It is in the northern part of the Atlantic Ocean near Greenland.

6 대화를 듣고, 여자가 남자에게 부탁하는 물건과 장소로 알맞게 짝지어진 것을 고르시오.

① 만화책 — 도서 대여점
② DVD — 비디오 가게
③ 책 — 도서관
④ DVD — 도서관
⑤ 책 — 지하철 역

W Are you taking a subway to go home?

M Yes.

W Could you _____ _____ _____ _____ then? Could you return these for me?

M It's across from _____ _____ _____, isn't it?

W Yes, I got these DVDs from the video shop across from the library.

M No problem, then. _____ _____ _____ _____ on the way to the subway station.

7 대화를 듣고, 의사가 말한 남자가 입원해 있을 기간을 고르시오.

① 1 day
② 1 week
③ 2 weeks
④ 2 months
⑤ 3 months

W Cheer up! You'll be better _____ _____ _____.

M Thanks for the kind words. I'll try to cheer up, but it was a really _____ _____ _____.

W I know. What did the doctor say?

M I will _____ _____ _____ on my back tomorrow. I can't walk for two weeks. And I will have to be in the hospital for more than two months, 12 weeks or so. I don't want to be in the hospital longer than two months.

W I hope _____ _____ _____ _____ soon.

8 다음을 듣고, 내용이 순서대로 나열된 것을 고르시오.

(A)　　　　(B)

(C)

① (A)–(B)–(C)　　② (A)–(C)–(B)
③ (B)–(C)–(A)　　④ (C)–(B)–(A)
⑤ (C)–(A)–(B)

M Saturday afternoon is the time I help my mom and dad around the house. The first thing I do is picking up the clothes on my bedroom floor. Then I _____ _____ _____ _____ on my desk. After cleaning my desk, I vacuum the whole apartment. I don't clean the floor _____ _____ _____. That's my sister's job. I just vacuum the floor. After vacuuming, I water the plants _____ _____ _____. After I do all these things, I _____ _____ _____.

---

9 대화를 듣고, 대화가 일어나고 있는 장소로 가장 알맞은 것을 고르시오.
① hospital
② hotel
③ airport
④ pharmacy
⑤ restaurant

M Can I have this _____ _____ ?
W Certainly, sir. Let me check your name.
M It's Phil Wright. W-R-I-G-H-T.
W OK. I'll have this filled for you _____ _____ _____.
　　[pause] OK. Mr. Wright, your prescription is ready.
M Thank you. How often should I take it?
W _____ _____ _____ _____, 30 minutes after meals.

---

10 다음을 듣고, 두 사람의 대화가 <u>어색한</u> 것을 고르시오.
①　　②　　③
④　　⑤

① **W** How tall are you?
　　M _____ _____ _____ _____ _____. I'm 175cm.
② **W** Please be quiet! You should not be _____ _____ _____.
　　M I know, but I have something to tell you right now.
③ **W** I've got a math test today.
　　M Good luck. I'm sure _____ _____ _____.
④ **W** Do you play a musical instrument?
　　M I don't listen to music.
⑤ **W** I'm going to go to a pop concert today.
　　M _____ _____. Who is singing?

11 대화를 듣고, 남자의 심정으로 가장 알맞은 것을 고르시오.

① proud
② surprised
③ frustrated
④ relieved
⑤ thankful

W Sorry, I can't _____ _____ _____ .

M It's OK. I don't expect you to. You're _____ _____ _____ _____ , though you're very good at math.

W Well, in two years I'll be able to do it.

M I've tried and tried, but I keep _____ _____ _____ _____ . And there's no one to show me how to do it.

W You'll have to ask the teacher.

M He's not here right now. We're at home and it's the day before the test.

---

12 대화를 듣고, 두 사람의 관계로 가장 알맞은 것을 고르시오.

① waiter ····· customer
② customer ····· customer
③ cook ····· waitress
④ customer ····· cook
⑤ waiter ····· waitress

M Are you ready to order? What do you want to eat?

W I'll have the chicken and pasta. It looks _____ _____ _____ .

M OK. And I'll have a steak.

W But we can share everything?

M Sure. Of course. I'd like to _____ _____ _____ , too.

W Good. _____ _____ _____ _____ .

---

13 다음을 듣고, 버스가 정차해 있을 시간을 고르시오.

① 20분
② 30분
③ 1시간 10분
④ 1시간 40분
⑤ 2시간

W Hello, everyone. This is Maria, your tour guide. We have been driving for over 2 hours and _____ _____ _____ _____ a rest stop. The bus will stop in one minute and _____ _____ _____ _____ . It's 1:10 right now and the bus will _____ _____ _____ _____ at 1:40 o'clock. Please make sure you are back on the bus by then.

---

14 다음을 듣고, 내용과 일치하는 것을 고르시오.

① 과식은 몸에 좋지 않다.
② 다이어트는 건강에 해롭다.
③ 가장 좋은 다이어트는 운동이다.
④ 적게 먹으면 지방이 연소된다.
⑤ 적게 먹고 운동을 해야 살이 빠진다.

M Many people _____ _____ _____ _____ . They eat less food and they do lose weight. Then they stop the diet, eat like they did before dieting and _____ _____ _____ _____ . This is crazy. I don't think we should worry about what we eat. To lose weight, _____ _____ _____ . When we exercise, _____ _____ _____ _____ . It is the only way to lose weight forever.

15 대화를 듣고, 남자가 햄버거 가게에서 하는 일을 고르시오.

① to cook the hamburgers
② to clean tables
③ to work as a cashier
④ to take an order
⑤ to do the dishes

W Do you like _____ _____ at Burger Heaven?

M It's OK. I've only been working for one month.

W Are you cooking the hamburgers?

M No. All I do is _____ _____, so it's not much fun. New employees clean tables first. After two months I can work _____ _____ _____.

W And cook? Will you cook food, too?

M Only if I work there long. But I don't think I will. When school starts, _____ _____ _____ _____.

16 대화를 듣고, 이어지는 질문에 가장 알맞은 답을 고르시오.

① 사고로 재활치료 중이기 때문에
② 오늘 컨디션이 좋지 않아서
③ 다른 선수가 다리를 발로 차서
④ 교통 사고의 후유증 때문에
⑤ 상대팀의 수비에 막혀서

M What's wrong with Peter? He is running very slowly. He is usually the best player on the team.

W Oh, he _____ _____ _____.

M When? At the start of the game?

W Yes, before you sat down. _____ _____ _____ _____. It was an accident, but that player kicked him hard _____ _____ _____.

M Oh, that's too bad.

Q Why is Peter _____ _____?

17 대화를 듣고, 남자의 마지막 말에 이어질 여자의 응답으로 가장 적절한 것을 고르시오.

① No, I'm an only child.
② That is really interesting.
③ Yes, I have two brothers.
④ Of course I do. Maybe 30.
⑤ No, he doesn't have any.

W You know what? I have _____ _____ _____ this weekend.

M That will be fun. How many people will _____ _____?

W My father has lots of brothers and sisters. He has seven brothers and sisters. And they will come _____ _____ _____.

M So do you have _____ _____ _____?

W _____

18 대화를 듣고, 남자의 마지막 말에 이어질 여자의 응답으로 가장 적절한 것을 고르시오.

① How about a dentist?
② I'd like to be an animator.
③ Why don't you try to be a doctor?
④ I agree. I will success as a businessman.
⑤ I think a lawyer could help the poor.

W It's hard to _____ _____ _____.

M I know. Everyone is always telling us what they think we should do _____ _____ _____.

W But I never want to be _____ _____ _____ _____ I should be. Mom says I should be a doctor. Dad says I should _____ _____ _____. Grandma says I should be a businessman. Grandpa says I should be a dentist.

M Ummm... I hope it's OK to ask. But what do you want to be?

W _____

19 대화를 듣고, 남자의 마지막 말에 이어질 여자의 응답으로 가장 적절한 것을 고르시오.

① Let's go have coffee together.
② My school is right near here.
③ I'm an elementary school teacher.
④ We are 25 years old.
⑤ I haven't gotten married yet.

M Excuse me, Suji, is that you?

W Wow, Namsu. _____ _____, _____ _____.

M It has been 10 years. How are you doing?

W Great. And you?

M Very good. _____ _____ _____ A-1 corporation. I am _____ _____ _____ _____. And what do you do, Suji?

W _____

20 다음을 듣고, 상황에 가장 어울리는 표현을 고르시오.

① Bye. I can't wait to get there.
② Vacations are never long enough.
③ I'm sorry not to have written you back.
④ I'll miss you while you're gone.
⑤ How can I get to your place?

W One of your best friends, Rachel, _____ _____ _____ for a long summer vacation. She is going to stay with her grandparents _____ _____ _____. You will not see her for 5 weeks. In this situation, what are you likely to say when _____ _____ _____?

1 대화를 듣고, 남자가 방금 한 일을 고르시오.

① ② ③ ④ ⑤

2 대화를 듣고, 음식이 배달될 시각을 고르시오.

① 10:05 p.m. ② 10:10 p.m.
③ 10:15 p.m. ④ 10:25 p.m.
⑤ 10:35 p.m.

3 대화를 듣고, 남자가 찾고 있는 곳을 고르시오.

Pine Street

4 다음을 듣고, 내용과 일치하는 것을 고르시오.

① 남자는 Bill Gates와 같이 일한다.
② 남자의 회사는 자금난에 부딪혀 어려움에 처해 있다.
③ 회사가 대단히 성장했지만, 지금은 직원수가 30명이다.
④ 남자는 천천히 꾸준하게 성장해야겠다고 명심하고 있다.
⑤ 남자는 회사가 더 이상 비대해지는 것을 원하지 않는다.

5 대화를 듣고, 여자가 올 여름에 캐나다에 가는 이유를 고르시오.

① 영어를 공부하려고 ② 사촌들을 만나려고
③ 배낭여행을 하려고 ④ 캠프에 참여하려고
⑤ 학교에 진학하려고

6 대화를 듣고, 여자의 현재 기분으로 알맞은 것을 고르시오.

① regretful ② well-rested ③ surprised
④ tired ⑤ hopeful

7 대화를 듣고, 여자가 전화를 건 목적으로 알맞은 것을 고르시오.

① Peter의 어머니가 전화를 해달라고 메시지를 남겨서
② Peter가 누구와 함께 있는지 물어보려고
③ Peter가 언제 학교에 나올 수 있는지 물어보려고
④ Peter가 어느 병원에 입원했는지 물어보려고
⑤ Peter가 왜 학교에 오지 않는지 물어보려고

8 다음을 듣고, 이어지는 질문에 대한 알맞은 답을 고르시오.

① They must tell their children not to watch TV.
② They must watch TV with their children.
③ They must do other things with their children.
④ They must get rid of the TV sets.
⑤ They must not watch TV themselves.

9 대화를 듣고, 두 사람의 관계로 가장 적절한 것을 고르시오.

① lawyer ····· client
② writer ····· journalist
③ librarian ····· student
④ professor ····· student
⑤ bookstore clerk ····· customer

10 대화를 듣고, 어제 여자가 한 일로 알맞은 것을 고르시오.

① 고기 잡이
② 수영과 선탠
③ 배 타기
④ 바닷가 청소
⑤ 인명 구조

11 다음을 듣고, 내용과 일치하지 <u>않는</u> 것을 고르시오.

① 폭풍으로 뉴욕에 착륙할 수 없다.
② 눈 때문에 필라델피아에 착륙할 수 없다.
③ 워싱턴에 불시착할 예정이다.
④ 원래의 목적지는 필라델피아였다.
⑤ 항공사에서 기차 값을 지불할 것이다.

12 다음을 듣고, 그림의 상황에 가장 어울리는 대화를 고르시오.

① ② ③ ④ ⑤

13 대화를 듣고, 남자의 직업으로 알맞은 것을 고르시오.

① doctor   ② photographer
③ hairdresser   ④ babysitter
⑤ painter

14 대화를 듣고, 여자의 주말 계획으로 알맞은 것을 고르시오.

① 음악회 보러 가기
② 아빠와 자전거 타러 가기
③ 아빠의 일을 좀 도와드리기
④ 아빠와 함께 여행가기
⑤ 친구와 함께 영화 보러 가기

15 대화를 듣고, 대화와 어울리는 속담을 고르시오.

① No news is good news.
② As the boy, so the man.
③ Better late than never.
④ Never too old to learn.
⑤ Make hay while the sun shines.

16 대화를 듣고, 무슨 내용인지 고르시오.

① 모국어를 말하는 시기
② 외국어를 공부하는 방법
③ 동시에 두 나라 말을 하는 방법
④ 외국어를 잘 배울 수 있는 시기
⑤ 어른들이 외국어를 공부하기 힘든 이유

17 다음을 듣고, 방송 내용과 <u>다른</u> 메모 내용을 고르시오.

> **Budget Airlines**
> ① Departure Time : 3 p.m.
> ② Flight Number : # 34
> ③ Non-stop Flight
> ④ Flight Time : 3 hours
> ⑤ Arrival Time : 7 o'clock

18 다음을 듣고, 내용과 일치하지 <u>않는</u> 것을 고르시오.

① 영어 글쓰기 대회에 관한 내용이다.
② 두 개의 표제가 주어진다.
③ 두 개의 표제에 대해 글을 써야 한다.
④ 사전을 이용할 수 없다.
⑤ 최종 교정지에 글을 수정할 수 있다.

[19-20] 대화를 듣고, 여자의 마지막 말에 이어질 남자의 응답으로 가장 적절한 것을 고르시오.

19

① I'm very thankful.
② I'm sorry to hear that.
③ It's my pleasure.
④ I had a pleasant time.
⑤ Thanks, but I can do it myself.

20

① I don't go swimming these days.
② Everytime I find some time.
③ For two weeks.
④ On Saturday at 1 o'clock.
⑤ That's quite often.

1 대화를 듣고, 남자가 방금 한 일을 고르시오.

① ② ③ ④ ⑤

W John, what were you doing? _____ _____ _____

_____ _____ .

M Don't worry, Mom. _____ _____ _____ before I come and eat.

W Were you playing soccer with your friends?

M No, baseball. It was a great game. But the field was _____

_____ _____ _____ .

W I can see that.

2 대화를 듣고, 음식이 배달될 시각을 고르시오.

① 10:05 p.m.
② 10:10 p.m.
③ 10:15 p.m.
④ 10:25 p.m.
⑤ 10:35 p.m.

[Telephone rings.]

M Hello. Beijing Chinese Food, the best Chinese food in the EastEnd.

W _____ _____ _____ _____ ?

M Well, it's almost _____ _____ . It's ten minutes before 10.

W It's Lucy Lutes in Palace Tower.

M Well, I guess it's no problem for one of our best customers.

W I _____ _____ _____ _____ very late and I am very hungry.

M _____ _____ _____ _____ ?

W Deep-fried pork, stir-fried vegetables and rice.

M OK. I'll be there in 25 minutes.

3 대화를 듣고, 남자가 찾고 있는 곳을 고르시오.

Pine Street

M Excuse me, where is the nearest supermarket?

W Well, _____ _____ _____ _____ _____ directly on your right.

M Well, isn't there a large supermarket around here?

W Yes, there is. _____ _____ _____ and turn right. There is a large supermarket _____ _____ _____

_____ of the road. It's next to a bank.

M Thank you.

4 다음을 듣고, 내용과 일치하는 것을 고르시오.

① 남자는 Bill Gates와 같이 일한다.
② 남자의 회사는 자금난에 부딪혀 어려움에 처해 있다.
③ 회사가 대단히 성장했지만, 지금은 직원 수가 30명이다.
④ 남자는 천천히 꾸준하게 성장해야겠다고 명심하고 있다.
⑤ 남자는 회사가 더 이상 비대해지는 것을 원하지 않는다.

M I started a computer company a few years ago. _____ _____ _____ _____. When I tell people I own a computer company, they think I am like Bill Gates. But I am not Bill Gates. My company is small, but _____ _____ _____. Three years ago we had 10 workers, now we have 20. I want to get bigger, but _____ _____ _____ _____ _____ _____ _____ about an old city in Europe whenever people think my company is too small. I know I must be careful and grow slowly.

5 대화를 듣고, 여자가 올 여름에 캐나다에 가는 이유를 고르시오.

① 영어를 공부하려고
② 사촌들을 만나려고
③ 배낭여행을 하려고
④ 캠프에 참여하려고
⑤ 학교에 진학하려고

M What are you going to do _____ _____ _____?
W I'm going to Canada.
M So I guess you'll be studying English.
W No, that's not why I am going. My family is going to Canada to _____ _____ _____ _____. We haven't seen them for a long time.
M Oh, _____ _____.
W We're only going for three weeks. _____ _____ _____ _____ see my cousins. By the way, what about you?
M I'm going to go English camp in Australia.
W Oh, that's great.

6 대화를 듣고, 여자의 현재 기분으로 알맞은 것을 고르시오.

① regretful
② well-rested
③ surprised
④ tired
⑤ hopeful

M How long have you been in the library?
W _____ _____ _____.
M Oh, my god! You've been studying for 15 hours.
W Yeah. I guess.
M Aren't you tired?
W Umm... Actually _____ _____ _____ for two hours. I just woke up _____ _____ _____.
M You fell asleep for two hours!
W Yeah. I was really exhausted, but now I feel better. I _____ _____ _____ to study.

7 대화를 듣고, 여자가 전화를 건 이유로 알맞은 것을 고르시오.

① Peter의 어머니가 전화를 해달라고 메시지를 남겨서
② Peter가 누구와 함께 있는지 물어보려고
③ Peter가 언제 학교에 나올 수 있는지 물어보려고
④ Peter가 어느 병원에 입원했는지 물어보려고
⑤ Peter가 왜 학교에 오지 않는지 물어보려고

[Telephone rings.]

M Hello.

W Hello. This is Karen Katts, Peter's homeroom teacher at JoongAng Middle School.

M Oh, hi. Ms. Katts.

W Peter was absent yesterday and _____ _____ _____ _____. Why is that?

M Oh, he's very sick. _____ _____ _____ _____.

W Oh, I didn't know.

M Didn't my wife call you yesterday?

W No. So _____ _____ _____.

M Oh, I'm sorry. She _____ _____ _____ I did it.

8 다음을 듣고, 이어지는 질문에 대한 알맞은 답을 고르시오.

① They must tell their children not to watch TV.
② They must watch TV with their children.
③ They must do other things with their children.
④ They must get rid of the TV sets.
⑤ They must not watch TV themselves.

M Most children and teenagers watch too much TV. Parents are very worried about this. _____ _____ is not to tell children they can't watch TV. The solution is for parents to do things with their children. They must _____ _____ _____. They must take them to other places. They must talk to them. They _____ _____ _____ _____ the TV and watch TV with them.

Q What should parents do _____ _____ _____ _____ watching too much TV?

9 대화를 듣고, 두 사람의 관계로 가장 적절한 것을 고르시오.

① lawyer ····· client
② writer ····· journalist
③ librarian ····· student
④ professor ····· student
⑤ bookstore clerk ····· customer

M Excuse me, I can't find a book. Can you check the computer for me?

W Can I have _____ _____ _____ of the book?

M *Roman History* by Riley Johnson.

W Hmm... It isn't here. _____ _____ _____ _____ in one week. Would you like us to reserve it for you?

M Yes, please. _____ _____ _____ _____.

W OK. When the book is returned, we will phone you.

10 대화를 듣고, 어제 여자가 한 일로 알맞은 것을 고르시오.

① 고기 잡이
② 수영과 선탠
③ 배 타기
④ 바닷가 청소
⑤ 인명 구조

M Hi, Jane. I called you yesterday, but you didn't answer.

W I was busy all day. I was at the beach.

M At the beach? Swimming, suntanning... Why couldn't you _____ _____ _____?

W I was helping clean the beach. _____ _____ _____ _____ and oil went on the beach.

M I know. So was it hard work?

W Yes, it was. But I feel good to _____ _____ _____ _____.

11 다음을 듣고, 내용과 일치하지 <u>않는</u> 것을 고르시오.

① 폭풍으로 뉴욕에 착륙할 수 없다.
② 눈 때문에 필라델피아에 착륙할 수 없다.
③ 워싱턴에 불시착할 예정이다.
④ 원래의 목적지는 필라델피아였다.
⑤ 항공사에서 기차 값을 지불할 것이다.

M This is the captain speaking. _____ _____ _____ _____, we cannot land in New York. We wanted to land in Philadelphia, but it is snowy there, too. So _____ _____ _____ _____ _____ in Washington, D.C. instead. Everyone will have to take trains to New York. The airline will _____ _____ _____ _____ _____ for all passengers. Please understand there is nothing we can do.

12 다음을 듣고, 그림의 상황에 가장 어울리는 대화를 고르시오.

① ② ③
④ ⑤

① W Excuse me, where is the bathroom?

　 M _____ _____ _____ _____. It's on your left.

② W I'll be working late tonight.

　 M What time will you be finished?

③ W What did you do yesterday?

　 M I went shopping _____ _____ _____ with my mom.

④ W I play tennis three times a week.

　 M You must be a good player.

⑤ W How is your bathroom decorated?

　 M My bathroom is _____ _____ _____ _____.

13 대화를 듣고, 남자의 직업으로 알맞은 것을 고르시오.

① doctor
② photographer
③ hairdresser
④ babysitter
⑤ painter

M Sit there, please. Just hold the baby in your arms.

W Like this?

M Yes, that's fine. Smile.

W _____ _____ a second. Is my hair OK?

M I think so. _____ _____ _____.

W Yes, it's fine.

M I want to take a picture of you and baby _____ _____ _____ now.

W OK.

14 대화를 듣고, 여자의 주말 계획으로 알맞은 것을 고르시오.

① 음악회 보러 가기
② 아빠와 자전거 타러 가기
③ 아빠의 일을 좀 도와드리기
④ 아빠와 함께 여행가기
⑤ 친구와 함께 영화 보러 가기

M There is a free concert in the park this Saturday afternoon. _____ _____ _____ _____ ?

W Oh, I'd love to go, but I can't.

M Why not?

W My dad and I _____ _____ . We are going for a bike ride together. He's usually too busy to go with me.

M Can't you _____ _____ _____ in the morning?

W Not really. My dad probably has to do _____ _____ _____ _____ in the morning. Our plan is for the afternoon.

15 대화를 듣고, 대화와 어울리는 속담을 고르시오.

① No news is good news.
② As the boy, so the man.
③ Better late than never.
④ Never too old to learn.
⑤ Make hay while the sun shines.

W John, you should study now. _____ _____ _____ _____ . Your little brother went outside to play.

M Why is he so noisy, Mom?

W He's only eight. _____ _____ _____ _____ . You were noisy when you were eight.

M Hey, it's 7:30, my favorite _____ _____ _____ _____ .

W No, John! You must study now! The house is quiet. He'll come back inside at 8:30 and the house will be noisy _____ _____ _____ _____ _____ .

M You're right, Mom. I must study now.

16 대화를 듣고, 무슨 내용인지 고르시오.

① 모국어를 말하는 시기
② 외국어를 공부하는 방법
③ 동시에 두 나라 말을 하는 방법
④ 외국어를 잘 배울 수 있는 시기
⑤ 어른들이 외국어를 공부하기 힘든 이유

M Children can _____ _____ _____ .

W Yes, I know. It's harder _____ _____ .

M It's easier when they're 6 or 7 years old.

W And it's very hard when they're our age, 50!

M But I think 3 or 4 years old is _____ _____ _____ _____ a second language.

W Yes, I agree. Children must speak their first language well. Then they can study another language.

17 다음을 듣고, 방송 내용과 <u>다른</u> 메모 내용을 고르시오.

> **Budget Airlines**
>
> ① Departure Time : 3 p.m.
> ② Flight Number : # 34
> ③ Non-stop Flight
> ④ Flight Time : 3 hours
> ⑤ Arrival Time : 7 o'clock

M Good morning. This is the captain speaking. Welcome to Budget Airlines Flight No.34 to Bermuda. Keep your seat belts fastened for about 30 minutes more. When I turn _____ _____ _____ _____ off, you may get up. The plane _____ _____ _____, so I want you to keep your seat belts on. _____ _____ _____ _____ and we will arrive in Bermuda in 3 hours. It will be 7 o'clock in Bermuda when we arrive.

18 다음을 듣고, 내용과 일치하지 <u>않는</u> 것을 고르시오.

① 영어 글쓰기 대회에 관한 내용이다.
② 두 개의 표제가 주어진다.
③ 두 개의 표제에 대해 글을 써야 한다.
④ 사전을 이용할 수 없다.
⑤ 최종 교정지에 글을 수정할 수 있다.

W Welcome to the Seoul City English Essay Competition for middle school students. There are two topics for you to choose from. Do not write _____ _____ _____. You have exactly one hour to write your essay. You can't use a dictionary, but you may use _____ _____ _____ _____ on the final paper you give _____ _____ _____.

19 대화를 듣고, 여자의 마지막 말에 이어질 남자의 응답으로 가장 적절한 것을 고르시오.

① I'm very thankful.
② I'm sorry to hear that.
③ It's my pleasure.
④ I had a pleasant time.
⑤ Thanks, but I can do it myself.

M Can I help you? _____ _____ _____.
W Oh, that would be nice. Can you _____ _____ _____ in my car?
M Yes. Right here in the back?
W Yes, right there. *[pause]*
M _____ _____ _____.
W Thank you. I really _____ _____ _____.
M _____

20 대화를 듣고, 여자의 마지막 말에 이어질 남자의 응답으로 가장 적절한 것을 고르시오.

① I don't go swimming these days.
② Everytime I find some time.
③ For two weeks.
④ On Saturday at 1 o'clock.
⑤ That's quite often.

W What are you doing this weekend?
M I'm going swimming.
W _____ _____ _____.
M Yes, I think so, too. And _____ _____ _____ _____.
W How often do you go swimming?
M _____

A Write down the definition of each word or phrase.

1	invention		11	difference
2	passenger		12	convenience store
3	blade		13	own (v.)
4	finalize		14	remind
5	celebrate		15	solution
6	well-developed		16	author
7	operation (on)		17	climb
8	rag		18	departure
9	family reunion		19	competition
10	get together		20	judge

B Match each word with the right definition.

1	in no time	_____	a	내리다
2	arrival	_____	b	활주로
3	reserve	_____	c	숙제
4	assignment	_____	d	여관, (작은)호텔
5	land	_____	e	방문하다, 들르다
6	corporation	_____	f	기운을 내라, 이겨라
7	pleasant	_____	g	곧, 바로
8	cheer up	_____	h	치우다, 간수하다
9	get off	_____	i	~에 물을 주다
10	inn	_____	j	(주식)회사
11	correction	_____	k	남겨두다, 예약해두다
12	water	_____	l	착륙하다, 도착하다
13	go by	_____	m	도착
14	runway	_____	n	수정
15	put away	_____	o	즐거운, 유쾌한

C. Choose the best answer for the blank.

1 His company is _____ bigger and bigger.

    a. having   b. getting   c. making

2 She reminds me _____ her mother.

    a. of   b. to   c. from

3 You should _____ this medicine three times a day.

    a. get   b. eat   c. take

4 I don't know why I can't fall _____ at night.

    a. sleep   b. sleepy   c. asleep

5 Make _____ that you turn the computer off when you leave home.

    a. sure   b. surely   c. to sure

6 Could you _____ me a favor?

    a. give   b. do   c. ask

D. Complete the short dialogues.

1 A: _____ do you do, Tom?

    B: I'm an elementary school teacher.

2 A: I'm gaining weight these days. My pants are getting tighter.

    B: Why don't you _____ _____ a diet, then?

3 A: Could I speak to Tom please?

    B: _____ on a second.

4 A: Wow, this painting is great. Where is my camera?

    B: Look, there is a sign. You can't _____ a picture of it.

5 A: I got a bad grade on my math test.

    B: Oh, that's too _____.

1 다음을 듣고, 설명하는 대상으로 알맞은 것을 고르시오.

①   ②

③   ④

⑤

2 대화를 듣고, 남자의 직업으로 가장 알맞은 것을 고르시오.

① 꽃가게 주인   ② 농부
③ 사업가   ④ 어부
⑤ 정육업자

3 대화를 듣고, Jennifer가 Andy에게 전화를 건 목적을 고르시오.

① 수학 공책을 빌리려고
② 수학 문제의 답을 물어보려고
③ 숙제가 무엇인지 물어보려고
④ 숙제를 같이 하자고 말하려고
⑤ 수학 시험 범위를 물어보려고

4 대화를 듣고, 남자의 충고로 가장 알맞은 것을 고르시오.

① 편지쓰기   ② 전화하기
③ 같이 쇼핑하러 가기   ④ 선물 주기
⑤ 집으로 초대하기

5 다음을 듣고, 부부가 믿었던 속담으로 가장 알맞은 것을 고르시오.

① As the boy, so the man.
② Blood is thicker than water.
③ It's no use crying over spilt milk.
④ A little knowledge is dangerous.
⑤ Don't count our chickens before they hatch.

6 대화를 듣고, 남자가 되려고 하는 것과 그 이유로 짝 지어진 것을 고르시오.

① 작가 – 문장력이 뛰어나서
② 교사 – 가르치는 일이 좋아서
③ 의사 – 아픈 사람들을 돕고 싶어서
④ 변호사 – 불쌍한 사람들을 돕고 싶어서
⑤ 음악가 – 사람들에게 좋은 음악을 들려주고 싶어서

7 대화를 듣고, 구두를 신고 키를 잴 경우 여자의 키가 몇 cm인지 고르시오.

① 162cm   ② 168cm   ③ 172cm
④ 178m   ⑤ 180cm

8 다음을 듣고, 상황의 순서를 바르게 나열한 것을 고르시오.

(A)    (B)

(C)

① (A)-(B)-(C)   ② (A)-(C)-(B)
③ (B)-(A)-(C)   ④ (B)-(C)-(A)
⑤ (C)-(A)-(B)

9 대화를 듣고, 대화가 일어나고 있는 장소로 가장 알맞은 것을 고르시오.

① restaurant   ② hotel
③ airport   ④ travel agency
⑤ tourist information

10 다음을 듣고, 두 사람의 대화가 <u>어색한</u> 것을 고르시오.

①   ②   ③   ④   ⑤

11 대화를 듣고, 여자의 심정으로 가장 알맞은 것을 고르시오.

① lonely   ② scared   ③ pleased
④ exhausted   ⑤ regretful

12 대화를 듣고, 두 사람의 관계로 가장 알맞은 것을 고르시오.

① 사진작가 – 모델
② 영화배우 – 팬
③ 화가 – 그림 애호가
④ 영화감독 – 라디오 진행자
⑤ 자서전 저자 – 비평가

13 다음을 듣고, 도표의 내용과 <u>다른</u> 것을 고르시오.

<Hours Spent Each Week Doing Homework>

	Minji	Jisung	Sanghyun
Math	6	8	10
Science	5	8	7
English	10	4	8

①   ②   ③   ④   ⑤

14 다음을 듣고, 내용과 일치하지 <u>않는</u> 것을 고르시오.

① 지하철이 역 사이에 멈춰 섰다.
② 지하철이 탈선했다.
③ 정상운행을 하려면 30분이 걸린다.
④ 다친 사람이 있다.
⑤ 버스 이용을 권하고 있다.

15 대화를 듣고, 남자가 식당에서 일하려는 이유로 알맞은 것을 고르시오.

① 학비를 벌기 위해
② 여행 비용을 마련하기 위해
③ 돈을 많이 벌 수 있어서
④ 아버지의 식당 일을 도와드리기 위해
⑤ 아버지의 경제적 도움을 받기 싫어서

16 대화를 듣고, 이어지는 질문에 가장 알맞은 답을 고르시오.

① He had a violin lesson.
② He did his math homework.
③ He copied her math homework.
④ He helped her with the math homework.
⑤ He went going to a special art high school.

17 다음을 듣고, 이어지는 질문에 가장 알맞은 답을 고르시오.

① 여자를 반으로 가른다.
② 모자에서 비둘기를 나오게 한다.
③ 여자를 눕혀서 공중에 띄운다.
④ 여자를 아주 작은 상자 안에 넣는다.
⑤ 여자를 상자에 넣고 사라지게 한다.

[18-20] 대화를 듣고, 남자의 마지막 말에 이어질 여자의 응답으로 가장 적절한 것을 고르시오.

18
① I think you'll have to have dinner.
② I guess we need some rest, rain or shine.
③ Let's go swimming in the sea, if weather permits.
④ No thanks, I'm too busy. Some other time.
⑤ I'm sure the weather is changing for the better.

19
① I'm not that funny.
② My favorite day is Sunday.
③ I'm so happy to hear that.
④ I play with my dog in the park.
⑤ My mom and dad travel in the countryside.

20
① You're welcome. Take care.
② No, turn around and go back.
③ No, turn left not right at the corner.
④ Yes, you've got it. It takes 3 minutes.
⑤ That's right. As you said, it's really close to here.

TEST 19

1 다음을 듣고, 설명하는 대상으로 알맞은 것을 고르시오.

① ② ③ ④ ⑤

M Every community has one of these buildings in it. There are always people inside this building prepared to go to work. Their work is _____ _____. These workers eat and sleep in this building. They must be ready whenever _____ _____ _____ _____. When the bell rings, they _____ _____ _____ _____ _____. The trucks race to where the event happens.

2 대화를 듣고, 남자의 직업으로 가장 알맞은 것을 고르시오.

① 꽃가게 주인
② 농부
③ 사업가
④ 어부
⑤ 정육업자

W What do you grow?
M Rice. And we have a small barn _____ _____ _____ _____.
W Is it hard work?
M Yes, but _____ _____ _____ _____ I'd like to do. I like to work outside.
W And will your son _____ _____ _____ _____ _____?
M I'm really sad about that. No, he won't. He has moved to the city. He would like to be a successful businessman.
W He doesn't want to be like his dad.
M No, I can understand him. _____ _____ _____.

3 대화를 듣고, Jennifer가 Andy에게 전화를 건 목적을 고르시오.

① 수학 공책을 빌리려고
② 수학 문제의 답을 물어보려고
③ 숙제가 무엇인지 물어보려고
④ 숙제를 같이 하자고 말하려고
⑤ 수학 시험 범위를 물어보려고

[Telephone rings.]
M Hi.
W Hi, Andy. It's Jennifer.
M Oh, hi, Jennifer. What's up?
W Have you finished all homework? I'm _____ _____ _____ _____ my math homework. I just came back from piano practice after school.
M Today's homework wasn't that hard.
W Good. But _____ _____ _____ _____ which questions he asked us to do.
M We have to do the exercises on pages 49 and 50.
W _____ _____ _____?
M Yes, all of them. But, like I said, they are not that hard.

4 대화를 듣고, 남자의 충고로 가장 알맞은 것을 고르시오.

① 편지쓰기
② 전화하기
③ 같이 쇼핑하러 가기
④ 선물 주기
⑤ 집으로 초대하기

W Cathy is really angry with me and I don't know what to do.

M Why is she angry?

W I _____ _____ _____ _____ last week when Min-ji and I went shopping. Cathy wanted to go shopping, too. _____ _____, but she wouldn't talk to me.

M I think you should write a letter. Tell her you made a mistake when you didn't call her. _____ _____ _____ on her desk. I'm sure she'll read it and understand.

W Good idea.

---

5 다음을 듣고, 부부가 믿었던 속담으로 가장 알맞은 것을 고르시오.

① As the boy, so the man.
② Blood is thicker than water.
③ It's no use crying over spilt milk.
④ A little knowledge is dangerous.
⑤ Don't count our chickens before they hatch.

M After Clara was born, her father died. Her mother was all alone. She decided she couldn't take care of Clara. She left the child _____ _____ _____ _____ another man and woman. The couple cared for Clara. The couple and Clara were happy. After a few years, Clara's mother _____ _____ _____. She was happy. She asked the couple to give Clara back. _____ _____ _____, but Clara wanted live with her mother. This is because the couple _____ _____ _____ _____.

---

6 대화를 듣고, 자가 되려고 하는 것과 그 이유로 짝지어진 것을 고르시오.

① 작가 - 문장력이 뛰어나서
② 교사 - 가르치는 일이 좋아서
③ 의사 - 아픈 사람들을 돕고 싶어서
④ 변호사 - 불쌍한 사람들을 돕고 싶어서
⑤ 음악가 - 사람들에게 좋은 음악을 들려주고 싶어서

W I have no idea _____ _____ _____ _____ _____ with my life.

M I do. I'm going to _____ _____.

W How can you be so sure? You're only 16.

M I used to hope to _____ _____ _____. But now I'm certain I want to help poor people. I can do that best as a lawyer.

W Do your parents want you to be a lawyer?

M No, they don't. They want me to be a doctor or teacher.

---

7 대화를 듣고, 구두를 신고 키를 잴 경우 여자의 키가 몇 cm인지 고르시오.

① 162cm
② 168cm
③ 172cm
④ 178m
⑤ 180cm

M You look taller today, Beth.

W _____ _____ _____. The shoes are 6cm high. I usually wear sneakers and jeans. But today I am _____ _____ _____ _____, so I wanted to wear nice shoes.

M Oh, I see. You look really great!

W I am only 162cm tall. But of course today _____ _____ _____ _____.

M I wish I were taller. I'm only 172cm. I wish I were 180cm.

8 다음을 듣고, 상황의 순서를 바르게 나열한 것을 고르시오.

(A)   (B)

(C)

① (A)-(B)-(C)   ② (A)-(C)-(B)
③ (B)-(A)-(C)   ④ (B)-(C)-(A)
⑤ (C)-(A)-(B)

M Last night my classmate, Peter, came to my house. _____ _____ _____ a school project together. After we finished our project, we played computer games for 30 minutes. Then my mother _____ _____ _____ _____. It was really delicious. Peter _____ _____ _____ _____ and I read my English storybook until it was time to go to bed.

9 대화를 듣고, 대화가 일어나고 있는 장소로 가장 알맞은 것을 고르시오.

① restaurant
② hotel
③ airport
④ travel agency
⑤ tourist information

[Telephone rings.]
M Hello, _____ _____. May I help you?
W Yes. I want to _____ _____.
M OK. I hope you enjoyed our service.
W Yes, I did. Would you _____ _____ _____? I'll be down in a minute.
M OK. No problem. Did you get your breakfast delivered?
W No, not yet. Can I have it at the restaurant _____ _____ _____ _____, instead of having it here?
M Sure. I'll have it ready soon. Would you _____ _____ _____ to help you with your bags?
W No, it's OK.

10 다음을 듣고, 두 사람의 대화가 어색한 것을 고르시오.

①   ②   ③
④   ⑤

① **W** I'd like to know if you can play the piano.
   M _____ _____ _____ it for five years.
② **W** Is it OK if I open the window?
   M Yes, I want _____ _____ _____, too.
③ **W** Where did you go to elementary school?
   M I went to Johnson Heights Elementary School.
④ **W** Would you like some more cookies?
   M Thanks, but I _____ _____ _____.
⑤ **W** You have to turn off the computer right now.
   M OK, Mom. _____ _____ _____ right now.

11 대화를 듣고, 여자의 심정으로 가장 알맞은 것을 고르시오.

① lonely
② scared
③ pleased
④ exhausted
⑤ regretful

M Hey, you _____ _____ _____ _____ Harry yesterday, didn't you? How was it?

W _____ _____, please!

M Don't ask? What do you mean? Did you do _____ _____ _____?

W Yes, I did. You know, every time I start talking to him I say something stupid. It's because I like him.

M What did you say this time?

W I said don't ask! He must think I am really stupid. I want to _____ _____ _____ _____.

12 대화를 듣고, 두 사람의 관계로 가장 알맞은 것을 고르시오.

① 사진작가 – 모델
② 영화배우 – 팬
③ 화가 – 그림 애호가
④ 영화감독 – 라디오 진행자
⑤ 자서전 저자 – 비평가

W _____ _____ _____ to meet you. I love all your movies.

M I'm happy to meet you, too. I want to _____ _____ _____ on the picture before _____ _____ _____.

W Oh, my name is Lebeca.

M There you go. There's an autographed photo of me.

W Thank you. I'll put it _____ _____ _____ in my bedroom. Can I _____ _____ _____ with you?

M Yes, of course.

13 다음을 듣고, 도표의 내용과 <u>다른</u> 것을 고르시오.

〈Hours Spent Each Week Doing Homework〉

	Minji	Jisung	Sanghyun
Math	6	8	10
Science	5	8	7
English	10	4	8

① ② ③
④ ⑤

W ① Sanghyun spends the most time doing homework each week _____ _____ _____ _____.

② Minji spends a longer time doing math homework each week than Jisung.

③ Jisung _____ _____ _____ _____ doing English homework each week than Sanghyun.

④ Jisung spends _____ _____ _____ of time doing homework each week in the three subjects.

⑤ Jisung spends the same amount of time doing math and science homework each week.

14 다음을 듣고, 내용과 일치하지 <u>않는</u> 것을 고르시오.

① 지하철이 역 사이에 멈춰 섰다.
② 지하철이 탈선했다.
③ 정상운행을 하려면 30분이 걸린다.
④ 다친 사람이 있다.
⑤ 버스 이용을 권하고 있다.

M Excuse me. May I _____ _____ _____, please? There has been an accident _____ _____ _____ _____. A subway train has stopped between stations. The subway train _____ _____ _____ _____. No one was hurt, but it will take 30 minutes to solve this problem. You'd better leave the subway station and take a bus. We are sorry _____ _____ _____.

15 대화를 듣고, 남자가 식당에서 일하려는 이유로 알맞은 것을 고르시오.

① 학비를 벌기 위해
② 여행 비용을 마련하기 위해
③ 돈을 많이 벌 수 있어서
④ 아버지의 식당 일을 도와드리기 위해
⑤ 아버지의 경제적 도움을 받기 싫어서

M I've got a summer job. A waiter in a restaurant.
W Do you think you'll _____ _____ _____?
M I don't know, but I hope so. I wish my dad could give me the money for the trip.
W Did you talk to him about that?
M _____ _____ _____ _____ with the money for school. But he said, other than that, I have to _____ _____ _____.

16 대화를 듣고, 이어지는 질문에 가장 알맞은 답을 고르시오.

① He had a violin lesson.
② He did his math homework.
③ He copied her math homework.
④ He helped her with the math homework.
⑤ He went going to a special art high school.

M Can I look at your math homework?
W No, _____ _____. You have to do your own homework.
M Hey, I had a violin lesson last night, so I didn't have time to do any math. I want to go to a _____ _____ _____ _____. But to get into the school, I must practice a lot.
W Well, _____ _____ _____ _____ and I'll help you before the bell rings, but I won't give you my homework. It's not right _____ _____ _____ _____.
Q What did the man do last night?

17 다음을 듣고, 이어지는 질문에 가장 알맞은 답을 고르시오.

① 여자를 반으로 가른다.
② 모자에서 비둘기를 나오게 한다.
③ 여자를 눕혀서 공중에 띄운다.
④ 여자를 아주 작은 상자 안에 넣는다.
⑤ 여자를 상자에 넣고 사라지게 한다.

M OK. Ladies and gentleman, _____ _____ _____. For this trick, I need _____ _____ _____. You remember her. I made her disappear, then I brought her back. Well, for my next trick I am going to _____ _____ _____ _____. Yes, that's right. She will lie down in this box and I will _____ _____ _____ _____ the middle of the box.
Q What kind of magic trick is he going to do?

18 대화를 듣고, 남자의 마지막 말에 대한 여자의 응답으로 가장 알맞은 것을 고르시오.

① I think you'll have to have dinner.
② I guess we need some rest, rain or shine.
③ Let's go swimming in the sea, if weather permits.
④ No thanks, I'm too busy. Some other time.
⑤ I'm sure the weather is changing for the better.

M What would you like to do _____ _____? Is it going to be sunny on Saturday?

W I don't know. I'll _____ _____ _____ _____. I like to go to the beach. How about you?

M I thought we can go to a Chinese restaurant and have a good dinner.

W Well, _____ _____ _____ a good idea, but...

M But, what?

W _____

---

19 대화를 듣고, 남자의 마지막 말에 대한 여자의 응답으로 가장 알맞은 것을 고르시오.

① I'm not that funny.
② My favorite day is Sunday.
③ I'm so happy to hear that.
④ I play with my dog in the park.
⑤ My mom and dad travel in the countryside.

M I just sleep _____ _____.

W I know _____ _____ _____ _____ hard, but you've got to do something.

M I do.

W You do?

M Yeah. I sleep.

W Ha! _____ _____.

M Well, what about yourself?

W _____

---

20 대화를 듣고, 남자의 마지막 말에 대한 여자의 응답으로 가장 알맞은 것을 고르시오.

① You're welcome. Take care.
② No, turn around and go back.
③ No, turn left not right at the corner.
④ Yes, you've got it. It takes 3 minutes.
⑤ That's right. As you said, it's really close to here.

M Excuse me, where is _____ _____ _____ _____?

W Turn left at the corner.

M And then?

W Walk to the end of the next block. You can see it _____ _____ _____, across from the Grand Supermarket.

M OK. _____ _____ _____. Turn right at the corner and walk to the end of the block.

W _____

1 대화를 듣고, 남자가 축제 때 할 일을 고르시오.

① ② ③ ④ ⑤

2 대화를 듣고, 남자가 모든 숙제를 하는 데 걸릴 총 시간을 고르시오.

① thirty minutes
② one hour
③ one hour and thirty minutes
④ two hours
⑤ two hours and thirty minutes

3 다음을 듣고, 소년에 대한 설명으로 일치하지 <u>않는</u> 것을 고르시오.

① 소년의 나이는 5살이다.　② 노란색 셔츠를 입고 있다.
③ 눈은 파란색이다.　　　　④ 머리는 갈색이다.
⑤ 파란색 바지를 입고 있다.

4 다음을 듣고, 그림과 일치하지 <u>않는</u> 것을 고르시오.

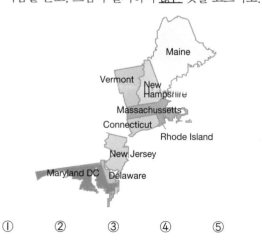

① ② ③ ④ ⑤

5 대화를 듣고, 남자가 MP3 player를 새로 산 이유를 고르시오.

① 옛날 MP3가 고장나서　② 디자인이 세련돼서
③ 가격이 저렴해서　　　　④ 색상이 마음에 들어서
⑤ 용량이 더 커서

6 대화를 듣고, 여자의 기분으로 가장 알맞은 것을 고르시오.

① encouraged　　　② nervous
③ uncomfortable　④ sympathetic
⑤ grateful

7 대화를 듣고, 여자가 남자에게 전화를 건 목적으로 알맞은 것을 고르시오.

① 음식을 미리 데워 놓으라고
② 직장에서 늦게 올 거라고
③ 혼자 저녁을 먹으라고
④ 요리법을 알려주려고
⑤ 아빠랑 같이 식사하라고

8 다음을 듣고, 이어지는 질문에 알맞은 답을 고르시오.

① 컴퓨터에 비밀번호를 걸어둔다.
② 자녀들의 컴퓨터 사용을 감시한다.
③ 집에 있는 컴퓨터를 치운다.
④ 차단 프로그램을 사용한다.
⑤ 아이들과 함께 인터넷을 이용한다.

9 대화를 듣고, 두 사람의 관계로 가장 적절한 것을 고르시오.

① flight attendant ····· passenger
② customs officer ····· visitor
③ tour guide ····· tourist
④ friend ····· friend
⑤ police officer ····· driver

10 대화를 듣고, 여자의 마지막 말의 의도를 고르시오.

① 비난 ② 충고 ③ 용서 ④ 불평 ⑤ 승낙

11 대화를 듣고, 내용과 일치하지 <u>않는</u> 것을 고르시오.

① 지금 비가 오고 있다.
② 남자는 오늘 밤에 숙제를 할 것이다.
③ 두 사람은 모두 내일 날씨가 맑기를 바란다.
④ 여자는 남자가 내일 집에서 숙제 하길 바란다.
⑤ 남자는 내일 하이킹을 계획하고 있다.

12 다음을 듣고, 메모지에 <u>잘못</u> 기록된 것을 고르시오.

① <Department Store>
② Special Sale : for one hour
③ Men's white T-shirts : 50% off
④ Toy department : 30% off
⑤ Women's socks : one+one

13 대화를 듣고, 여자가 주말에 한 일을 고르시오.

① 집에서 축구경기를 시청했다.
② 경기장에 가서 축구시합을 보았다.
③ 경기장에서 축구 시합을 했다.
④ 축구선수의 사인을 받았다.
⑤ TV가 고장 나서 수리했다.

14 대화를 듣고, 여자가 Rachel의 집에서 하려고 하는 것을 고르시오.

① 영화 보기
② 공부하기
③ 이야기하기
④ TV 보기
⑤ 식사하기

15 대화를 듣고, 내용과 어울리는 속담을 고르시오.

① A friend in need is a friend indeed.
② Seeing is believing.
③ Good words cost nothing.
④ Don't judge a book by the cover.
⑤ Every dog has his day.

16 대화를 듣고, 이어지는 질문에 알맞은 답을 고르시오.

① 빌린 돈을 갚으려고
② 구입한 물건의 값을 지불하려고
③ 선물 살 돈을 내려고
④ 돈을 빌려주려고
⑤ 불우이웃 성금을 내려고

17 다음을 듣고, 이어지는 질문에 알맞은 답을 고르시오.

① school bags
② electronic devices
③ textbooks
④ dictionaries
⑤ food

[18-20] 대화를 듣고, 남자의 마지막 말에 이어질 여자의 응답으로 가장 적절한 것을 고르시오.

18

① Don't worry. I'll be fine.
② You must be careful.
③ Yes, I want you to walk with me.
④ Where are you going?
⑤ I'm so sorry to bother you.

19

① why are you so sad?
② I'm sorry to hear that.
③ you have to be more careful.
④ don't mention it. It's nothing.
⑤ you should go to the hospital.

20

① I don't like exams.
② I don't watch TV.
③ I'd like to have a bike.
④ They will buy me a bike.
⑤ I go to bed late.

TEST 20

1 대화를 듣고, 남자가 축제 때 할 일을 고르시오.

① ② ③ ④ ⑤

W What are you doing this weekend, Peter?

M I've got to practice _____ _____ _____ _____.

W _____? I didn't know you were singing a song.

M I am not. I want to, but they already had too many singers.

W Are dancing or _____ _____ _____ _____ then?

M No, I'm doing a magic show. I've been _____ _____ _____ for three months now and I'm ready to do tricks for students.

2 대화를 듣고, 남자가 모든 숙제를 하는 데 걸릴 총 시간을 고르시오.

① thirty minutes
② one hour
③ one hour and thirty minutes
④ two hours
⑤ two hours and thirty minutes

M I'll have thirty minutes of Korean homework.

W So _____ _____ _____ _____ by 7.

M No, I've got _____ _____ _____ to finish, too. I have to read 15 pages and answer 20 questions. It'll be about one hour and a half work.

W Can we go out after that?

M _____. There's the math homework. It will take about 30 minutes. Why does everyone give homework _____ _____ _____ _____?

W All right. I'll just let you do your homework.

3 다음을 듣고, 소년에 대한 설명으로 일치하지 <u>않는</u> 것을 고르시오.

① 소년의 나이는 5살이다.
② 노란색 셔츠를 입고 있다.
③ 눈은 파란색이다.
④ 머리는 갈색이다.
⑤ 파란색 바지를 입고 있다.

W Attention, shoppers. We're looking for _____ _____ _____. His mother is very worried. His name is Brandon and he is five years old. He is _____ _____ _____ _____ and blue pants. He has _____ _____ _____ and brown eyes. If you see this boy, please bring him to the store's _____ _____ _____.

4 다음을 듣고, 그림과 일치하지 <u>않는</u> 것을 고르시오.

Maine
Vermont New Hampshire
Massachussetts
Connecticut
Rhode Island
New Jersey
Maryland DC Delaware

① ② ③
④ ⑤

M ① Vermont is west of New Hampshire.
② New Hampshire _____ _____ Maine _____ Massachusetts.
③ Rhode Island is west of Connecticut.
④ Delaware is _____ _____ _____ _____ .
⑤ Massachussetts is north of Connecticut.

5 대화를 듣고, 남자가 MP3 player를 새로 산 이유를 고르시오.

① 옛날 MP3가 고장나서
② 디자인이 세련돼서
③ 가격이 저렴해서
④ 색상이 마음에 들어서
⑤ 용량이 더 커서

W Hey, is that a new MP3 player?
M Yeah. I just got it.
W It's got a nice design _____ _____ _____ _____ . I guess that's why you bought it. Your old MP3 didn't have a _____ _____ .
M No, I bought this one because it has _____ _____ _____ . 80GB.
W Oh, you didn't like _____ _____ _____ on your player every few weeks.
M Exactly! I wanted one with a really large storage space.

6 대화를 듣고, 여자의 기분으로 가장 알맞은 것을 고르시오.

① encouraged
② nervous
③ uncomfortable
④ sympathetic
⑤ grateful

M Sarah, can you do me a favor?
W Yes, _____ _____ .
M Actually, I don't want to ask this, but I have no choice.
W What is it?
M It's not easy to ask, but can you lend me some money? I'll try hard to _____ _____ _____ _____ .
W You know I don't like to _____ _____ . I don't feel good if I have to ask for it back.
M I know, but...

7 대화를 듣고, 여자가 남자에게 전화를 건 목적으로 알맞은 것을 고르시오.

① 음식을 미리 데워 놓으라고
② 직장에서 늦게 올 거라고
③ 혼자 저녁을 먹으라고
④ 요리법을 알려주려고
⑤ 아빠랑 같이 식사하라고

[Telephone rings.]

M Hello.

W Andrew, it's Mom.

M Oh, Mom. Where are you?

W I'm still at aunt Susie's house. And she needs to keep talking to me.

M So you won't be home soon?

W No. You have to _____ _____ _____. Dad is working late, too.

M I really don't want to eat alone, but I guess I have _____ _____ _____.

W Just take soup out of the refrigerator and _____ _____ _____. There are plenty of side dishes _____ _____ _____.

M OK. I'll go ahead and do that.

8 다음을 듣고, 이어지는 질문에 알맞은 답을 고르시오.

① 컴퓨터에 비밀번호를 걸어둔다.
② 자녀들의 컴퓨터 사용을 감시한다.
③ 집에 있는 컴퓨터를 치운다.
④ 차단 프로그램을 사용한다.
⑤ 아이들과 함께 인터넷을 이용한다.

M The Internet is dangerous. There are many bad web sites. _____ _____ _____ _____ your children. But you can't always watch them whenever they use the computer. And you can't take the computer _____ _____ _____ _____. But there is a computer program, *Childsafe*, that can stop children from going to bad web sites. _____ _____ _____ today. It really works.

Q How can parents protect children from bad web sites?

9 대화를 듣고, 두 사람의 관계로 가장 적절한 것을 고르시오.

① flight attendant ····· passenger
② customs officer ····· visitor
③ tour guide ····· tourist
④ friend ····· friend
⑤ police officer ····· driver

M Can I _____ _____ _____?

W Yes, here it is.

M Are you here _____ _____, Ms. Peterson?

W No, I've come to Korea _____ _____ _____. I met them when they were living in America. And now they've invited me to Korea.

M So how long _____ _____ _____ _____ here?

W Just two weeks.

10 대화를 듣고, 여자의 마지막 말의 의도를 고르시오.

① 비난
② 충고
③ 용서
④ 불평
⑤ 승낙

M Oh, no. *[Crash!]* Oh, are you OK, ma'am?

W Well, I don't know.

M I'm sorry. I think I _____ _____ too quickly.

W You should have been more careful.

M _____ _____ _____ about this. Well, did you hurt yourself?

W No, I am fine.

M Well, do you want me to _____ _____ _____, in case?

W I don't think that's necessary. Maybe I wasn't careful enough, either.

---

11 대화를 듣고, 내용과 일치하지 <u>않는</u> 것을 고르시오.

① 지금 비가 오고 있다.
② 남자는 오늘 밤에 숙제를 할 것이다.
③ 두 사람은 모두 내일 날씨가 맑기를 바란다.
④ 여자는 남자가 내일 집에서 숙제 하길 바란다.
⑤ 남자는 내일 하이킹을 계획하고 있다.

W A boring, lazy Friday! We can't do much when it is _____ _____. I hope tomorrow is sunny.

M So do I. I'm planning to go hiking, then _____ _____ _____ _____ _____.

W Sounds like fun. What about your homework?

M I'm going to do that tomorrow night.

W No, you should do it tonight. It's only 7. You still have _____ _____ _____.

M OK. You're right. I'll do it right now.

---

12 다음을 듣고, 메모지에 <u>잘못</u> 기록된 것을 고르시오.

① 〈Department Store〉
② Special Sale : for one hour
③ Men's white T-shirts : 50% off
④ Toy department : 30% off
⑤ Women's socks : one+one

W Hello, shoppers! We have a special one-hour sale _____ _____ _____. Men's white T-shirts are 50% off. And in the toy department, Terry, the Train sets are 30% off. And in women's wear if you buy _____ _____ _____ _____, you will get a third pair for free. Hurry before _____ _____ _____ _____. Thank you.

---

13 대화를 듣고, 여자가 주말에 한 일을 고르시오.

① 집에서 축구경기를 시청했다.
② 경기장에 가서 축구시합을 보았다.
③ 경기장에서 축구 시합을 했다.
④ 축구선수의 사인을 받았다.
⑤ TV가 고장 나서 수리했다.

M Did you watch the soccer game on the weekend?

W _____ _____ _____ _____?

M What?

W I didn't watch the game at home on the television. I went _____ _____ _____.

M Wow! It must have been fantastic.

W It was great. My favorite player _____ _____ _____.

M Are you sure?

14 대화를 듣고, 여자가 Rachel의 집에서 하려고 하는 것을 고르시오.

① 영화 보기
② 공부하기
③ 이야기하기
④ TV 보기
⑤ 식사하기

M Are you going out? I thought Mom said you can't _____ _____ _____ _____.

W I'm not going to a movie. When I told Rachel I couldn't go to the movie, she asked me _____ _____ _____ to her house.

M Mom and I want you to study, not visit a friend.

W Dad, she invited me to study with her.

M Won't you _____ _____ _____ or maybe watch a movie on TV?

W No, Dad. _____ _____. I'm just going to study with Rachel.

M OK, I'll trust you and tell your Mom.

15 대화를 듣고, 내용과 어울리는 속담을 고르시오.

① A friend in need is a friend indeed.
② Seeing is believing.
③ Good words cost nothing.
④ Don't judge a book by the cover.
⑤ Every dog has his day.

W Look at the children. They are wearing _____ _____.

M Clothes are not important.

W But expensive clothing and shoes look better.

M I know that family. They don't _____ _____ _____. Their father is sick, too.

W I don't know. _____ _____ _____ _____.

M Come and talk to them. You will see they are good people. Their mother works hard.

16 대화를 듣고, 이어지는 질문에 알맞은 답을 고르시오.

① 빌린 돈을 갚으려고
② 구입한 물건의 값을 지불하려고
③ 선물 살 돈을 내려고
④ 돈을 빌려주려고
⑤ 불우이웃 성금을 내려고

M Do you know that Friday is Sam's birthday?

W No, I didn't. I must _____ _____ _____ for him.

M Well, I want to collect money from all his friends and buy one big present.

W Sounds like a good idea.

M Do you think you can _____ _____ _____ _____ now?

W How much?

M $5 will be fine.

W OK. Here you go. What are you buying him?

Q Why did she give him some money?

17 다음을 듣고, 이어지는 질문에 알맞은 답을 고르시오.

① school bags
② electronic devices
③ textbooks
④ dictionaries
⑤ food

M Good morning, students. We are getting the classroom ready. It will be ready in a minute. You are here to _____ _____ _____ _____ to get into Seoul High School. You can _____ _____ _____ into the classroom but, as the school is an electronics-free zone, make sure there is _____ _____ _____, MP3 players or electronic dictionaries in the bag. Also, be noted that food is not allowed _____ _____.

Q What can't you bring into the testing area?

18 대화를 듣고, 남자의 마지막 말에 이어질 여자의 응답으로 가장 적절한 것을 고르시오.

① Don't worry. I'll be fine.
② You must be careful.
③ Yes, I want you to walk with me.
④ Where are you going?
⑤ I'm so sorry to bother you.

M Finally we have finished this project. _____ _____ _____ _____ to our office, isn't it?

W Yes, it's really _____ _____ _____.

M Are you going to walk home?

W Yes, it's only 15 minutes away.

M Yes, but it's dark. Do you want me to walk with you?

W No, it's OK. _____ _____ _____ _____.

M Are you sure?

W _____

19 대화를 듣고, 남자의 마지막 말에 이어질 여자의 응답으로 가장 적절한 것을 고르시오.

① why are you so sad?
② I'm sorry to hear that.
③ you have to be more careful.
④ don't mention it. It's nothing.
⑤ you should go to the hospital.

W You look sad. What's wrong?

M _____ _____ _____. We all knew he was very sick.

W Excuse me, but who are you talking about?

M My grandfather. Umm... _____ _____ _____ last week. He loved me very much. I'll _____ _____ _____.

W Oh, _____

20 대화를 듣고, 남자의 마지막 말에 이어질 여자의 응답으로 가장 적절한 것을 고르시오.

① I don't like exams.
② I don't watch TV.
③ I'd like to have a bike.
④ They will buy me a bike.
⑤ I go to bed late.

W I'm trying to study _____ _____ _____ _____ these days. My parents promised me to _____ _____ _____.

M Good. Our final exams are in two weeks.

W That's right. I hope to _____ _____ _____. So I don't do other things. I only study.

M So what don't you do anymore?

W _____

A Write down the definition of each word or phrase.

1	community	11	assistant
2	race	12	disappear
3	apologize	13	sword
4	invite	14	storage space
5	saying	15	lend
6	certain	16	protect
7	check out	17	trust
8	autograph	18	cost
9	dresser	19	collect
10	trick	20	entrance

B Match each word with the right definition.

1	bring	-------	a	기르다, 재배하다
2	put through	-------	b	결정하다, 결심하다
3	break	-------	c	~을 좋아하다, 돌보다, 걱정하다
4	work	-------	d	~을 …에게 가져오다, 데려오다
5	present	-------	e	과목, 주제
6	decide	-------	f	괴롭히다, 폐를 끼치다, 성가시게 하다
7	grow	-------	g	베끼다, 복사하다
8	care for	-------	h	눕다
9	allow	-------	i	통과시키다, 꿰뚫다
10	trouble	-------	j	잃어버린, 길 잃은
11	subject	-------	k	냉장고
12	copy	-------	l	작용하다, 잘 듣다, 효과가 있다
13	fridge	-------	m	선물
14	lost	-------	n	허락하다, 허용하다
15	lie down	-------	o	잠깐의 휴식 시간

C Choose the best answer for the blank.

1 She watched TV instead _____ studying.

   a. of   b. on   c. at

2 I want you to _____ the dishes.

   a. clean   b. do   c. brush

3 I wish I _____ younger.

   a. am   b. were   c. have been

4 I _____ to practice for the school festival.

   a. got   b. must   c. have got

5 Would you like to go _____ a movie on Saturday night?

   a. to   b. for   c. on

6 I want to help the poor people. I can do that best _____ a lawyer.

   a. for   b. as   c. by

D Complete the short dialogues.

1 A: Will the show be canceled if it rains tomorrow?

   B: No, the show will be held, rain or _____.

2 A: What are you going to do tomorrow?

   B: I'll go to the beach if the weather _____.

3 A: Are you here _____ business?

   B: No, I've come to Korea to visit my friend.

4 A: If you buy two pairs of socks, you will get a third pair _____ free.

   B: Then I'll buy them.

5 A: My grandfather died yesterday.

   B: I'm sorry to _____ that.